D1519416

THRIVING IN E-CHAOS

Discover the Secrets of 20 Companies That Have Conquered a Turbulent Marketplace

JAMES D. UNDERWOOD

PRIMA VENTURE
An Imprint of Prima Publishing
3000 Lava Ridge Court • Roseville, California 95661
(800) 632-8676 • www.primalifestyles.com

To H. Igor Ansoff, Distinguished Professor of Strategic Management at U.S. International University, San Diego, California

---

Library of Congress Cataloging-in-Publication Data

Underwood, James D.
Thriving in e-chaos : discover the secrets of 20 companies that have conquered a turbulent marketplace / James D. Underwood.
p. cm.
Includes bibliographical references and index.
ISBN 0-7615-3117-3
1. Leadership. 2. Organizational learning. 3. Electronic commerce—Management. 4. Success in business. I. Title.
HD 57.7.U53 2001
658—dc21 2001018522

01 02 03 04 05 06 HH 10 9 8 7 6 5 4 3 2 1
Printed in the United States of America

How to Order

Single copies may be ordered from Prima Publishing, 3000 Lava Ridge Court, Roseville, CA 95661; telephone (800) 632-8676. Quantity discounts are also available. On your letterhead, include information concerning the intended use of the books and the number of copies you wish to purchase.

Visit us online at www.primalifestyles.com

CONTENTS

ACKNOWLEDGMENTS

From the beginning, and throughout the process of writing *Thriving in E-Chaos,* my agent, John Willig, has been a partner in this work. I have truly appreciated his insight and wisdom throughout this endeavor.

I want to thank the staff at Prima Publishing for their commitment to excellence. First and foremost must be David Richardson, my editor. He graciously endured my questions (as well as an occasional practical joke at his expense) and the challenges of taking my manuscript and making it better. Andrew Vallas has been a charm to work with as we edited the book. Hilary Powers, the copy editor, can only be described with one word: genius. Her help with crafting the theme and the various nuances of the book enhanced the final product immeasurably.

There have been a lot of people who gave me access in the writing of this book. There were a number of executives who really went out of their way to provide some of their own personal insights into organizational success. I was impressed with their warmth and openness as I worked with them. I am sure that those are two of the characteristics that have made them successful executives.

A foundation is important for any work of this type. I am grateful for the work done by Dr. H. Igor Ansoff's students over the years in over 1,000 research studies. I also owe a debt of gratitude to the 100 or so executives of Fortune 500 companies that have allowed my graduate students from Dallas Baptist University to complete strategy studies for their firms. I have also been blessed by some exceptional students that carried out those studies.

I am truly grateful for a loving God, who encouraged me in times of discouragement. I cannot fail to mention Patsy, my wife, who has never failed to support the writing of this book. Lastly, who can write a book without the constant reassuring visits from the likes of Harvey (the Golden Retriever), Becky (the Golden Retriever), Boo (the Sealyham Terrier), Tuffy (the Sealyham Terrier), and of course Moses (the cat)?

INTRODUCTION

THE PAST TWENTY YEARS HAVE INVOLVED NUMEROUS CHALLENGES for the managers of global enterprises. The dominance of Japanese companies was prevalent in the 1980s. In the 1990s, the emergence of the Internet, the digital revolution, and the development of wireless communication caused the technological explosion that changed the world. The cooling of the e-revolution of the early 2000s has likewise had challenges of its own.

The lessons learned from the last two decades of the 20th century are many. One of these lessons is not that "change is the only constant," but rather that the new technology-driven world will be one of unpredictable rates of change, as well as continual cycles of complexity variations. Another lesson learned is that the use of historic distinctive competencies as a basis for projecting the future of the firm is quite suspect. In fact, the issue for organizations has ceased to be "What do we do well?" and has become "What do we need to become to maximize 'return on investment' tomorrow?"

As a number of people have pointed out, the management theories of the last hundred years that were based upon the equilibrium theory of economics no longer work. Thus the idea of the competitive world as a complex, dynamic system has begun to creep into the minds of many leading thinkers.

Paradigms, or how managers think about or perceive their world, have everything to do with corporate success. Those who understand that they are managing in a sea of varying rates of change and complexity tend to do substantially better than those who do not. Additionally, managers who take a "complex dynamic view" of the world, often also take a "complex adaptive system" view of the firm. That means that they understand that each aspect of the firm must be in balance with the emerging external environment if the firm is to be successful in the future.

While this approach is rarely taught in academic settings, it is alive and well in the companies that are thriving in the new economy. These are companies that seem to adapt to economic downturns with a plan for accomplishing exceptional goals, and not just surviving. They are also firms that are led by executives who value organizational learning and, most important, value their people.

This book is about one simple idea: It is possible to choose to be one of those exceptional companies. It is not a matter of luck or economic happenstance; it is a decision to stay on the leading edge of learning and to purposefully drive transformation into the firm on a continual basis. It is not about a seminar or a staff retreat. It is about changing the way that a company thinks and acts.

I have been privileged to observe some of these companies and their executives in action. I have learned that people want to work at such companies. More than that, these companies are winners. That's what is exciting for me to see.

What I hope to provide in this book is two-fold: First, I want to offer a new way of thinking about competitive environments and the challenges that organizations will face in the future. Second, I want to provide a logical, understandable way of creating organizational strategies that will lead to long-term success.

CHAPTER 1

STRATEGIC BALANCE

A LOT OF PEOPLE OFTEN TURN TO THE LAST CHAPTER OF A book to find out how it ends. To save you that effort, here it is, in summary form:

The End

- The e-chaos of the new economy is changing the rules of the game.
- What has worked in the past will no longer work in the future.
- Sustained success in the 21st century will belong to those firms that:

  Have leaders obsessed with the future, committed to organizational learning, and able to continually transform organizations.

Understand the critical role of the CEO in organizational success.

Base their philosophy of management and strategy on complex reality and avoid simplistic approaches.

Understand the critical importance of balancing organization with environment.

- It is possible to design an organization that will consistently out-perform competitors.

That's it. Success is not about trying to copy successful companies. It is about learning how to develop an organization that will maximize profit by adopting a profile that maximizes performance in the competitive environment.

If managers are going to understand how to change the future prospects for their companies, most will have to change the way they think about management and strategy. E-chaos is the reality of the new competitive world. Further, e-chaos is global. Managers can choose to move their organizations toward sustainable profitability, or they can choose the status quo. Effective performance enhancement begins with changing almost every traditional concept about management. Those who are able to make the change will set new standards of performance and growth for their organizations.

Each year thousands of business books hit the shelves. In essence, each one proposes that it offers the perfect solution to business success. Nonetheless, other than their authors, few believe that the solution for business success has yet been discovered. So business practitioners are left to continue their search for a way of leading a business to success. In the end, those who search for a single solution will always be disappointed, for the real profit solution for organizations is a balance of attributes. I call this blending of profit-critical solutions to fit the competitive environment *strategic balance.*

Numerous companies score well using one of the scorecard or best practices approaches but are not doing well. That is because they fail to have appropriate strategic balance for their competitive environment. Having great quality is not enough. Being a great marketer or having a strong brand is not enough. Building a wonderful culture or having a great CEO is simply not enough. Companies that win in the new economy and companies that will thrive beyond the new economy will be those that possess strategic balance.

A BROAD VIEW OF SUCCESS

Success is never simple. Nonetheless, businesses that enjoy long-term success seem to follow a fairly understandable approach. This means it is important to understand two things: successful managers' view of management, and what behaviors successful managers drive into their organizations.

From a practical standpoint, those who create organizations that enjoy long-term success reject the traditional view of management. They depart from the traditional planning-organizing-leading-controlling view and adopt one of learning-transformation-performance. The first definition has no provision for the future. The second is based on the future. The first is simplistic. The second is about complexity, about fitting the organization to the future emerging environment. Almost all the senior executives interviewed for this book made a comment that boiled down to this: "Learn to profit from the future."

Besides taking a different view of their jobs, successful managers focus on driving behaviors in the company that differ sharply from the ones their less successful counterparts promote. Rather than obedience and unquestioning loyalty, successful managers want to see widespread leadership, learning, and agility. These three broad areas of organizational behavior translate readily into long-term performance.

The first attribute of businesses that enjoy long-term success is that of *leadership*. Leaders of successful companies tend to be driven toward excellence, while understanding that organizations must be dynamic, just like their environments. They understand the need to constantly focus on the future and foster an internal environment that has a healthy balance of creativity and risk-taking.

The second attribute of companies that enjoy long-term success is *learning*. From top to bottom, the company team is all about learning. At companies like Southwest Airlines, for example, one of the rules is "there are no bad ideas." People there understand that their future depends on their ability to gather information as an organizational family and then translate that learning into knowledge. Learning becomes knowledge and knowledge becomes profit through transformation. Organizations that learn well are those that understand when (and why) to move from familiar products into uncharted territory. Organizations that learn well are those that are willing to go anywhere knowledge leads them in order to maximize profit.

The third attribute of successful organizations is *agility*, both proactive and reactive. Successful firms are those that can both seize opportunities offered by unexpected events and minimize the damage caused by such events. Successful firms live with a commitment to continually be the first mover in their chosen arena.

These three attributes—leadership, learning, and agility—are the building blocks of what I call the "Triad of Success."

It takes all three. Further, the three must be in balance if the organization is to change in harmony with the emerging environment. Figure 1.1 portrays each of the three attributes of the triad, and shows how the triad is the driver for the processes of strategy, organizational transformation, and performance.

It is useful to notice the internal relationships created in successful organizations by the synergistic effect of the attributes of the triad. Leadership fosters learning that drives the firm to

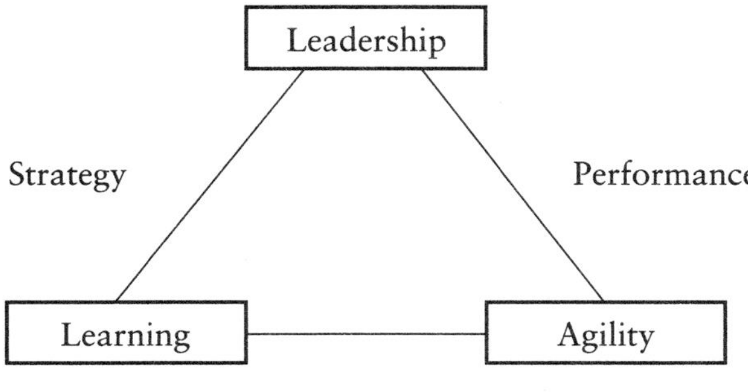

FIGURE 1.1. The Triad of Success.

highly profitable strategy and management of the firm's assets. Learning fostered by effective leadership becomes knowledge, which provides a continual understanding of what the firm must become (transformation). Finally, the ability to move proactively and reactively based on knowledge allows the firm to be first in transforming itself into what it must become. It also allows the firm to respond to environmental discontinuities effectively. The key point here is that is something that companies can *choose* to do. Companies can (and should) choose to have the proper strategic balance. Companies that manage that reap some important benefits:

- Companies with strategic balance tend to enjoy long-term success.
- Companies with strategic balance have enthusiastic workforces—people love to work there.
- Companies with strategic balance understand exactly what they are doing and why.
- Companies with strategic balance typically have ROIs (returns on investment) of 100 percent higher than firms that do not proactively manage their strategic balance.

EVER WONDER WHY?

There is more to the triad than meets the eye. Did you ever wonder why some companies seem to be excellent for a while, then mysteriously drop off the radarscope? How is it that supposedly excellent companies are featured in one year's bestselling management books as "best in class" only to emerge as companies in serious trouble a few months or years later?

The answer to that question is "the environment." The organization failed to account for environmental changes and its once-best-in-class practices were not suited for the new environment. That is why those who define management as learning-transformation-performance have an edge over everyone else. They understand the urgency of creating a learning organization, as well as that of fostering effective transformation. Simply put, that is a philosophical foundation for success. Managers who view their job in that manner create companies that practice the Triad of Success. Companies that continually apply the triad are companies that achieve long-term sustained profitability and growth.

Therefore, the objective of organizational learning is to create an organization that fits the environment into which it is moving. In other words, the objective is to balance all aspects of the organization with its environment. This is called strategic balance. That is why some best-in-class companies dropped off the radarscope. They did not have the leadership, the organizational learning, and the agility to allow them to find the future first. Their strategic imbalance thus cost them dearly.

THE BEGINNINGS OF THE NEW ECONOMY

In the late 1980s and early 1990s, evidence of the emergence of a new and quite different world began to appear. During the 1991 presidential campaign, President Bush declared that a new explosion of the economy had already begun. The American people did not believe George Bush. Many had experienced job losses due to the massive downsizing initiatives conducted by American companies as a result of Japan's new prominence in global commerce. As often happens, the American people voted their pocketbook and changed presidents.

Consider the changes that occurred under the last three U.S. presidents. It is interesting to look at the changing environment through the eyes of a typical computer user:

> In the early 1980s, you finally bought one of those Apple computers so you could do spreadsheets on a program called Visicalc.
>
> In the mid-1980s you were introduced to a new type of machine that used a different type of protocol called "DOS." It even had a monstrous storage capability of 20 megabytes.
>
> In the early 1990s you bought a machine that featured a new concept called "Windows" by a company called Microsoft. Now you had a 100-megabyte hard drive.
>
> By the mid-1990s, you found out about something called the Internet and decided to get an account with an Internet Service Provider (ISP). By then, your storage had exploded to 500 megabytes.
>
> By 2000, your computer was a virtual rocket ship, but it was becoming obsolete every six months as even faster computers appeared. You'd been rating storage in terms of gigabytes for the last two or three years. Further, your Internet connection was working at near the speed of light... and it was looking likely that connections would reach the speed of light in the near future. (In 1999 a company called Media Fusion was already talking about doing just that.)

It turns out that George Bush was right. Most economists maintain that the introduction of a "new economic boom" began around 1988 or 1989. What most people (including George Bush) did not understand is just how massive and rapid the impact of these economic changes on the global economy would be. Perhaps even more astounding is what happened to the nature of life itself in the years from 1990 to 2000. During that 10-year period, the complexity as well as the pace of life accelerated drastically.

At the beginning of the decade, getting an urgent proposal to a client from Los Angeles to New York was expensive and took at least 24 hours. At the end of the decade, that same proposal could be electronically transferred for free in a matter of minutes. At the beginning of the decade, foreign competitors used traditional espionage approaches to steal U.S. companies' secrets. By the end of the decade, they could achieve their goals by penetrating the competitor's computer from the other side of the world.

As the decade began, a start-up company would expect to take decades to reach the Fortune 1000. By the end of the decade, companies were reaching the Fortune 1000 in a few short years. At the same time, companies were finding that accelerating change and complexity were making it difficult to maintain profitability. One of those companies was the Boeing Company of Seattle, Washington.

During the mid-1990s, Boeing encountered numerous problems involving a multitude of internal and external issues. It is important to understand the history of Boeing in order to understand just how unbelievable the problems became.

Boeing got its start as an aircraft pioneer when the industry was quite young. Over the years, Boeing had become what a lot of pilots called the Cadillac of commercial aircraft. Each decade from 1950 on involved the introduction of at least one more commercial aircraft winner. Boeing stayed ahead of the global competition by building the highest-quality, most innovative products in its industry.

In the 1990s, Boeing's global leadership began to decline. Europe's Airbus began to make significant inroads into the U.S.

market. By 2000, Airbus had become a major player in the global commercial aircraft market by beating Boeing in a number of competitive battles.

Boeing's inability to effectively reduce internal costs and its inability to anticipate global challenges were the major contributors to Boeing's problems. When the European Common Market introduced new requirements for aircraft design, Boeing suffered from its failure to anticipate design changes needed to comply with the new regulations.

The meltdown of the Japanese banking system had been the focus of numerous articles and books in the United States throughout the 1990s. A number of companies, armed with the knowledge of the impending disaster, took action to avoid being caught by it. After years of stories about Japan's banking problems, in the mid-1990s it became apparent to the world that if Japan's banks were operating under U.S. regulations, many would be insolvent. In spite of all the warnings, Boeing suffered badly in the economic recession that hit the Japanese economy in the 1990s.

The casual observer might ask about how such a thing can happen. How can a world-class company like Boeing fall victim to so many almost catastrophic events in such a short time? The answer lies in two places: Boeing's external environment and in Boeing itself. Boeing's new chairman and CEO seems to agree: "We're in a different world," he says.[1]

THE NEW ECONOMY: FAST WINNERS AND FAST LOSERS

Pilots understand the problems related to changing from one aircraft to another. A small training aircraft usually operates at a slow airspeed and is quite forgiving of minor mistakes. When one moves up to a heavier propeller aircraft, the rules begin to change. Approach speeds for landing are faster and the aircraft sinks faster, so the pilot must begin to think ahead of the airplane and anticipate corrections or changes much earlier. When the pilot moves to a large commercial aircraft such as a Boeing 767, the speeds and other flight characteristics change again. The same is true when the pilot moves to a supersonic fighter. Each change involves a change in the rules of the game.

In the same way, the rules of the game of the new economy are substantially different from what they were just a decade ago. In fact, they have changed substantially in the last five years. Just like pilots who move from single-engine training aircraft to supersonic fighters, the managers of companies beyond the year 2000 must learn absolutely new rules of the game.

To understand the new game, it is first necessary to understand the drivers of changes in the rules. That is best grasped by way of what I regard as the 10 basic forces of business life.

The 10 Forces

1. Economic
2. Ideological
3. Government and Political
4. Legal
5. Media
6. Psychological and Sociological
7. Moral
8. Environmental
9. Technology
10. Market (competitive)

In looking at the problems of Boeing, it is possible to quickly recognize three of the ten forces that had a significant impact on the firm: government, economic, and market. It isn't enough to stop with the list, though—the information becomes useful as you assess the manner in which the 10 forces interact to create a compounded effect on business.

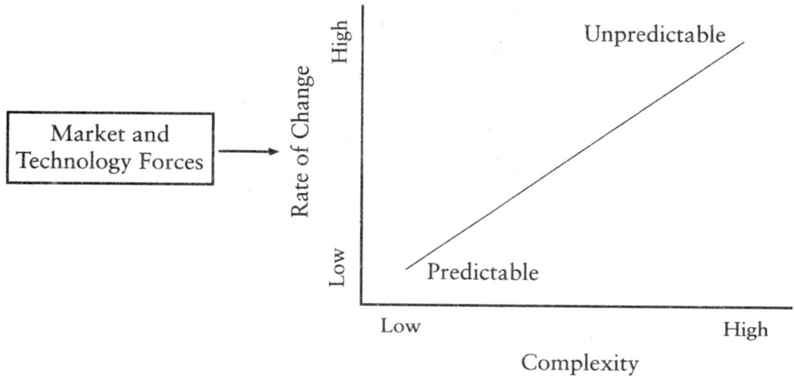

FIGURE 1.2. The Interaction of the 10 Forces in Accelerating Change and Complexity.

Business managers are dealing with two major dynamics in the competitive environment: *complexity* and *rate of change.* Both have an impact on the effectiveness of management planning and decisions. A second perspective on the 10 forces helps explain these two dynamics better. Figure 1.2 portrays the forces that drive rate of change on one axis, and the forces that drive complexity on the other. Although it is possible for either set of forces to accelerate faster than the other, generally they tend to change equally as shown in the figure.

The figure reveals the underlying reasons behind much of the frame-breaking change that characterizes the new economy.[2] As long as the rate of change (driven by technology and market forces) is slow to moderately slow and the complexity (driven by the other eight forces) is low to moderately low, the combined result is still an environment characterized by incremental change. Incremental change is unlikely to require fast, complex responses on the part of the organization.

At the same time, as the rate of change and complexity pass the moderate level, the organization is dealing with two extremely negative combinations. First, the rate of change exceeds the normal rate of change that is comfortable for the organization. Second, the complexity of the issues is such that it may be overwhelming to the organization (as with Boeing) because both the speed of challenges and the number of challenges have exponentially changed.

Ralph Stacey, in his book *Managing the Unknowable,* suggests that the environment may become so chaotic that a manager is unable to mentally process information about the environment due to its speed and complexity. He calls this "bounded rationality."[3] He goes on to suggest that companies that do well in chaos are not those that manage the future (with strategy), but rather are those that simply respond to the environment as events occur.

CYCLES OF CHANGE, LOSERS, AND WINNERS

In business environments where the 10 forces interact such that moderate to high levels of complexity and rates of change are created, a phenomenon that some writers call "frame-breaking change" occurs. A look at the past century will show why frame-breaking change has become such an important issue for business managers.

In 1900, technology diffusion (penetration) into the world was fairly slow. Each decade through 1970 experienced an increasing rate of technological diffusion. By 1970, however, technology began to diffuse at much higher rates each decade (see Figure 1.3). By the 1990s, the diffusion rates exploded. That trend is not expected to reverse itself—or even taper off—in the 21st century.

The Diffusion of Technology Changes

As many observers have noted, the 1950s brought in a time during which each decade involved a major cycle of change. By the 1990s, the cycles of change had shortened considerably, and

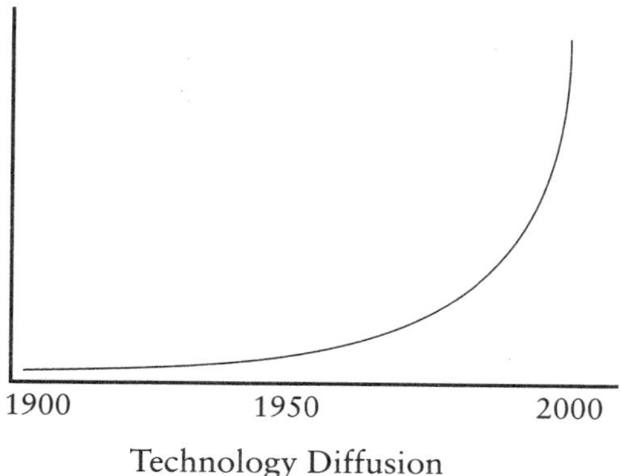

FIGURE 1.3. The Increasing Rate of Technology Diffusion: 1900–2000.

business leaders found themselves challenged by frequent discontinuous changes in their competitive environment.

I like to use "the tsunami effect" to describe the results of rapid change and increasing complexity in business life. Those familiar with other parts of the world understand the tsunami, a giant wave generated far from shore by an undersea earthquake. By the time it reaches the coast, it is a wall of water that seems to appear out of nowhere with no warning, wiping out entire villages before anyone can escape.

The business-life tsunami effect is much the same. As the complexity forces (eight of the basic forces) change, and the other two (market and technology forces) accelerate the rate of change in the environment, the result is an unexpected tsunami of change. These massive, rapid change events, seemingly out of nowhere, may inflict serious damage on global competitors. The emergence of the new economy has signaled the introduction of the tsunami effect.

Once companies get past the terror of the tsunami effect, they are left with another reality: As the competitive environment grows more and more turbulent, it becomes increasingly difficult to achieve or maintain profitability.

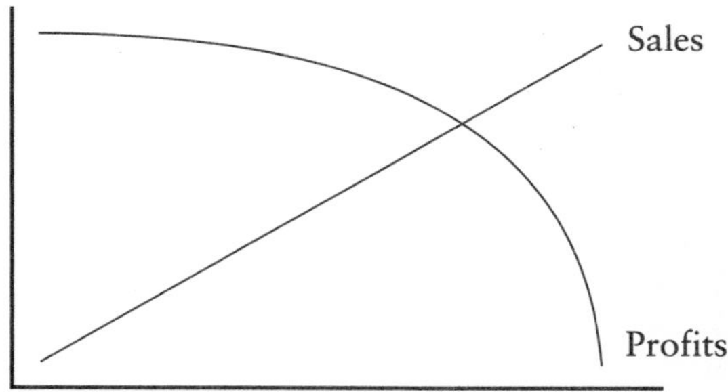

FIGURE 1.4. New Results in the New Economy.

Figure 1.4 conveys the reality of the new economic world. Historically, as sales increased profits usually kept pace. In the new economy, sales may well go up while profits go down. Things just do not work the same way in a rapidly changing environment.

When a tsunami event occurs, historical relationships deteriorate. For example, a company's sales may be related to population growth, but when a tsunami event occurs, the revenue trend may continue but the rapid change in the rules of the game may mean that profitability takes a nosedive.

Even the casual observer can spot companies that have suffered from a tsunami event. Those same observers can also see that there are companies that seem to encounter the same tsunami event and do quite well. What is the difference between companies that struggle or die in successive cycles of change and those that do well?

Losers

Losers tend to be characterized by three behaviors. First, they almost always have leadership problems. Here is the contradiction of leadership: The skills that get a leader to the top (operating skills and political skills) are not the ones required for

CEO success. In fact, a CEO who focuses on operating issues and internal political success is a disaster waiting to happen.

Second, losers don't learn well. Losers are the last to perceive impending change in their environment. They tend to think of change as bad for the organization. (There is research to support this contention, since change disrupts the organization. At the same time, change is the way in which the organization takes advantage of profit opportunities.) Losers value internal organizational knowledge more than external knowledge. In most cases, losers tend to think that fads (the latest and greatest management book) will save them. Losers are organizations that seem to chase at least one major fad each year. After years of total quality management (TQM), process reengineering, downsizing, getting back to basics, open book management, and lean thinking, losers are worse off than before they started chasing the fads.

Despite these sweeping assertions, I'm not actually slamming all the research done over the past 25 years. Although the management tools listed here can be treated as fads—and often are, to the cost of those who misuse them in that fashion—they each have an important place in organizational performance. Quality (TQM) is the table stakes if a firm is to even be able to get into the game of competition. Process reengineering is a phenomenal tool for understanding and changing cycle times. It's just that any one of these tools by itself is not effective in dealing with the complex challenges of a turbulent environment. (Chapter Ten returns to these tools in more detail to show how they can be used and misused in the pursuit of success.)

The third characteristic of losers is that they have no agility. They are neither proactive enough to achieve first-mover advantage on a new product nor reactive enough to respond effectively to the surprises or discontinuities characteristic of turbulent environments.

One company that was able to understand its past mistakes and take drastic action to change itself is IBM Corporation.

Certainly the hiring of Lois V. Gerstner Jr. as CEO marked a turning point in the company's history.

Winners

Some firms seem to withstand the effects of the tsunamis they encounter. When analyzed, these firms turn out to operate much like successful symphony orchestras. They seem to be on the same page as an organization, even though the page frequently turns. While they appear to have clear, charismatic direction, at the same time they are characterized by an internally generated life created by leading-edge knowledge. How are those firms different from the losers? The Triad of Success, discussed at the beginning of this chapter, captures the essence of the differences between winners and losers. Figure 1.5 shows the Triad of Success adjusted to reflect organizational strategic balance as well as the enhanced role of technology in the new economy. When the Triad of Success is reframed in the context of the new economy, there is an unavoidable reality that technology now affects everything. From brick-and-mortar to click-and-mortar companies, technology will have a continuing impact. Technology has an impact on leadership, learning, and transformation. It is about speed. As a result, it has a major role in relation to the environment, and to an organization's ability to achieve and maintain strategic balance.

The organization that does well in any environment, but especially well in a turbulent or tsunami-like environment, is one that holds onto the Triad of Success. It is important to realize that success cannot be achieved by excellence in just one area. A great leader, absent organizational learning or agility, will not be successful. The triad is like a three-legged stool. Without all three legs, it cannot stand.

Leadership is the first leg. The CEO is responsible for leadership. How the CEO spends the day is of primary importance. As I noted earlier, leaders destined to be unsuccessful spend their

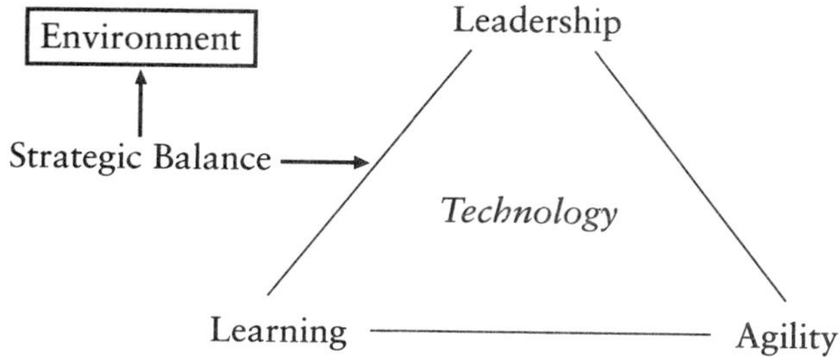

FIGURE 1.5. The Triad of Success Revisited.

time on operational issues and internal politics. It makes a kind of sense to do that, because in most cases it's what got them to the top. That is, they were excellent at negotiating internal political minefields and were great at achieving operating results.

In their 1995 article in *Harvard Business Review,* Sumantra Ghoshal and Christopher Bartlett reveal one of the key ideas behind leadership that produces adaptive organizations:

> *Perhaps the most widespread and deleterious effect of the growth of bureaucratic structures in corporations has been the erosion of management entrepreneurship—the externally oriented, opportunity-seeking attitude that motivates employees to run their operations as if they owned them.*[4]

When a manager assumes the role of CEO, day-to-day behavior must drastically change. There are three major jobs that CEOs must accomplish on an ongoing basis.

1. They must demand that the organization excel in learning about and responding to future challenges and opportunities. They must insist that the organization is a dynamic learning organization. They must be the CIO, the Chief Innovation Officer of the organization.
2. They must be adept in understanding and communicating the importance of empowerment, creativity, and

risk-taking in the organization. They are the only force in the organization that can ensure that subordinate managers are accountable for supporting the behaviors that create dynamic, renewing organizations. They must become the CEO, that is, the Chief Entrepreneurship Officer.

3. They must set the standard as excellence. A leader understands that performance is driven by an expectation of excellence. That is, they must become yet another CEO, the Chief Excellence Officer.

This may seem to be contradictory in some ways. How can a CEO be simultaneously directive and empowering when it comes to people?

When Les Carter and I wrote *The Significance Principle,* we analyzed a lot of writings related to motivation and human behavior. The underlying idea of all of those writings was that if managers want high levels of performance and creativity from individuals, they must learn how to communicate their value and appreciation for those individuals. At the same time, they must establish extremely clear boundaries for excellence and creativity.

Recently, the idea of "self-organizing companies" has become popular in the business literature. The concept is based on Darwinian evolution and states that companies left to self-organize will out-perform those with strong leaders. I have two responses to that idea.

First, there is no substantive body of evidence to support any links between self-organizing behavior and performance. Second, it is quite apparent that the most dynamic, growing companies in the world are characterized by visionary leadership. That is, they have leaders who are both obsessed with excellence and determined to find the future before the competition. Additionally, they manage their organizations to achieve those objectives. Certainly, the reality of those companies contradicts the ideas that underlie the assumptions related to self-organizing companies.

It turns out that leadership is the first and possibly the most important aspect of success. Successful CEOs often characterize themselves as being "paranoid" or obsessed. Bill Gates, founder of Microsoft, put it best: "I spend every waking moment worrying about the next Bill Gates out there."

Leaders who sustain organizations are simultaneously structured and directive, while at the same time they excel in the people side of the equation. They understand that when the structure of learning and being first mover is combined with the recognition of the value of each contributor, great things can happen to an organization.

Learning is the second major contributor to success in organizations. Learning involves understanding the future. It has to do with anticipating not only competitor moves but also shifts in the 10 forces.

As organizations encounter a tsunami event, it is their ability to learn that directly relates to their ability to respond. As organizations encounter data or signals from the environment, the first challenge is to get the data into the organization for analysis. At that point, the data becomes knowledge. Knowledge has little value unless it is attached to power. Absent power (usually the power associated with the senior executive level) the knowledge rarely leads to action.

Learning is what defines what the organization must become. Often there is talk about the organization's core competencies or competitive advantage. What a company does well or has done well in the past is irrelevant. What is critically important is what the company needs to do well in the future. The process of asking that question and translating the answer into action may be the most critical of all processes for a company.

Agility is the third critical aspect of the triad. There are two types of agility: proactive and reactive. Both are important. Proactive agility may also involve a number of areas of the firm. For example, the structure of the firm has a lot to do with the flexibility and thus the speed with which it can operate. The proactive agility of the firm may be revealed in the marketing area and the ability to be the consistent first mover in highly turbulent environments. Proactive agility also affects organizational learning. Firms that proactively focus on over-the-horizon issues have significantly more time to deal with potential problems than do firms that simply react to things happening at the present moment.

Unavoidably, tsunami events will create situations or crises that the organization could not anticipate or predict. That is where (and when) the reactive ability of the firm is critical. Since turbulent environments create unpredictable events by their very nature, a company need not wonder whether it will have to deal with such events. The only issue is reactive agility, or recovery time.

Two things happen to organizations with low reactive agility or recovery time. The chart in Figure 1.6 describes the impact of agility on profit. First, the magnitude of the dollar cost of the event is significantly higher for the sluggish firm than for the highly reactive one. Second, the length of time that the event costs the sluggish company money is extended.

Again, it is important to observe that companies with excellent proactive abilities anticipate future change and profit opportunities. They are consistent first movers. Those with high levels of reactive agility minimize the impact of surprises by minimizing the time it takes before they can implement a response and correction.

Firms with high reactive agility usually limit internal political traps (or the blame game) when discontinuous events occur. Instead, they focus the power of the organization on problem resolution. Low-reactive-agility organizations will often politicize a discontinuous event to the point that they may take months (in some cases years) to begin to take action. Often, there is a tendency to scapegoat the event, that is, to place

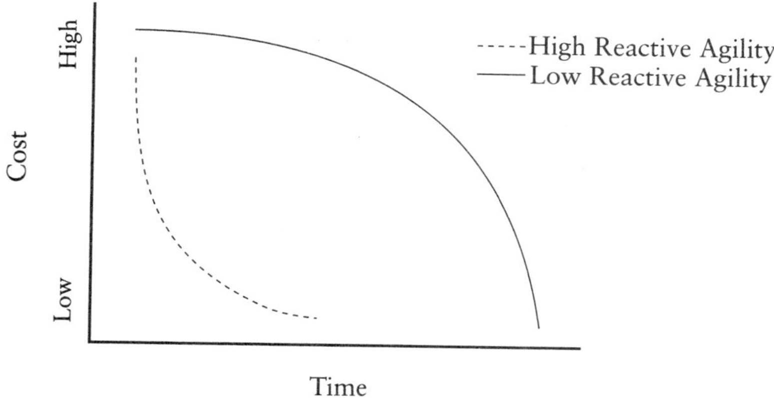

FIGURE 1.6. Agility and Profit.

blame on factors other than the root-cause event. In fact, it is the scapegoating of events that often leads to the application of fads such as so-called rightsizing as a solution. Obviously, if the firm has a learning problem, which then leads to a marketing (product) problem, no amount of downsizing will resolve the problem.

Ultimately, the Triad of Success must be seen as a system. Leadership alone cannot drive an organization. Learning cannot be effective, or even occur, unless the power associated with the senior leadership position is behind the learning. Agility cannot exist without both learning and executive drive to support it. That is why managers often fail. They focus on operational issues as the root cause and fail to understand that organizational success depends on their own ability to create an agile learning organization.

THE TRIAD: A SYSTEMS VIEW

Leaders of companies that produce long-term success usually have a strong ability to *contextualize,* that is, to understand the emerging future environment and how to put their company

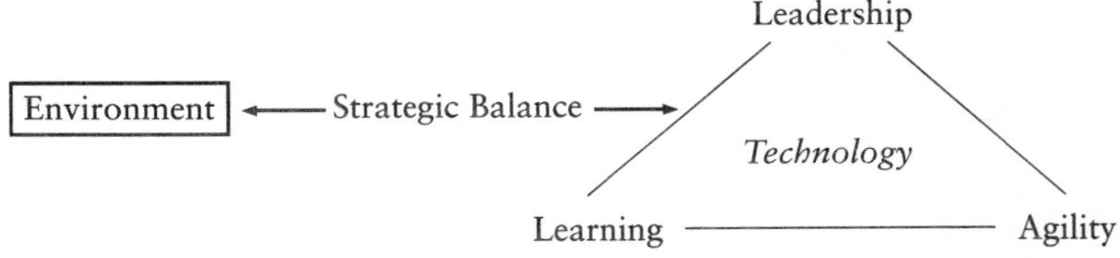

FIGURE 1.7. Understanding Strategic Balance in the Triad of Success.

into the context of that environment. Another phrase for this process is "strategic balance." In other words, exceptional managers understand how to create strategic balance between their organization and its competitive environment. These same managers tend to have entirely different views of management than do their lower-performing counterparts. Successful managers in the 21st century are different in another way. They understand the role that technology will play in the future, regardless of the industries in which the firm is competing. Figure 1.7 reveals the key issues managers must deal with, both inside the firm and out.

During the 1960s, the basic makeup of the triad began to change. Of the basic forces, technology began to significantly change the rules of the game. At first, the changes were slow. By the early 1990s, however, technology-driven change was extremely fast. For that reason, the triad must now include technology as its center. While technology is often transparent in the process, it is playing an increasingly important role in the global marketplace.

The rate and complexity of change went through a major shift in the early 1990s. The result of that shift is that the rules of the game are now changing frequently. That means that an organization's rules of engagement (including operations) must change each time the environmental rules of the game change. Thus, the organization is forced to take its strategy from the environment. As change accelerates and becomes more complex, the firm's leadership must change their role to that of leading complex organizational change.

TECHNOLOGY: A COMPLEX PERSPECTIVE

It is important to understand that technology has become the key driver among the forces when it comes to business management. On one hand, technology is often a part of the product. That means that technology must be applied creatively in the development of products. On the other, technology is an enabler.

Also, technology enables a company to respond faster and with more efficiency. On one hand, technology is involved with the learning aspects of the triad. On the other, it is involved in the agility aspects of the triad. Simply put: Technology can play a major role in every aspect of the organization.

STRATEGIC BALANCE

Nothing is ever simple. That is true of the Triad of Success as well, for while it may be synthesized into three broad areas, in actuality it is composed of a number of key attributes. It is the successful balancing of these attributes with the competitive environment that provides the company the opportunity to do well. Strategic balance, therefore, is the process of successfully managing the attributes that make up the triad (see Figure 1.8).

Throughout this book, interviews with executives of companies that will do well in the new millennium are featured. All these companies featured are excellent at maintaining their strategic balance. It is important to note how each firm is balanced not only in its relationship with the competitive environment but in its internal structure and operations. Each of the 12 factors that make up the triad is equally valued by the firms. Notice also the critical role that technology plays in both the learning and the competitive agility of the firm.

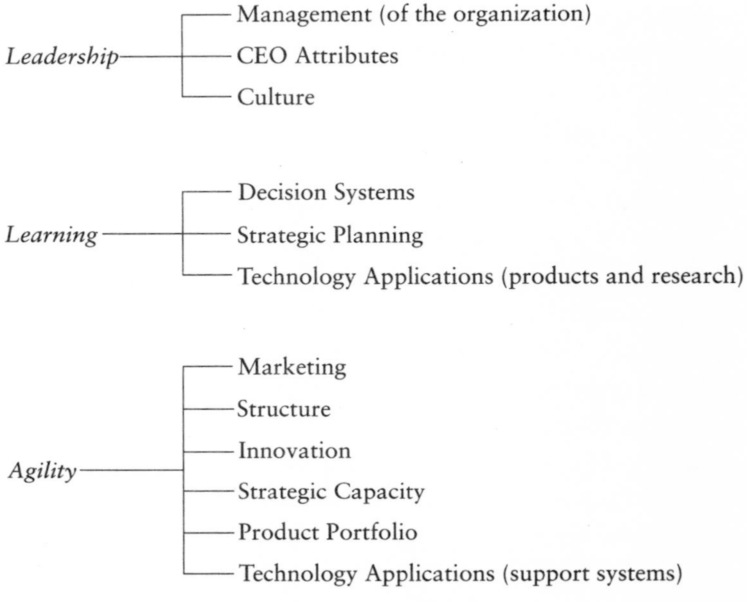

FIGURE 1.8. The Triad of Success Revealed in the Organization.

GE: A TRIAD ORGANIZATION

When Jack Welch took over General Electric in 1981, it was an old-line company that had continued to enjoy growth. Once Welch arrived, he began to radically change the company. He realized that the global environment had become extremely competitive and that the command-and-control system that most companies—including GE—used just no longer worked.[5]

Jack Welch would be the last to adopt an ecological view of an organization. As he puts it, he is a "kick rear and hug" kind of manager. He created a meritocracy, one that rewards people who discover and create the future. Each year every person in the corporation is evaluated and ranked. The lowest 10 percent, he suggests, are counseled to look for jobs at other companies.

Welch brought an obsession for organizational learning to the company. That has been most obvious in his preoccupation with the firm's product portfolio. When he joined the firm, he sold off a lot of companies. He called them "yesterday's businesses." That is a very telling comment about Jack Welch. It reveals his continual focus on the future and on organizational learning (which results in new, high-growth product opportunities).

Another observation about Jack Welch's preoccupation with learning is revealed in the diversity of the firm's holdings under his leadership. GE has holdings that include everything from high-tech companies to a major television network. He is relatively unconcerned with what the firm used to do and is most concerned about leading the firm into industries that have high future growth and future profit opportunities. It is obvious that Welch cares little about the firm's core competencies; he focuses on the profit opportunities discovered by organizational learning.

Jack Welch's insistence on excellent performance fosters organizational agility. By rewarding people for discovering and taking advantage of opportunity, the firm is able to consistently be the first mover among competitors.

In the late 1990s, Welch concluded that if GE were to go digital, it could own the future. He directed that all of GE's 350,000 employees begin moving their business onto the electronic highways of the world. As a result, GE is now doing much of its business on the World Wide Web. The result is a faster, more efficient, more competitive organization.

Jack Welch provides the umbrella of leadership that creates a learning organization. He also makes sure that the firm is agile, that it is quick to respond to discontinuities and fast enough to be first mover on opportunity. He has a highly developed skill to keep the balance between organization and environment. Additionally, he has insisted that the firm adapt technology in both internal and external product areas. He has truly created a company that exemplifies the Triad of Success.

Is it any wonder that a $10,000 investment in GE when Welch took over in 1981 is now worth over $750,000?

CONCLUSION

Companies that achieve and maintain strategic balance are successful. The balance that effective leaders create between external environment and the firm results in substantial profit opportunity for the firm. The leaders provide the thrust to continually discover the future. At the same time, they provide the umbrella of power to support creativity and risk-taking. Learning creates knowledge that can be turned into performance. Agility enables the organization to preemptively move to obtain first-mover advantage, as well as the ability to minimize costs related to unexpected events.

Some companies seem to think that technology will provide a magic bullet for success, but others understand how to blend their organizations into the increasing levels of e-chaos of the 21st century. It is those companies that will achieve long-term success.

Organizations that continue to thrive over time are those that achieve this strategic balance. They attract the brightest and most creative people to work for them, because they are organizations that take pride in affirming the value of people who discover the future. In reality there is no such thing as a competitive advantage. There is, however, a group of companies that are entering this millennium with the brightest of futures. These are the companies that will thrive beyond the new economy. The reason? They are constantly involved in the dynamic process of becoming what the future demands. They understand that the sizzle of the wired world may sell for a while, but in the end the company that figures out how to blend excellent business principles with leading-edge technology is the one that will achieve long-term, sustainable performance and growth.

The companies featured in this book generally fit the Triad of Success. They are different from most companies. Not only are they run differently, they have the ability to make people want to work for them. But there is more than that. Most of the companies featured are growing rapidly. In many cases, they are doubling in size every five years. They are enjoying much higher profits than do their competitors. They are different because their leaders have an entirely different view of how companies create long-term value growth.

CHAPTER 2

THE LADDER OF PERFORMANCE

THE IDEA OF CREATING SIGNIFICANTLY MORE PROFITABLE companies is exciting, but it's not all that obvious how to put it into practice. Just exactly how is it possible to create a company that will consistently out-perform its competitors? When expanded, the principles presented in the first chapter answer that question. Figure 2.1 provides a useful snapshot of the concept: *Strategic balance,* that is, creating a maximum profit profile for the firm, involves adjusting the firm to suit the environment.

The emerging environment is complex—and growing increasingly fast-moving and still more complex—in the

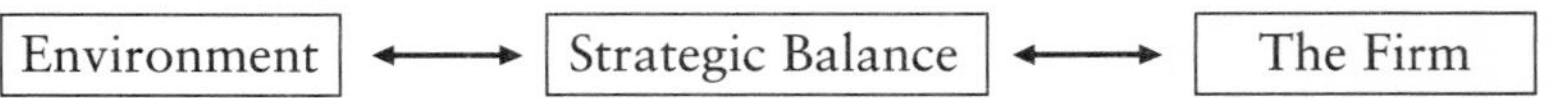

FIGURE 2.1. Maximizing Profit with Strategic Balance.

e-chaos of the 21st century. If a firm is to match itself with the environment, each aspect of the organization must match. In essence, that means that sales, advertising, public relations, management, and the other controllable aspects of the firm must each be carefully designed to mirror the speed and complexity of the environment. As illustrated back in Figure 1.8, 12 broad areas of a firm must be considered if strategic balance is to be achieved: management of the organization, attributes and skills of the CEO, culture, decision systems, strategic planning, applications of technology to products and research, marketing systems, organizational structure, innovation, strategic capacity, product portfolio, and applications of technology to internal support systems.

At the heart of this book is the "ladder of performance," which is derived from a unique, profit-enhancing approach for organizational strategy that was developed by H. Igor Ansoff, whom Henry Mintzberg calls "The Father of Strategic Management."[1] Ansoff and his associates have conducted almost 1,000 studies, uniformly finding that companies that achieve strategic balance have ROIs (returns on investment) 100 percent to 300 percent higher than those in strategic imbalance. I have supervised more than 100 studies at the graduate business school level myself with similar results, accurately predicting the future earnings of a number of Fortune 500 companies—and the future bankruptcy of a number of other companies.

Across the board, companies that scored well on strategic balance were significantly more profitable than those that did not score well.

What is it that makes an approach based on Ansoff's work significantly more powerful than other approaches? There are a number of explanations, but it all begins with understanding the environment and your frame of reference.

PREDICTIVE MODELING

Most strategy or planning approaches focus on the past or the present. In developing his approach to strategy, Ansoff concluded that although it is not usually possible to predict future events, it is certainly possible to predict the nature of the future environment. He was especially interested in issues related to the level of chaos and the rate of change in the future.

While working at the Rand Corporation, a well-known think tank, he encountered the *Delphi panel,* a technique developed at Rand that is extremely accurate in developing accurate predictions when the future is moderately or highly unpredictable. A Delphi panel usually comprises six content experts who address specific questions that relate to some future issue. The objective of the Delphi panel is to investigate specific slices of the future that will lead to an accurate, reliable understanding of the emerging environment. Ansoff structures his research questions to explore levels of change and competitiveness in the future market, and the effectiveness of this technique is supported by the results of his years of research.

Ansoff's approach to assessing the future of a firm involves reviewing relevant research as well as questioning the firm's internal managers. Internal managers tend to see the future as much less turbulent than it looks to content experts in the area (as well as what the literature reveals). This difference is extremely important, and I will return to it at length in Chapter Eleven, "The Process of Strategic Balance."

The slices of the future to measure focus on the following issues:

- Level of complexity
- Rate of change

- Length of product life cycles
- Level of competition
- Rate of technological change
- Industry capacity versus product demand

Returning to the "10 forces" illustration as expanded in Figure 2.2, it is possible to begin quantifying the results of this approach. Market and technology forces generally drive the level of the rate of change. The other eight forces generally drive the level of complexity of change. Although the figure portrays equal levels of acceleration in each of the two groupings, it is possible that one could accelerate more than the other. However, historically they have increased at the same relative rate.

The index numbers in the figure convey an idea of the rapidity of change and growing complexity. Ansoff uses a similar five-point scale to represent what he calls "environmental turbulence." The following is a modified version of the future factors that Ansoff considers. *(The complete Ansoff Model is proprietary. However, the general attributes presented here provide an accurate summary of the larger model.)* He uses two broad areas as components of his environmental turbulence index.

Figure 2.3 presents the area of future marketing and innovation turbulence, using a five-point scale to represent levels of turbulence from very low to extremely high. The left-hand column identifies the specific aspect of the environment being measured, and the index numbers for levels of turbulence appear across the top row. Detail rows include narrative descriptions for levels of turbulence in specific environmental areas. For example, if the sales aggressiveness of competitors in the future market was expected to be aggressive (between competitive and highly aggressive) the analyst might choose level "4" to describe that future aspect of the environment. After each as-

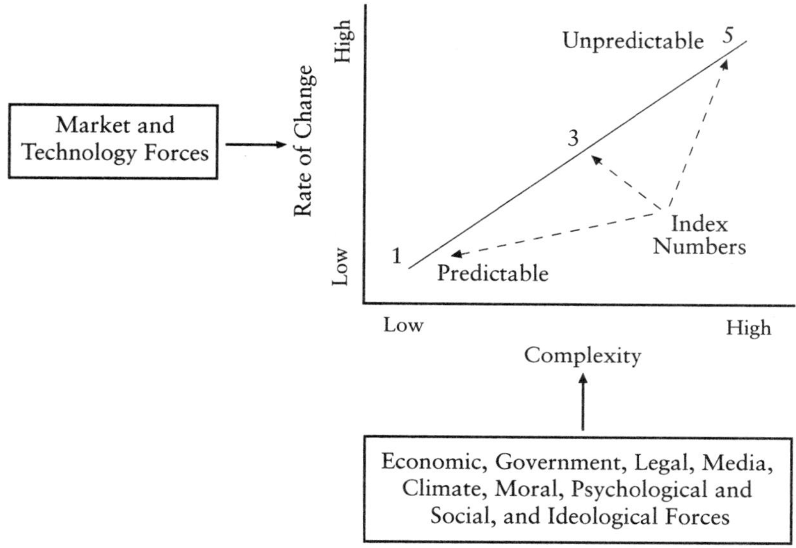

FIGURE 2.2. Indexing the 10 Forces.

pect has been rated, an average is computed that describes future marketing turbulence.

The same process is followed in computing future innovation turbulence. The two different levels of turbulence are then averaged to determine "future environmental turbulence."

It is important to understand that any point on the scale may be used. For example, if the sales aggressiveness of competitors is expected to be "moderate" in the future, that would mean that a level of 2.0 would be chosen. If it was going to be slightly higher than that, 2.5 would describe it—and any point on the scale that represented the future level of that attribute could be chosen. A good way to understand the approach is a real example. In early 2000, broadband (digital subscriber line, known as DSL) Internet access was introduced in the United States. Figure 2.4 shows an assessment of that market for the year 2004, developed from information obtained in 2001.

Future Marketing Turbulence

Market Behavior (Competitors)	1	2	3	4	5
Sales Aggressiveness	Low		Competitive		Highly Aggressive
Marketing Aggressiveness (Advertising and PR)	Low		Moderate		Very High
Market Strategy	Serve Customers		Grow Market		Expand Share
Industry Capacity vs. Demand	Excess Demand		Equilibrium		Capacity Significantly Exceeds Demand

Future Innovation Turbulence

Innovation Behavior (Competitors)	1	2	3	4	5
Innovation Aggressiveness	Low		Competitive		Highly Aggressive
Technological Change	Slow		Moderate		Extremely Fast
Innovation Strategy	Follower		Product Improvement		Product Innovation
Customer Strategy	Meet Needs		Stay Close to Customer		Anticipate Unrealized Needs
Product Life Cycles	Long		Moderate		Very Short

FIGURE 2.3. Future Marketing and Innovation Turbulence Computation. Adapted from H. Igor Ansoff's Strategic Diagnosis procedures. Used with permission.

Once future marketing and innovation turbulence were determined, they were averaged to indicate the future environmental turbulence of that market segment. The computation came up with a future turbulence of 4.55.

Broadband technology might best be described as the new digital communications highway in the United States. It is often thought of as the fiber-optic cables that carry data between cities. However, new developments are going to change the landscape for broadband over the years 2001 to 2004. Companies like Terabeam (of Seattle, Washington) are developing wire-

Future Marketing Turbulence

Future Innovation Turbulence

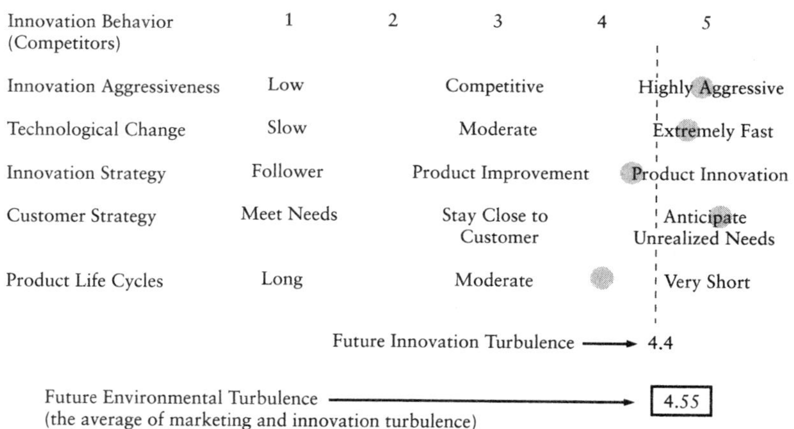

Figure 2.4. Future Turbulence of U.S. Broadband Industry. Adapted from H. Igor Ansoff's Strategic Diagnosis procedures. Used with permission.

less technologies that will compete with the wired broadband networks. Cellular providers such as Sprint PCS and AT&T are also developing broadband capabilities. Add to that the reality of new "light spectrum" technology currently under development for fiber optics, and the result is a virtually unlimited supply (or capacity) for broadband applications such as DSL.

What does this mean, and why is it important to a manager? First, the future assessment approach is extremely accurate. That means that it is information that has power. Second, once the future turbulence of a segment is understood, the complex challenge the organization faces becomes readily apparent. A future turbulence level of 4.55 like the one predicted here for broadband three years out has some serious implications for a manager:

- Some level of vertical integration will occur (excess of capacity). That also means that industry consolidation is highly probable by the year 2004.
- Broadband will become commodity priced (no opportunity to use price differentiation as a strategy . . . this was becoming obvious as early as 2000).
- It will be nearly impossible to predict technology winners. Companies will need to remain highly flexible and avoid totally committing to one technology as the final solution. (The research did indicate that a significant winner would be the fiber-based applications.)
- The future environment will be highly unpredictable, rapidly changing, and extremely complex.
- The level of competitiveness in the market will be almost overwhelming.
- Product life cycles will be extremely short.

The future turbulence index provides a metaphorical description of the coming environment. Rather than a simplistic extension of historical data, it provides a complex, nonlinear assessment of the future competitive environment.

The predictive power of the turbulence model is extremely high. Working for EDS in 1994, a graduate research team predicted significant change in the client-server segment by 1997. In 1997, all of the team's predictions proved true. In 1993, I used the turbulence model (combined with the detailed ladder of performance assessment introduced later in this chapter) to accurately predict changes in a major market segment for IBM Corporation. The client developed strategies for the changed environment and the result was extremely beneficial. The bottom line, predictive modeling works. It can be extremely accurate and can allow an organization to begin making changes long before discontinuous events in the market have an impact on the firm. And it gets better.

TURBULENCE AND PERFORMANCE

Research confirms that managers who have a good understanding of turbulence are more successful than those who do not. Further, firms that are led by managers who have a good understanding of emerging turbulence are more profitable than those who do not.[2] Also, managers who perceive changes in future turbulence early are significantly more successful in leading discontinuous change initiatives than are their counterparts.[3]

Senior executives who have a good understanding of future turbulence also seem to be much better at understanding the necessity for driving technological change into the organization. And executives who have a better understanding of future turbulence are significantly more insightful in understanding the importance and role of information technology in their company's future.[4]

The research certainly affirms the validity of the view of management that underlies the Triad of Success. Notice that managers who learn about the future are also better at transformation, which leads to maximum performance. Consider also the triad and the issue of agility. Those managers who have a good understanding of future turbulence tend to be able to take that information and understand how leading-edge technology systems directly affect the ability of the organization to compete at the appropriate speed, that is, its agility.

If leaders who correctly perceive turbulence lead more profitable companies, that is important. More important, however, is the real driver of profitability: strategic balance. Notice that turbulence describes levels of competition, change, innovation, and so forth. The issue for managers has to be what the firm does in response to impending change in the turbulence-driven rules of the game. *Managers who understand that the entire organization must be balanced with the environment are those who will lead companies to substantially higher profitability.*

ARTHUR ASHE WAS A CHEATER (NOT REALLY)

I once had the opportunity to take a tennis clinic from Arthur Ashe. For those who don't remember him, Ashe was one of the leading tennis professionals in the world for a number of years. After watching Ashe returning serves from another professional at the clinic, I concluded that he must be cheating, because nobody could be that good! Ashe was returning 110-mph serves as if they were sitting ducks. He did not even seem to break a sweat.

It looked as though he and his opponent had worked out exactly where each ball would go so that Ashe could look really, really good for the trainees. But it wasn't like that at all. What Arthur Ashe had done was develop his game to a very high level indeed. Before his opponent served, Ashe would begin to move to the right or left as he saw the angle of the server's shoulder. When his opponent tossed the ball up to hit it for his serve, Ashe would continue to adjust his position. Before the opponent's ball crossed the net, Ashe already had his racket back on the appropriate side. If the server put spin on the ball, Ashe was able to make minor adjustments in order to get a solid return.

Arthur Ashe did not cheat—he didn't need to collude with his opponent to know where the ball was going. He just had a marvelous combination of proactive, anticipatory skills and reactive skills. Ashe was able to begin moving before his opponent served the ball because he could anticipate where the ball was going as he picked up signals or cues from the opponent. Once the ball came across the net, he was equally reactive in responding to any surprises he might encounter.

Playing tennis with a beginner is simple. You can hit the ball slowly, and there is little need for complex strategies or speed. As you move up the ladder of competition, the need for anticipation, speed, and complexity increases. When you get to a guy like Arthur Ashe, you have discovered your worst competitive nightmare. That is, unless you are able to mirror his abilities of anticipation, complexity, and speed with your own. The same is true of companies.

Turbulence defines the nature of competition that a company will face in the future. Once turbulence is determined, it can become a competitive road map for the manager. There are two ways to balance an organization with its environment. The first is to hire a manager who has the intuitive skills. There are some managers that understand how the complex parts of the company must be uniquely balanced with the future competitive environment. Those are the people like Jack Welch (GE), Dave House (Bay Networks and Nortel), and Andy McKelvey (TMP Worldwide) to mention just a few. The problem is, there are not a lot of people like them. That leads to the second way a firm can achieve strategic balance: the ladder of performance. The ladder of performance is a profile that any manager can use to create a high-performance organization. You do not have to have natural intuitive skills to do this—it gives you a way to create organizations like the ones created by Jack Welch and people like him.

BUILDING THE LADDER OF PERFORMANCE

I have adapted Igor Ansoff's approach to what I call the "ladder of performance." As I said earlier, it is possible to accurately predict the level of turbulence of the future environment.

It is also possible to measure different aspects of an organization. For example, there are different types of leadership, ranging from highly controlling to highly empowering. Also, there are different types of organizational structures, and each one produces a different level of flexibility. Hierarchies are inflexible while cross-product/cross-functional organizations are highly flexible. There is a body of research that has developed over the years that has revealed the following:

- In low-turbulence environments, controlling managers can do quite well.
- In high-turbulence environments, controlling managers will not do well, but empowering managers will produce high levels of performance.
- In low-turbulence environments, a steep hierarchy will serve a company well.
- In high-turbulence environments, cross-relationships (such as matrix structures) produce higher performance.

The ladder of performance recognizes the reality that for each different type of environment (or turbulence), an entirely different type of organization is required. This becomes clear if you picture turbulence as a five-level ladder. If you pictured each aspect of the organization in the same way, each level of change in the environment would require a change in the level of the organization. Figure 2.5 illustrates the idea.

The idea is simple: Notice that as the turbulence goes up the ladder from "2" to "4" that the type of organization (in this case leadership) changes correspondingly from "2" to "4."

It is possible, as you will see, to measure many aspects of an organization. In the case with the original Ansoff approach there were eight broad areas of the firm that he measured. I have expanded that to twelve. The important thing to remember is that each area of the organization must ascend to the same level on the ladder as does the turbulence.

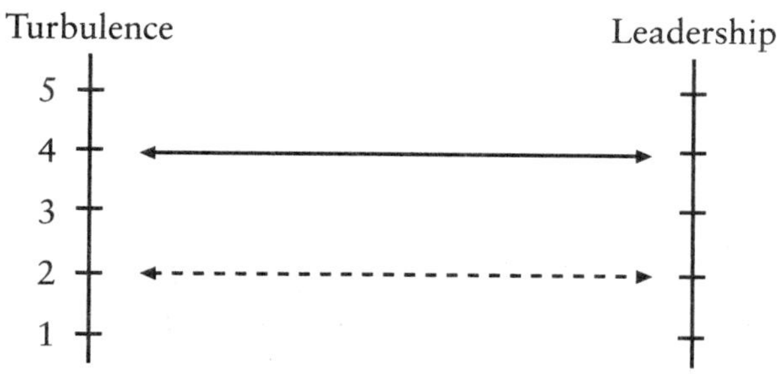

FIGURE 2.5. The Ladder of Performance.
Adapted from H. Igor Ansoff's Strategic Diagnosis procedures.
Used with permission.

The ladder of performance requires two elements. First, you need a logical way of splitting up the firm into performance drivers. Remember that the process of management is defined as learning-transformation-performance. That is the underlying driver of the Triad of Success. The triad in its expanded form allows the organization to assess its ability in the areas of leadership, learning, and agility.

Second, you need a way of assessing the gaps in each performance area. The same five-point scale used in Ansoff's turbulence assessment turns out to work very well for gap assessment with each of the 12 factors of the triad as presented in Figure 1.8.

Another key concept here is the "requisite variety theorem," developed by W. R. Ashby almost half a century ago:

> *For a successful response to the environment, the complexity and the speed of the firm's response must match the complexity and speed of environmental challenges.*[5]

That is, the successful organization is one that mirrors its competitive environment. To do that, a firm must have two basic agilities: the proactive agility to look forward and anticipate the future, and the reactive agility to dynamically cope with surprises, or discontinuous events. The good news is that the process of understanding environmental turbulence helps the manager understand the future environment. The key is to design the firm so that it does both processes well.

If it is possible to use a five-point scale to describe the future environment, it stands to reason that the same scale could be used to measure the organization. For example, if the future turbulence of a market segment is expected to be 4.0, it would be reasonable to assume that the firm's marketing would need to be very aggressive (say, 4.0). At the same time, if the marketing aggressiveness of the firm was moderately low (2.0), it would seem obvious that the firm needed to increase its marketing aggressiveness to compete in the future environment. That is the basis of strategic balance.

USING THE LADDER OF PERFORMANCE TO GET RESULTS

Don't let the numbers and the projections put you off—this isn't just another academic theory unlikely to work in the real world. The beauty of the concept is just how logical and practical it really is. I always enjoy watching how fast executives adopt this idea at seminars. Once they understand the idea of turbulence, a quick drill brings out the importance of balancing the organization with the environment. For example:

Assume that the turbulence in three years will be at level 2.0. That means that change will be slow, there will be little complexity, and the level of competitiveness will be low. This understanding of the environment invariably leads executives to create an organization that looks like this:

> **Marketing:** A follower strategy will work; advertising can be limited; little advertising and PR will be required. Price differentiation will be effective (selling higher quality for a higher price).
>
> **Innovation:** Low levels of research and development will be required. Internally, the firm should assume that product life cycles will be long.

CEO Attributes: An operationally focused CEO who is risk-averse will be effective.

Management: Managers who focus on operational efficiency will work well. High levels of empowerment are unnecessary. Risk-taking should be minimized.

Similar observations are made for the other eight attributes, but these four are enough for clarity here. Notice what happens to these four attributes when the future turbulence is perceived to be level 4.6:

Marketing: Follower strategies kill competitiveness; the firm must be a first mover in all areas. Highly aggressive advertising and PR efforts will be imperative. Pricing will be commodity-based (no ability to differentiate . . . except that the first mover will have a short window in which differentiation will be effective).

Innovation: Product life cycles will be extremely short. Due to the uncertainty of the environment (there will be failures), high levels of R&D will be required. Product bundling (products and services as one product offering) will be common.

CEO Attributes: The CEO selected for this organization will need to be obsessed with change. The CEO will need to focus on maintaining a high level of excellence, risk-taking, creativity, and first-mover status.

Management: The organizational management will need to be highly empowering. A strong support for a creative, risk-taking culture will be critical.

Notice the difference between the two organizations! One is designed to mirror or balance a slow, predictable environment. The other is designed for a highly uncertain, overwhelmingly competitive environment.

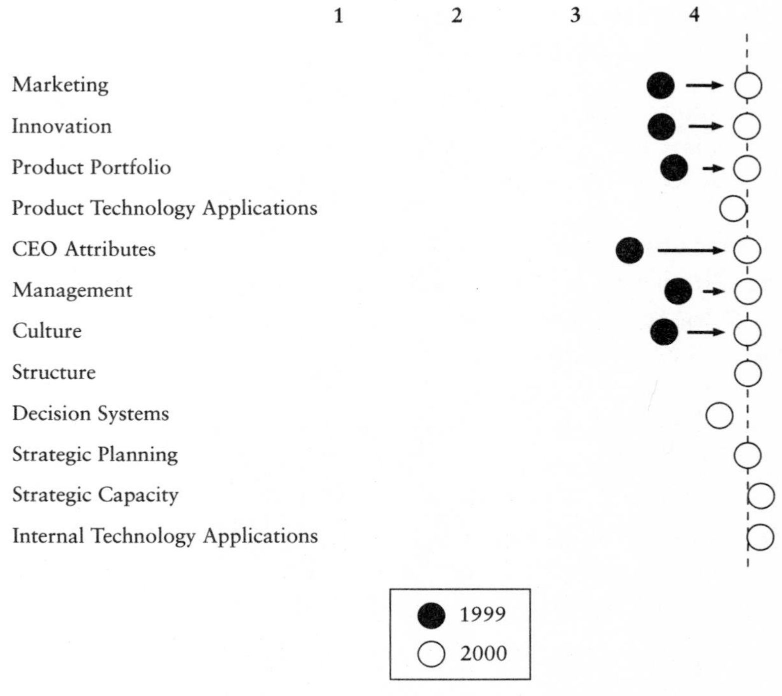

FIGURE 2.6. A Comparison of HP and the Environment: 1999 and 2000. Adapted from H. Igor Ansoff's Strategic Diagnosis procedures. Used with permission.

Now it should be obvious as to why companies featured in *In Search of Excellence* or *Built to Last* encountered periods of diminished performance.

Hewlett-Packard was one of the companies featured in *In Search of Excellence.*[6] The company prospered in the early 1980s by being an effective follower in product innovation. The idea was to wait until a competitor produced a product, get customer feedback on the product, then come out with a better one. That strategy fit the level 3 environment of the early 1980s, but it led to trouble as turbulence increased.

Figure 2.6 presents the profile of Hewlett-Packard and its environment in 1999 and then later, in 2000. The general attributes of the firm are listed on the left margin, and each attribute's level is represented by a circle. The vertical line represents environmental turbulence, which remained at a constant high level in both years. The closer the circle for an attribute comes to the vertical line, the better the firm's strategic balance for that area. (This pattern is used for figures comparing profiles of various firms with their environment throughout the rest of the book.)

The general environment the firm faced was rapidly changing, highly uncertain, and extremely complex. The black circles in the figure show that in mid-1999 the CEO attributes were not quite matched to the environment. The same is true for internal management and the marketing aggressiveness of the firm.[7] Notice also that the firm's ability to be a first mover from an innovation standpoint fell well short of what the environment demanded.

The difference between what a firm needs (turbulence defines what the firm must mirror if it is to be in balance) and the current level of an attribute is called a *gap*. For example, in the case of HP illustrated in Figure 2.6, the CEO attributes were at 3.3 in mid-1999, a gap of –1.1 with the turbulence of 4.4. Ansoff and his associates have consistently found the following statistical relationships between gaps and organizational performance:

Range of Gap	*Profit Impact*
0 to –0.5	Maximum Profit
–0.51 to –1.0	Marginal Profit Impact
–1.1 to –1.50	Serious Profit Impact
–1.51 and above	Critical Profit Impact

What changed the profile of Hewlett-Packard? In July 1999, faced with HP's declining performance, CEO Lew Platt decided it was time for a new CEO. Carly Fiorina was appointed his successor. As one publication put it, HP was a great "built to last" organization, but it was no longer competitive enough for the new e-chaos environment.[8] Carly Fiorina set about to change all that. When asked what sets great companies apart from others, she has one reply: "Balance."

Fiorina believes that the year 2000 was the "renaissance of the information age." When she accepted the job as CEO, she immediately began changing many of the ways that HP did business. She departed from the "HP way." In an effort to create a new, balanced HP, she made some significant changes:

- Established new rules of behavior for the firm:

  "Preserve the best . . . reinvent the rest."

  "No politics, no bureaucracy."

  "Radical ideas are not bad ideas."[9]

- Increased the innovation level to balance with the environment.
- Focused on nonlinear innovation (disruptive technologies).
- Changed the culture to reward risk-taking.[10]

The result was a CEO-driven change approach that took the firm from a strategic imbalance in 1999 to strategic balance in 2000. The results of the changes became evident by the second quarter of 2000:

- Revenue growth went from less than 5 percent to 15 percent.
- Unix server revenue grew by 26 percent.
- Printer revenues grew by 9 percent.

The concept of balance is complex. Notice that changing internal values (culture) toward a more risk-taking mentality (as well as market aggressiveness) enhanced the overall marketing aggressiveness. HP's increased focus on innovation produced a more timely introduction of products to the market. Additionally, that led to a substantially better portfolio of products.

DEVELOPING THE DETAILS

Organizational learning about complexity generally involves eight of the ten forces. Those are issues related to customer preferences, markets, government, and the like. Organizational learning about the rate of environmental change centers on market forces and technology forces. The 21st century will be one in which technology forces will play a major part.

Figure 2.6 illustrated a way of profiling a company and assessing its strategic balance with the environment. But if you are the manager responsible for such things, what you need to know is how to derive each attribute. It turns out to be enough to discuss only a couple of the factors involved in each attribute and to break each attribute into just a few factors. Although the version I present here is smaller and simpler than Ansoff's original model, I have seen it used effectively hundreds of times in the field.

The following sections discuss each of the 12 broad aspects of the firm, and further subdividing them into individualized segments. Figures in each section provide a parallel view of the segments and how they relate to increasing turbulence.

Marketing (Aggressiveness)

As the environment becomes more turbulent, the behavior of the firm must become more aggressive. Turbulence describes or predicts market behaviors—including the aggressiveness of competitors—and it is essential to match those behaviors. It might seem tempting to *overprofile* the firm, that is, to be more aggressive than the turbulence level indicates is desirable. However, that would not be advisable because the extra aggressiveness would decrease profits (since the firm would be spending more money than it needed to). Overaggressive behavior is also

Marketing (Aggressiveness)

Factor	1	2	3	4	5
Sales Aggressiveness	Low	Moderately Low	Competitive	Moderately High	Highly Aggressive
PR and Advertising Aggressiveness	Negligible	Moderate	Competitive	Aggressive	Highly Aggressive
Market Strategy	Maintain Market	Maintain Market	Grow with Market	Expand Market	Increase Market Share

FIGURE 2.7. Marketing.
Adapted from H. Igor Ansoff's Strategic Diagnosis procedures.
Used with permission.

likely to drive the turbulence up, making the environment more difficult for the firm to operate in.

Figure 2.7 breaks up marketing aggressiveness into sales aggressiveness, public relations and advertising, and market strategy. Again, provision is made to depict turbulence and compare the firm's profile with the turbulence.

Innovation (Aggressiveness)

Innovation involves creating new products and ideas at the right speed. If the firm's leadership thinks that product life cycles will be five years in the future when they will in actuality be three, the firm would underinnovate, resulting in declining sales and profit.

Figure 2.8 breaks out innovation aggressiveness in terms of R&D spending, planned product life cycles, and customer focus.

Product Portfolio

As the environment becomes more turbulent, two product areas become critical. First, the need to diversify out of familiar prod-

Innovation (Aggressiveness)

Factor	1	2	3	4	5
R&D Spending	Low	Moderately Low	Competitive	Moderately High	Highly Aggressive
Product Life Cycles Plan	Very Long	Long	Moderate	Short	Very Short
Customer Focus	Respond to Demands	Meet Demand	Stay Close to Customer	Anticipate Needs	Anticipate Unrealized Needs

FIGURE 2.8. Innovation.
Adapted from H. Igor Ansoff's Strategic Diagnosis procedures.
Used with permission.

uct areas becomes more important as the turbulence goes up. Second, the balance of products at each level of the product life cycle needs to change. Figure 2.9 sketches the life cycle curve.

Figure 2.10 traces the effects of turbulence on product diversification and life cycle balance, using the reference points on the curve in Figure 2.9.

Product Technology Applications

Technology is one of the key driving forces in the new economy. As the speed of the economy continues to increase as a result of e-chaos, the importance of the role of technology will also increase, both in companies' internal operations and in the products they make and sell. Product technology applications have to do with technology as a singular product or the bundling of technology into some aspect of a product.

This applies far outside the obvious high-tech realm—consider the use of technology in the pizza industry. Research indicates that there is a significant trend toward what is called home meal replacement, with pizza being one of those meals. Consumer studies are revealing that speed and ease are key

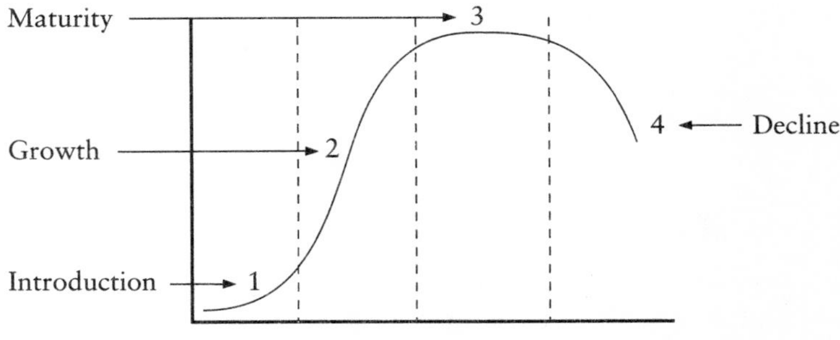

The Four Stages of Products
(Life Cycle)

FIGURE 2.9. The Four Stages of the Product Life Cycle.

Product Portfolio

Factor	**1**	**2**	**3**	**4**	**5**
Diversification (Product)	None	Limited	Moderate	High	Very High
Product Life Cycle Balance	Mostly 3 & 4	Mostly 3 & 4	Balance of 1–4	Skewed Toward 1–3	Skewed Toward 1&2

FIGURE 2.10. Product Portfolio.
Adapted from H. Igor Ansoff's Strategic Diagnosis procedures.
Used with permission.

aspects of delivered pizza. That is why a number of competitors in the pizza business are investigating the role of technology in the pizza market. It appears that the reason the home meal replacement business is growing so much is the time issue. People do not feel they have enough time. That's where technology comes in. Pizza companies realize that cell phones, the Internet, and even interactive television may become the preferred way for people to get their pizza where they want it, when they want it.

Product Technology Applications

Factor	1	2	3	4	5
Technology Applications (Product)	None	Limited	Moderate	High	Very High
Technology Philosophy	None	Last In	Adapt with Competition	Seek Early Adaptation	First Mover

FIGURE 2.11. Product Technology Applications.
Adapted from H. Igor Ansoff's Strategic Diagnosis procedures.
Used with permission.

Figure 2.11 shows how increasing turbulence affects the applications of technology to products themselves, and to a company's philosophy about technology.

CEO Attributes

The Hewlett-Packard story illustrates the success that companies can enjoy when they have the right CEO. As with other attributes of strategic balance, as the environment changes, the type of CEO needed changes. Figure 2.12 shows how with increasing turbulence, the CEO's attitude toward change and focus upon creativity become more and more important, as does the CEO's attitude toward subordinates. At the highest level, that adds up to charismatic leadership. Another issue, integrity, is the same at all levels of turbulence. A CEO who is not trustworthy cannot be effective on a long-term basis.

Management of the Organization

The internal management of an organization is the support system for the CEO. If the internal management team lacks the commitment to the appropriate direction as necessitated by the

CEO Attributes

Factor	1	2	3	4	5
Attitude Toward Change	Reject	Resist	Slow Adaptation	Drive Change	Aggressively Drive Change
Attitude Toward Creativity and Risk	No Value	De-Value	Necessary Evil	Drive Creativity	Aggressively Promote

FIGURE 2.12. CEO Attributes.
Adapted from H. Igor Ansoff's Strategic Diagnosis procedures.
Used with permission.

Management

Factor	1	2	3	4	5
Leadership Style	Controlling	Moderately Controlling	Results Oriented	Empowering	Inspirational
Attitude Toward Risk	Reject	Discourage	Tolerate	Encourage	Expect

FIGURE 2.13. Organizational Management.
Adapted from H. Igor Ansoff's Strategic Diagnosis procedures.
Used with permission.

turbulence, the organization will become disorganized and ineffective. Figure 2.13 shows the effects of turbulence on management's leadership style and attitude toward risk.

Culture

Organizational culture relates to values that the organization holds, both its institutional values and the value it places on its people. Additionally, it relates to the rewards and incentives of the organization. The culture of an organization may involve a number of other aspects. It may involve rituals and core beliefs. Culture is one of the keys to maintaining an open, creative, and aggressive organization. At the same time, culture is extremely dependent upon CEO attrib-

Culture

Factor	1	2	3	4	5
Values	Defend the Status Quo	Support the Status Quo	Maintain the Status Quo	Challenge the Status Quo	Create the Future
Value of Employees	Little	Minimal	Moderate	High	Very High
Rewards and Incentives	Historic Performance	Accuracy and Efficiency	Productivity	Solutions Development	Creativity

FIGURE 2.14. Culture.
Adapted from H. Igor Ansoff's Strategic Diagnosis procedures.
Used with permission.

utes and organizational management. Figure 2.14 shows how increasing turbulence affects all these aspects of culture.

Structure

The structure of an organization is defined by its formal reporting relationships and rules, and by the way things actually get done. As the environment becomes more turbulent, the organizational structure must change to a more flexible form. Additionally, the distribution of power must change. Figure 2.15 traces the effects of turbulence on the type of structure that works for an organization, and on its distribution of power.

Decision Systems

Decision systems are the organization's techniques for making choices. As Figure 2.16 shows, turbulence affects the speed of decision making as well as the need for early warning systems. As decision systems improve, the organization becomes better able to anticipate competitive discontinuities in the future

Structure

Factor	1	2	3	4	5
Formal Structure	Hierarchy	Functional	Divisional	Matrix	Matrix
Power Focus	Senior Executive	Bureaucracy	Executive and Bureaucracy	Distributed CEO Team	Bi-Centralized*

* A bi-centralized focus on power involves a high level of creative leadership at the top and highly empowered teams at the competitive level.

FIGURE 2.15. Structure.
Adapted from H. Igor Ansoff's Strategic Diagnosis procedures.
Used with permission.

(proactive agility) as well as to be highly reactive to discontinuous events.

Internal Technology Applications

As noted earlier, the increasing speed of the economy is placing increasing emphasis on the role of technology in companies' internal operations. Internal technology applications can have a direct impact on customers as well as on a firm's own employees, often through the use of CTI (computer telephony integration) or information systems. Internal technology systems can enhance both the quality of the firm's processes and the speed at which it can operate.

Figure 2.17 traces the impact of turbulence on a company's internal technology strategy and on its need for *redundancy*—that is, the value that must be placed on the ability to take over for an operating system. Although it is true that any system worth having is worth backing up, in many conditions (especially at lower levels of turbulence) not all functions need the ability to stay in operation if the main system were to go down. Obviously, there are some systems that must be redun-

Decision Systems

Factor	1	2	3	4	5
Speed of Decisions	Very Slow	Slow	Moderate	Fast	Extremely Fast
Early Warning Systems	None	Limited	Competitive Intelligence	Strategic Intelligence	Multiple Systems

FIGURE 2.16. Decision Systems.
Adapted from H. Igor Ansoff's Strategic Diagnosis procedures.
Used with permission.

dant regardless of the turbulence of the environment (health, safety, and the like).

Strategic Planning

Strategic planning can involve either linear or nonlinear systems. A budget-based system, for example, is linear because it is based on assumptions related to the past and extrapolated to the future on a straight-line basis. A nonlinear system might be based on scenarios or futuristic thinking, or—as in this chapter—on a careful assessment of the multiple effects of anticipated changes. Technology applications are particularly important in the strategic planning area.

Figure 2.18 traces the impact of turbulence on the planning model and planning technology a company needs. As the figure shows, when the turbulence passes level 3, linear planning models no longer work. In the figure, the *competency-based model* is the traditional strategic model based on historic core competencies, competitive advantage, and mission. *Strategic balance* refers to the modified Ansoff model presented in this chapter, which is a nonlinear model. That is, it involves developing strategy from the future back. This model is often supported by other nonlinear tools such as scenarios.

Internal Technology Applications

Factor	1	2	3	4	5
Technology Strategy	Very Slow Adaptation	Slow Adaptation	Stay with Competition	Leading Edge not Bleeding Edge	Consistent First Mover
Redundancy	Unnecessary	Unimportant	Important	Serious	Critical

FIGURE 2.17. Internal Technology Applications.
Adapted from H. Igor Ansoff's Strategic Diagnosis procedures.
Used with permission.

Strategic Capacity

Strategic capacity refers to the depth of a firm's ability to do creative strategic work. A number of companies train their executives in the area of creativity. Others are known to conduct "complexity training" as a part of their executive training programs. Figure 2.19 traces the impact of increasing turbulence on the need for strategic capacity at the senior executive and lower management levels.

NO "ONE TRUE WAY" WORKS ALL THE TIME

A number of excellent books attempt to develop links between certain types of organizational strategy and organizational behavior and performance. One of those books is *In Search of Excellence*, which is valuable because it opens the door to looking at an organization as a system. In the end, however, it fails to deliver an appropriate system for sustainable performance.

Built to Last is another book that has proposed that the organization is a competitive system (that is, a complex system). The authors of that exceptional book suggest that there are consistent core principles that create sustainable performance.

Strategic Planning

Factor	1	2	3	4	5
Planning Model	Budgeting	Business Analysis	Competency Based	Strategic Balance	Strategic Balance
Planning Technology	Manual	Computer Projections	Complex Budgeting	Artificial Intelligence	Artificial Intelligence

FIGURE 2.18. Strategic Planning.
Adapted from H. Igor Ansoff's Strategic Diagnosis procedures.
Used with permission.

Strategic Capacity

Factor	1	2	3	4	5
Senior Executive Team	Very Low	Low	Moderate	High	Very High
Staff and Managers	Very Low	Low	Moderate	High	Very High

FIGURE 2.19. Strategic Capacity.
Adapted from H. Igor Ansoff's Strategic Diagnosis procedures.
Used with permission.

It is an excellent contribution toward building an understanding of the complex set of corporate attributes that produce long-term profitability.

The concept of strategic balance adds the critical issues of environment, future-based thinking, and organizational profiling to provide a clear road map to sustainable profit. By explaining the need to balance the organization with the environment and how to do just that, strategic balance perfectly supplements the work done by those excellent writers. Strategic balance or imbalance increasingly affects organizational performance as turbulence increases. Nonetheless, even in low to moderate turbulence environments it is important for firms to be in balance with the environment. The following table traces the effects of balance and turbulence that I've noted in my research.

Organizational Strategic Balance	*Turbulence 1–3*	*Turbulence 4–5*
Serious Imbalances	Under-performance	Drastic under-performance
Marginal Imbalances	Performance below industry	Marginal under-performance
Strategically Balanced	Performance above industry	100–300 percent higher ROI

Senior managers who have an accurate understanding of environmental turbulence are able to lead their organizations to higher profits than those that do not understand it. In addition, organizations that maintain strategic balance are significantly more profitable than those that fall into strategic imbalance. As turbulence goes higher, strategic imbalances have a much larger impact on the performance of the organization. That brings up a critically important issue: What is the impact of strategic imbalance in an e-chaos environment?

E-Chaos and Strategic Balance

As previously noted, the digital revolution has created a major paradigm shift in the global environment. Technology change has drastically increased the rate of environmental change and has also contributed to the increase in the level of complexity. That means that achieving strategic balance may be the most important goal any organization needs to set.

It is important to remember that the companies featured in *In Search of Excellence* were in a much less turbulent environment when they went into strategic imbalance. They had time to change because the environment was changing relatively slowly. The same case can be made for companies featured in *Built to Last.* The authors point out that all of the excellent companies cited in the book have had some significant down periods in their history. A look back at those companies reveals that the companies had substantial asset bases to sustain them and additionally, they were in an environment that was changing at a rate slow enough to allow the firm to make incremental adjustments to catch up.

The new e-chaos environment has created an environment in which the failure to plan from the future back can threaten the existence of the organization. Further, in the higher turbulence of the e-chaos world, strategic mismatches can be devastating.

A Lesson Learned: Oxford Health Plans

In the mid-1990s Oxford Health Plans enjoyed a soaring stock price with a soaring membership. Then the bubble burst. Within a few months, the stock of the firm fell from 87 to 6. It even made the headlines at the *New York Times:* "Insurer in Agony: Behind the Bleeding at Oxford." So what was the problem? A bad business model? No, the company had a great business model. Bad marketing? No, sales were growing nicely. The problem: computer systems. The firm had failed to grow its systems applications in balance with the changing market and membership growth.[11]

The story of Oxford's decline reveals how a simple (that's an understatement) computer problem led to delinquent payments to physicians in their health care system. Before it was all over, the symptoms created by the computer problem convinced the market that Oxford had become a management nightmare. The result was a crisis that threatened the company's ability to do business.

The crisis was driven by numerous changes in the external environment. In reality, the company's agility was critically damaged. On one hand, it lacked the technological agility to

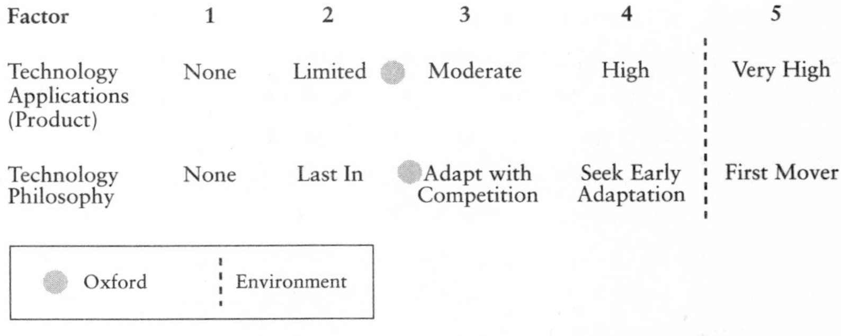

FIGURE 2.20. Oxford's Product Technology Applications. Adapted from H. Igor Ansoff's Strategic Diagnosis procedures. Used with permission.

change with the external environment and meet the demands that change was forcing on it. On the other, it lacked the internal agility to do business. In short, the change of the speed of the environment (driven by technological change) exceeded the ability of the organization to operate at the new speed of the environment (a technology applications problem).

The technology profiles of Oxford shown in Figures 2.20 and 2.21 clearly reveal the problem the firm had when its stock cratered. This did not happen in a vacuum. Inadequate levels of strategy, culture, management, and CEO attributes also contributed. The supersonic speed of the environment resulted in a crisis that threatened the firm—and all that happened in a matter of a few months.

Snatching Defeat from the Jaws of Victory at AT&T

The disappointing outcome of AT&T's acquisition of NCR is widely known. A debate as to why the acquisition was so disappointing has gone on in the academic community as well as in the popular business press. Perhaps the most notable comment was by Michael Porter of Harvard Business School, who suggested that the acquisition was a failure because AT&T lacked the "core competencies" to compete in the computer business.

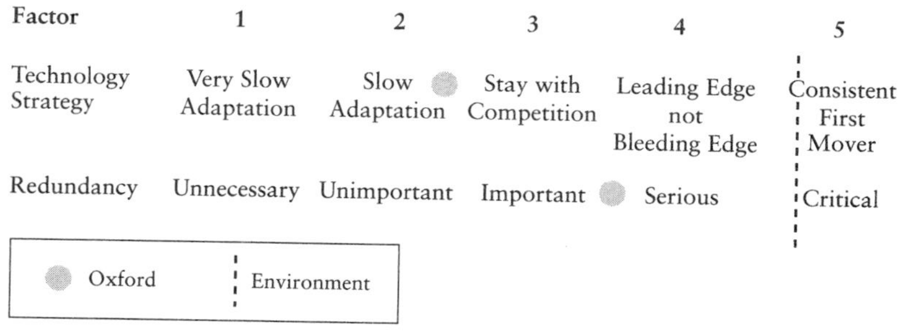

FIGURE 2.21. Oxford's Internal Technology Applications. Adapted from H. Igor Ansoff's Strategic Diagnosis procedures. Used with permission.

I put together a graduate research team and set out to discover the reason the merger failed to meet AT&T's expectations. We used the turbulence model presented in this chapter to assess the turbulence in NCR's segment at the time of the acquisition. Additionally, the team was able to access sources who enabled them to develop a strategic profile of NCR after the AT&T acquisition. The results, shown in Figure 2.22, are quite telling.

We found that AT&T imposed its strategic profile on NCR at the time of the acquisition. At that time, AT&T was still trying to shake off its old "regulated" mentality. Notice what happened. Instead of creating an autonomous organization that was suited to a high-churn, highly competitive environment, AT&T chose to profile NCR for a much slower, less competitive environment. The failure of the acquisition was a fait accompli before the work began.

WINNING IN E-CHAOS

A number of conclusions can be reached at this point. First, it is possible to predict the nature of the future environment. Second, by applying the strategic profiling concept of the ladder of performance, it is possible to design an organization that will

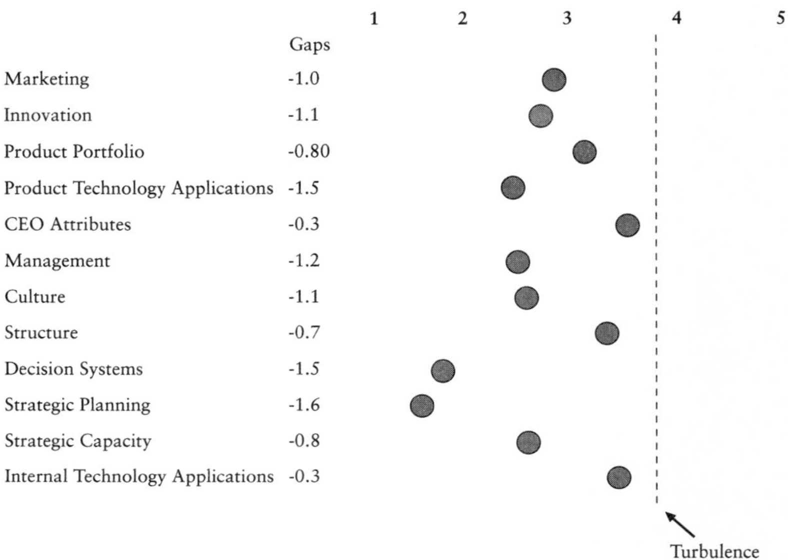

FIGURE 2.22. NCR's Post-Acquisition Profile.
Adapted from H. Igor Ansoff's Strategic Diagnosis procedures.
Used with permission.

be highly profitable. Third, it is possible to predict the future performance of an organization by comparing its present profile with the future environment, that is, assuming that the firm's management chooses not to correct strategic imbalances.

There is more. The technology revolution of the 21st century has created a new world. The rules of the game have shifted drastically. That means that the corporate rules of the game must also shift just as drastically. Technological change has created a supersonic digital environment in which being slightly late or slow can mean failure. At the same time, it is just as obvious that it is possible to choose success. It is possible to choose to be a winner. That is what this book is all about!

CHAPTER 3

LEADERS FOR THE NEW MILLENNIUM

OVER THE PAST FEW YEARS, THE TERM "FRAME-BREAKING change" has been used as a way of describing what happens when an industry or environment undergoes a massive transition. Frame-breaking change involves a drastic shift in the rules of the game. A good illustration of such a shift occurred in the late 1970s and 1980s. Armed with an intelligence capability that allowed them to capture U.S. companies' product secrets long before the products were released, Japanese companies introduced a new approach to competition: quality.

The Japanese competitors also brought another strategic shift to the competitive arena by adopting a long-term view of product strategy. In the 1980s, for example, they realized that flat screen panels were going to be the future in computers and other applications that required a monitor display. With the backing of the Japanese government, Japanese companies led a coordinated assault on any U.S. company that attempted to develop a flat screen product. The Japanese companies were willing to sell flat screen products below their cost as long as required to ensure that no U.S. company was able to enter the flat screen market. Additionally, the Japanese companies were able to control the U.S. trade representative's office well enough to ensure that their predatory trade practices were not restricted.

AN AMERICAN DISASTER

American companies were totally unprepared for this drastic shift in the rules of the game. A number tried to copy the Total Quality Management approach applied by the Japanese, but most failed to achieve the same level of quality as their Japanese counterparts. The U.S. automobile industry lost over a million jobs during this period. Japanese companies, armed with their massive profits, began buying up American companies. The future prospects of U.S. companies did not look good.

It was during this time that an entire new service industry grew up. Change management consulting exploded overnight, with change management teams at the major consulting firms and a host of new players in the market. The publishing industry exploded with change books. The Fortune 1000 inundated their employees with pamphlets on the topic of change. *(Much of the teaching about managing change has historically been ill-founded. See Chapter Seven, "Managing Change in Supersonic Environment," for research-based insight into the effective management of change.)*

NEW MANAGERS, NEW WAYS OF COMPETING

While many CEOs of U.S. companies seemed powerless to cope with the frame-breaking change of the 1980s, a number of companies seemed to have the ability to meet the challenges of the foreign competition and win. As the 1980s drew to an end, companies such as Intel, Microsoft, and Texas Instruments appeared to be significantly different from other firms that were struggling to keep up with their environment.

Many boards of directors began to try to understand why some companies were doing better than others were. A lot of boards ended up going through a series of CEOs over a relatively short period in hopes of finding the perfect champion. Most involved in these situations agreed that successful CEOs had a different focus and style from that of the underperforming CEOs. The consensus that developed was twofold:

1. The CEO is extremely important in creating sustainable profit.

2. Successful CEOs are different from their counterparts at unsuccessful companies.

The reality is that Jack Welch (GE), Bill Gates (Microsoft), David Novak (Tricon), John Chambers (Cisco), and other CEOs who enjoy long-term success are simply different. What makes them different?

Figure 3.1 revisits the 10 forces to help in understanding how they are different. Notice the shift in the environment that took place between 1980 and 2000.

Prior to 1980, senior executives were given the task of dealing with predictable, incremental change. In the early 1980s, the global Japanese challenge created a need for managers capable of managing frame-breaking change. At that time, however, most expected that the environment would stabilize once the massive changes driven by the Japanese were dealt with. The idea was

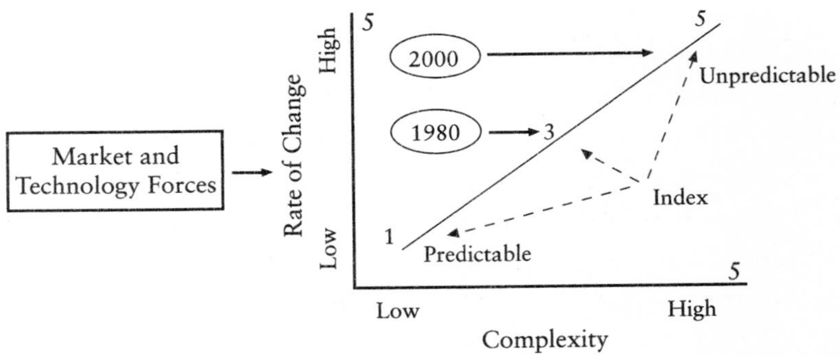

FIGURE 3.1. The 10 Forces: 1980–2000.

that once a company adapted to the new quality-oriented environment, life would again be characterized by predictable, stable change. But just the opposite was true. Technological change was just beginning to affect the environment in the early 1980s at the same time that the Japanese were changing the rules of the game. By 1990, a new and different environment characterized by technological discontinuities had taken shape. When the year 2000 arrived, technological changes (as well as market forces) were creating an environment in which frame-breaking change was much more frequent and persistent.

Between 1980 and 2000 frame-breaking shifts (complete cycles of change) began to occur over shorter time periods. By the year 2000, as Figure 3.2 shows, the businesses were facing a rapid succession of frame-breaking shifts—and there was no end in sight.

The shifts in the environment created different types of demands upon organizations. Not only did corporate behavior need to change, executive leadership did too, as summarized in Figure 3.3.

Prior to 1980, the CEO had to be concerned with efficiency and control issues. In the late 1970s and early 1980s, the CEO had to be able to manage the major paradigm shift driven by the new Japanese competition, but the actual rate of change

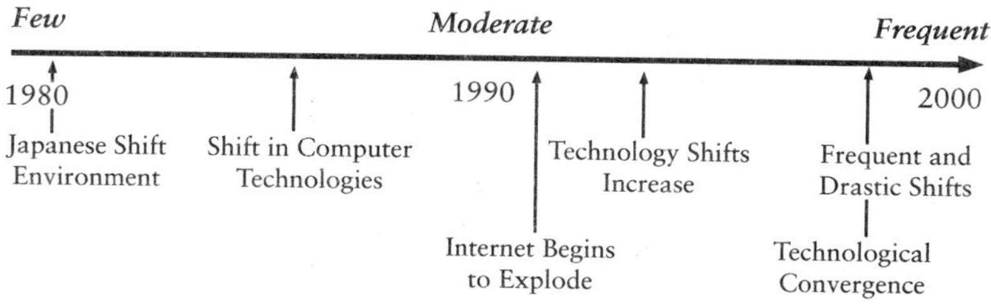

FIGURE 3.2. Increasing Frequency of Frame-Breaking Shifts: 1980–2000.

	1980	1990	2000
Corporate Success Behaviors	Simple adaptability	Moderate speed; moderate adaptability	High speed; complex adaptiveness
CEO Success Behaviors	Drive change; efficiency and stability	Foster creativity; excellence	Foster speed, risk-taking, creativity, excellence, and iconoclastic behavior

FIGURE 3.3. The Changing Roles of Executives.

was moderate, as was complexity. That meant that many of the success behaviors of the companies need not change once they had dealt with the quality initiative of the Japanese companies. In the 1980s, there was really only one cycle of frame-breaking change. In the first five years of the 1990s, there was another. By the end of the decade, technological change (as well as market conditions . . . much of that driven by technological change) had begun to create change cycles about every two to two-and-a-half years. In other words, by the year 2000, technological change had created an environment that never really reached stability. It was in accelerating, continuous, dynamic change.

As the rate of technology and market change drove significant changes in the nature of the environment, every organization needed to be able to mirror that change with its strategies

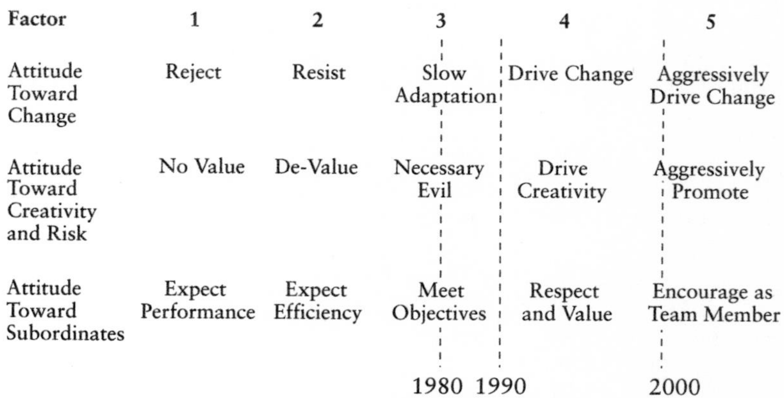

CEO Attributes

Factor	1	2	3	4	5
Attitude Toward Change	Reject	Resist	Slow Adaptation	Drive Change	Aggressively Drive Change
Attitude Toward Creativity and Risk	No Value	De-Value	Necessary Evil	Drive Creativity	Aggressively Promote
Attitude Toward Subordinates	Expect Performance	Expect Efficiency	Meet Objectives	Respect and Value	Encourage as Team Member
			1980 1990		2000

FIGURE 3.4. Linking CEO Attributes, Profit, and Environment. Adapted from H. Igor Ansoff's Strategic Diagnosis procedures. Used with permission.

and its capabilities. Those changes meant that the basic attributes and skill sets of executives needed to be drastically different from what they had been over the preceding two decades.

A look at the changing profile requirements for CEOs on the "ladder of performance" is equally revealing. As shown in Figure 3.4, between 1980 and 2000, executives needed to move from reluctantly accepting change to championing it. Notice also that the attitude that executives had toward subordinates was also a critical area of change. That explains why companies like Southwest Airlines did so well in the turbulent 1990s and early 2000.

HOW SUCCESSFUL CEOS DIFFER FROM UNSUCCESSFUL CEOS

Successful CEOs understand the necessity of continually driving learning, transformation, and performance. That is how they view the art of management. It is that view of management that drives an organization to achieve strategic balance. The leader of an organization creates expectations of excellence and uses positional power to ensure that the company is a learning organization and has the agility to match the speed of the environment (thus maintaining the Triad of Success). All exceptional CEOs whose companies do well in the new economy will score about the same (very high . . . near level 4.5 to 5) when assessed. At the same time, the CEOs of companies that are not doing well in the new economy will score in the 3.0 to 3.5 range, for two reasons:

- They do not understand the environmental turbulence of their industry.
- They hold an old view of management (planning, organizing, leading, and controlling) instead of the more adaptive modern view of management (learning, transformation, and performance).

To put it another way, some CEOs create nonadaptive, slow organizations and others create fast, adaptive organizations. The case for this argument can be made by looking at some level 5 CEOs and their companies. A good company to start with is Cisco Systems.

"IS JOHN CHAMBERS THE BEST CEO ON EARTH?"

The May 2000 edition of *Fortune Magazine* asked that question on its cover. Chambers, CEO of Cisco Systems, has done a remarkable job since taking the helm of the company. As with all CEOs who lead successful companies in the turbulent 2000s, John Chambers has a management profile in the level 5 range of the CEO Attributes scale, as shown in Figure 3.5.

Since the company went public in 1990, its stock has increased an astounding 100,000 percent in value.[1] During that time the company vied with the likes of Microsoft to become the most valuable company on earth.

Factor	1	2	3	4	5
Attitude Toward Change	Reject	Resist	Slow Adaptation	Drive Change	Aggressively Drive Change
Attitude Toward Creativity and Risk	No Value	De-Value	Necessary Evil	Drive Creativity	Aggressively Promote
Attitude Toward Subordinates	Expect Performance	Expect Efficiency	Meet Objectives	Respect and Value	Encourage as Team Member

FIGURE 3.5. CEO Profile of Cisco's John Chambers.
Adapted from H. Igor Ansoff's Strategic Diagnosis procedures.
Used with permission.

Chambers does have a reputation for being tough, especially when it comes to the company's customers. He will accept nothing less than excellence. He also likes to make sure that Cisco is constantly involved in anticipating and discovering the future. That attitude includes working with the Justice Department to ensure that the firm stays clear of any possible antitrust actions.[2]

Working at Cisco, as with other excellent companies, is not a walk in the park. The Cisco culture is one of winning and hard work. It is also similar to the cultures of Southwest Airlines and Pizza Hut, where everyone in the organization matters. John Chambers insists on this. In one case, he wanted to promote Barbara Beck from director of HR to senior VP. She suggested that she might not be the right person for the job, since she had three young children and often needed to be available for them. His response: "Barbara, if we can't figure out how to do it for you, we aren't worth much as a company."[3]

Chambers spends a lot of time making sure that Cisco's values and culture are sustained. He ensures that the firm maintains its focus on excellence in dealing with the customer. He was late to his first board meeting as CEO because he stopped to help solve a customer problem. His management style is most often characterized as "coaching."

As with many other executives who are extremely successful, John Chambers learned some important lessons at another company (IBM, in this case) before he joined Cisco. He was frustrated with the internal focus that IBM had adopted during the 1980s as well as with its inflexible nature. Chambers brought those lessons to Cisco. (One interesting practice at Cisco is that the executives don't take the outside window offices. Those go to the team. Chambers, just like all the top managers, has a modest inside office.)

Cisco gives a lot of its annual stock incentives to nonmanagers—42 percent in 1999. Chambers makes sure that managers understand the importance of empowerment in creating success in the rapidly changing technology environment. He has little patience with managers who are controlling and directive. He works very hard to keep the company focused out of the box, instead of on whatever it is currently doing. "Our core competency is our people," he states.[4]

He suggests that Cisco might have one real skill or competence, which he describes as "IP" or Internet protocol. He also suggests that whatever the company does well today (the standard definition of core competencies) is irrelevant. Chambers believes that if Cisco is to be successful in the future, it has to be willing to go wherever the environment leads.

Chambers's attitude might be described as "discontinuous adaptation." That is, he is not concerned with the past or staying in any specific segment of the market. He will go anywhere and do whatever the environment demands. Under Chambers's leadership, Cisco has paid some high prices to obtain new technologies. He views such acquisitions as having a twofold importance: bringing in new, emerging technology, and—what he regards as most important—taking over the intellectual capital of the acquired firm, that is, its people. Chambers is obsessive about open communication and recognition. That may be why

Cisco typically loses less than 5 percent of the employees of acquired companies.[5]

John Chambers walks the talk when it comes to the culture and leadership style he regards as critical in supporting supersonic levels of technological change. As already noted, he keeps the company on the leading edge of technology developments in the product area. He also makes sure that the internal technology applications of the organization keep the company in the lead as well. By 2000, the company was taking 85 percent of its orders over the Internet. That amounts to $40 million dollars a day![6]

John Chambers illustrates an interesting reality of leadership in a technology-driven world. Chambers has a law degree and an MBA. A lot of people just did not think he could be successful in leading a high-tech company. The reality is, level 5 leaders will generally do quite well (as Chambers has proven), regardless of the industry.

Strategic balance is the goal and outcome of every move Chambers makes. He is the corporate enforcer of learning and agility. He makes sure that the company gets to the future first. He does that by setting a standard of excellence in everything that the company does. From its product portfolio (balancing it to achieve leadership in technology) to its people (building a really happy team), he has created an organization designed to succeed in a high-speed environment.

STRATEGIC BALANCE: A YACHT-RACING ANALOGY

Yacht racing is one of the most challenging and complex sports around. A good skipper must be part meteorologist, part psychologist, part physicist, a good teacher, excellent at geometry, extremely patient, and totally committed to win. Nonetheless, skippers do not win races, crews do. No matter what other skills may be brought to the race, if the skipper can't build and hold a cohesive, trained, and motivated crew, victory is almost impossible.

A well-trimmed yacht cuts through the water with a special sound like a rushing train. When each member of the crew—from the helmsman to the sail trimmer—is on the job, the yacht takes on a life of its own. The result is a synergistic effect that drives the boat faster and more efficiently than any amount of micromanagement could give it. The skipper whose crew does best at finding its ideal balance is apt to beat out competitors' boats even when those boats have advantages of hull or rigging design that ought to have given them an edge.

A company that achieves strategic balance is quite similar to a fine-tuned yacht. Each part of the organization is working in harmony. There is no battle between different functions because each respects and values the contribution made by the others. An organization "in tune" is one that has the appropriate balance between marketing, innovation (R&D), sales, production, technology, and many others. Much as with a winning yacht, it is the skipper who is responsible for maintaining the balance among the roles of all the players. Without that balance, it is impossible to win.

Successful companies do not just do one thing well. They do many things well. Companies that reach a level of high learning and agility do not get there by accident. Organizational learning and agility are the result of careful planning and maintenance of those attributes. It is the senior executive of the firm who must proactively drive complex, high-performance organizations.

E-chaos creates continual tsunami events that can roll over an organization without notice. The challenge of meeting change can no longer be left to an organization's planning department—it must be shared by the entire organization. What that means is that an organization must weave learning into every activity. Organizational learning that leads as well as protects a company's future must be as closely managed as any other area of the firm.

Certainly, excellent companies sometimes do use self-organizing teams—if they achieve the appropriate combination of factors such as culture, valuing of risk, rewards, and so on, virtual teams will often form, solve a problem, and then disappear. That fact does not, however, make the case for ecological management or establish that companies do not really need excellent leadership at the top. As I see it, it actually defeats the idea that all a company needs is to be left alone and it will evolve to some higher state.

Racing yacht crews often make independent adjustments during the progress of a race. The crew members trimming the jib (foresail) may work in conjunction with the crew handling the main sail to experiment with different combinations of sail trim to deal with changes in sea or wind conditions. In most cases, the skipper of the yacht is the one who creates the on-board environment that fosters such behavior. Often when such adjustments are made, the crew will suggest that the skipper (who is usually at the helm) also make adjustments in how the boat is steered or tacked (turned). It becomes a ballet on water. A group of people working together, often passing strategies to the top, yet the entire group never forgets that it is the skipper who must make the final decision.

Experience has shown the following: Yachts that win some of the time have skippers that make almost all the decisions. Yachts that self-organize (no strong leadership from the skipper) always lose. Yachts with skippers that display strong leadership skills (especially those listed earlier) are consistent winners. Companies are no different. It is the CEO who leads the systematic balancing of all aspects of the organization who will win. And just as on a yacht, there must be balance.

A number of theorists have suggested that the senior executive is relatively unimportant when it comes to organizational success. That is simply not true. In just the same way that winners in the new millennium will deploy technology effectively, those same companies will understand the critical role of the executive. It takes more than the latest technology and more than just a good product. It takes balance among all the drivers of success. It takes strategic balance, and it is the CEO who is responsible for creating that balance.

DAVE HOUSE: A GREAT SKIPPER

A casual observer who managed to get into one of Dave House's staff meetings at Bay Networks in the late 1990s would have been in for a shock. Imagine walking into the room and seeing Dave House and one of his subordinates standing toe to toe, in an animated argument over a product decision. The two engage in a heated debate and when the smoke clears, Dave House congratulates the subordinate for sticking to his guns.

Some executives like to make sure that everyone knows who is the boss. They abhor even the thought that someone would disagree with them—after all, they're the CEO. Not so with Dave House. Can you imagine having a CEO who expected you to disagree openly? At Bay Networks, if you worked with Dave House, disagreeing with the CEO was part of your job description.

Dave House is a creative individual. He is the one who came up with the "Intel Inside" idea when he was an executive with Intel. Under his leadership, Intel's Microprocessor Division went from $40 million in 1978 to $4 billion in 1991.[7]

When Dave House accepted the job as CEO of Bay Networks, all was not well with the company. As he described his immediate priorities, "The first was to set the company's organizational structure and establish a culture. Then we refurbished the product line in 1997."[8]

One of the most important things that House did was to emphasize the need for organizational learning. Each executive at Bay Networks received a daily briefing that summarized competitor strategies and technology trends. House wanted to be sure that the whole team understood the challenges of the emerging environment.[9]

In planning growth at Bay Networks, House paid a lot of attention to two critical areas: people and technology. As part of the company's growth and innovation strategy, House and his team went after specific technologies that would allow them to better balance their product portfolio. They also realized (as do the people at Cisco) that intellectual capital is extremely important. That's why in each acquisition, Bay Networks went out of its way to bring the acquired company's team into the Bay fold.[10]

When asked to describe his management style in three words or less, Dave House replied, "Customers, employees, innovation."[11] Making these three elements into priorities is the key to maintaining strategic balance. In 1999, after assuming the presidency of Nortel (Nortel acquired Bay Networks in 1999 for $9.1 billion), House wrote an article that appeared on the Novell Web site. The article reveals clearly that Dave House concentrates on the future. In that article, he predicted that the new world of communication would be primarily a wireless world. He also predicted that it would be seamless. That is, office sites and residences would have wireless microcells allowing the integration of voice, data, messaging, and so on. Those small networks would be seamlessly connected to the public network. He also predicted that it would be possible for an individual to have just one phone number that would work regardless of location (work, home, anywhere) and that voice, faxing, e-mail, and so on would be unified.[12] A short year and a half after Dave House made his predictions, a Richardson, Texas, company named Telecom Technologies announced that it had developed a technology called a "soft switch." The device allows individuals to use one phone number for all their communications and effectively unifies voice, data, messaging, e-mail, and the rest.

Personal Reflections on Nortel

In 1994, Nortel was characterized by a lot of silos. That is, the various technology areas were isolated from each other. One of the company's research managers asked me to facilitate a two-day planning session for a team of managers from all parts of the company, including the wireless group, the traditional wired applications group, and the Internet group. We first developed a turbulence prediction for 1998, which indicated extremely high levels of competition, high rates of change, and very high levels of unpredictability. Next, the group split into teams including members from each of the three technology areas, and challenged each team to develop different scenarios of the future. As the teams progressed through their analysis, they each began to see that the telecommunications world was about to converge . . . wired, wireless, and Internet into one.

In 1995, I conducted a number of studies within Nortel. Using predictive modeling, it became apparent that the implications of the new digital revolution were massive. It became clear that telephony applications as they existed at that time would undergo a radical shift to digital applications. That meant that the real threat to telephony manufacturers was from computer manufacturers, not from each other.

One study uncovered some fairly significant strategic imbalances within Nortel related to its ability to compete effectively in the new digital environment. The study also revealed that the technology base of the client division would become obsolete in the digital revolution. Not surprisingly, the client organization rejected the findings of the study.

When John Roth was promoted from president to chairman of Nortel, he recognized the problem and immediately took steps to make sure that Nortel became a leader in the digital revolution. The $9 billion acquisition of Bay Networks was a significant step in regaining their leadership in the new digital economy. Under Roth's leadership, Nortel Networks (as it is now known) has become a leader in numerous technology areas—including optical technologies, which have the potential to drive yet another major shift in the world of communications.

BILL MITCHELL AND TEXAS INSTRUMENTS

Bill Mitchell, who retired as vice chairman of Texas Instruments in 1996, had the opportunity to watch many of the massive changes of the 1980s and 1990s with a much different perspective from what U.S. executives could bring to bear. In an interview for this book, he told me he had begun his career with TI as an engineer in 1961. In the 1980s Bill was involved in defense department technologies, including the so-called *black projects* (top secret defense initiatives that appear as a black box on the U.S. budget). He witnessed the fall of the Soviet Union and how that led to a significant shift in defense-related industries.

Bill was also involved in the U.S.–Japan technology battles. Texas Instruments was one of the premier U.S. companies in developing partnerships with Japanese companies and at the same time protecting vital technologies. As he neared the end of his career, Bill was involved in another issue: the coming digital revolution.

Throughout the years, TI had a highly diversified base of product families. That is, it had a massive defense group, a semiconductor group, a geophysical group, and numerous consumer products groups. With the assistance of people like M. Scott Myers, a consultant, TI built an organization that valued intellectual capital. Further, it developed a culture and values that emphasized the importance of every individual in creating the future of the organization.

As a result, TI created one of the first digital watches. It was a leader in hand-held calculators. It had a PC group, and also created a notebook computer that received worldwide acceptance as a best-in-class product. Its people were leaders in the area of pure research also. The semiconductor was invented at Texas Instruments.

In the early 1990s, the TI executive team spent a lot of time assessing the company and its product families. They realized that they had a company that could be expected to produce consistent growth and profit. At the same time, when they compared their product families with those of other companies, their products did not have the future growth and profit attractiveness they saw in those of other companies that they investigated.

Bill Mitchell suggests that a lot of thought went into TI's consideration of changing the focus of its products. On one hand, he suggests, TI had a nicely diversified product balance. When the chip business was down, it could count on the defense business to maintain company profits. The same was true for the other areas. When one was down, another would be up. That strategy avoided what Mitchell calls "focus risk." Focus risk means that the product focus is so narrow that when a downturn occurs in the segment, the entire company endures a downturn because there is no offsetting income from diversified products.

At the same time, the executive team foresaw another problem. They realized that the turbulence of the environment was increasing (though they did not use those exact words). They also realized that as turbulence increases, so does critical mass (the amount of money it takes to develop a product and get it to the break-even point). That reality put the TI executives into a quandary. On one hand, the turbulence of the emerging environment meant that diversification could shelter the company's earnings from drastic swings. On the other, if the firm was to have the money to reach critical mass in its chosen product areas, it would have to liquidate slow-growth product areas in favor of more attractive opportunities.

During the first half of that decade, the executive team also caught a glimpse of the massive changes that digitization could bring to the world. "We realized that we had to drastically change our culture and values if we were to compete in the digital revolution," says Mitchell. "We started changing our culture 10 years before we anticipated that shift. We knew it would take time to make such a change. We also knew we could not effectively compete unless we were successful in making that change."

As the executive team continued to investigate the future world, they concluded that digitization was going to drastically shift the role of technology by the end of the decade. They foresaw a convergence of analog applications into digital applications (telephony, computing, communications, the Internet). It was then that they realized the explosive nature of the digital revolution. The company's leadership set out to make it a leader in that new digital world. They made the decision to divest slow-growth product families to meet the critical mass requirements of the future, turbulent environment. They also set out to change the culture, structure, management, and product portfolio philosophy of the firm so as to achieve strategic balance. Figure 3.6 illustrates TI's profile and how it compared with the environment by 2000.

"I think that when any firm loses its balance it's in trouble," says Mitchell, replying to a question about how some firms allowed their focus on EVA (capital-budgeting-based assessments) to dominate the thinking of the firm's leadership. He went on, "The marketing, finance, and accounting people may have different information. It's the blending or balancing of that information that provides appropriate strategy and quality decisions. Unless the value of all parties is recognized, the output will be flawed."

Mitchell had another response to a question that seems to be similar to executives from almost all of the top performing companies in the world. The question involved the issue of how people are treated. A lot of the best companies seem to think that an organization's performance is directly linked to how well people are treated or valued by their superiors. His response was powerful and insightful:

> *I think it goes a lot further than that. I could never see myself as an individual at the top of anything. I viewed myself as a member of a team, while at the same time, accepting my personal responsibility for performance excellence.*

Product Technology Applications

Factor	1	2	3	4	5
Technology Applications (Product)	None	Limited	Moderate	High	Very High
Technology Philosophy	None	Last In	Adapt with Competition	Seek Early Adaptation	First Mover

CEO Attributes

Factor	1	2	3	4	5
Attitude Toward Change	Reject	Resist	Slow Adaptation	Drive Change	Aggressively Drive Change
Attitude Toward Creativity and Risk	No Value	De-Value	Necessary Evil	Drive Creativity	Aggressively Promote
Attitude Toward Subordinates	Expect Performance	Expect Efficiency	Meet Objectives	Respect and Value	Encourage as Team Member

Management

Factor	1	2	3	4	5
Leadership Style	Controlling	Moderately Controlling	Results Oriented	Empowering	Inspirational
Attitude Toward Risk	Reject	Discourage	Tolerate	Encourage	Expect

FIGURE 3.6. CEO and Management Profiles of Texas Instruments: 2000. Adapted from H. Igor Ansoff's Strategic Diagnosis procedures. Used with permission.

> *That suggests that I needed to treat people more as equals and that was the way the organization became a winner. I would have to agree: How you treat people goes straight to the bottom line.*

I go into more detail about TI's strategy development during this time period in Chapter Eight, "Product Management and

Complex Environments." For the moment, it is enough to say that the real key to the global technology leadership of the firm was its senior executive's foresight in creating an organization that achieved strategic balance with its environment. That achievement allowed the company to take the lead in the technological revolution.

SPRINT PCS: DESIGNED TO WIN

Another company that had a lot to do with the digital revolution is Sprint PCS. An interview with Keith Paglusch, the second employee hired by the company, reveals many of the secrets of winning in the new economy. At the time of the interview, Paglusch was executive vice president of Sprint PCS.

In October 1994, Sprint Corporation joined forces with three major cable television companies to form Sprint Spectrum, L.P., now known as Sprint PCS. By 2000, the company was the largest 100 percent digital nationwide wireless network in the United States. By that time, the firm served more than 4,000 metropolitan areas in the country, and continued to be the fastest-growing U.S. wireless carrier. In October 1998, Sprint bought out its partners in Sprint PCS and took the firm public. By October 2000, the firm had grown to 26,000 people.

Keith Paglusch clearly recognizes the reasons for the phenomenal success of the company, which was designed for success from day one. "We knew we wanted to break the mold from the beginning," he says, adding, "We knew that we had to be the most innovative and aggressive firm going if we were going to be able to effectively go after this market and win." He went on to describe how the wireless market at the time his company entered the market was somewhat fragmented. There were a lot of regional carriers, but there really wasn't one national player.

"We broke the wireless paradigm," says Paglusch. The company set out to be a marketing innovator from the beginning. It began by building caller ID and voice mail into its system, and in 1999 introduced wireless data capability.

When they started the company, the senior executives knew that they needed to be different if they were to become the innovation force in the market that they wanted to be. From the beginning, they focused on developing a modest, collaborative, almost "Internet-like" organization. The executives also felt that they had to create an internal atmosphere of excellence. That meant that they would treat their people as well as their customers extremely well. It also meant that the standard for everything they did was "excellence."

They paid a lot of attention to their culture. From the beginning, the executive team spent a great deal of time in making sure that the company's culture was open, supportive, and fostered creativity as well as risk-taking. "We place a lot of value on our culture," says Paglusch. "It's the oil that greases the creative wheels of the company." According to Paglusch, the management team also spent a lot of time in avoiding what some call "silos." *Silos* are segments of the company, often divisions or product areas, that find themselves competing with each other. Siloing is usually the result of bureaucracy. "We began with the idea that we wanted to create an organization that had a 'cross-functional attitude,'" says Paglusch. "We also spend a lot of time making sure that it continues."

At one point during the interview, I asked if Keith Paglusch was aware of the differences between his company—especially its understanding of how the emphasis on leadership and culture fosters high levels of technological excellence—and the way that the majority of companies were run. (Sprint was in the 10 percent of companies that understood the importance of empowerment and open communication.) His response: "Most of us had worked at those companies [the other 90 percent] and we knew from that exactly what we did not want to be and what we wanted to be."

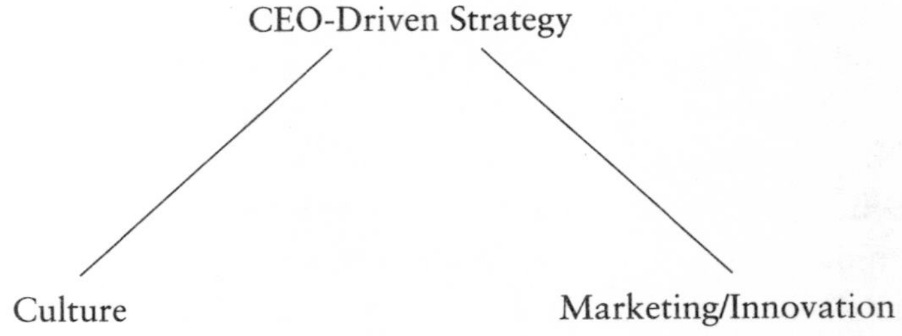

FIGURE 3.7. Key Success Drivers at Sprint PCS.

Strategy at Sprint PCS

Sprint PCS obviously spends a lot of time in making sure that the organization is capable of sustaining entrepreneurial behavior. It does that with structure, leadership, and culture. It also spends a lot of time in maintaining the levels of aggressiveness of innovation and marketing. "If I were to draw a picture of how we view our organization, it would look like this," says Paglusch, sketching the graphic shown in Figure 3.7.

"We get a lot of our ideas from our people," Paglusch says. "We view our people as our 'intellectual capital.' The senior executive team would be the first to say that a lot of the really good ideas generated in this organization start at the bottom. Our job is just to make sure that we maintain that attitude in the organization—26,000 people have a lot more intellectual horsepower than a few senior executives. We try to never forget that."

From a strategy standpoint, the firm fully intends to be the first mover in any market that it targets. Keith Paglusch says, "The future market is the driving force of our strategy. You can't stay ahead by resting on your historic success." Thinking back to the preceding example, I can't resist noting that Nortel Networks has been one of Sprint PCS's major partners in creating its network—further evidence of the emerging leadership of Nortel Networks in the digital economy.

If Sprint's competitors think they are going to rest on their historic successes, they had better think again. Sprint has already announced that it is expanding its involvement in wireless Internet access. Further, it has announced that in 2001 or early 2002, it will offer 2.4MB/second data streaming on its network. That may sound technical to some, but it's very practical indeed. It will make all sorts of flashy digital applications possible—just for starters, think what you could do with high-resolution video conferencing between notebook computers.

Sprint PCS is a company that knows how to succeed in the new digital world. Its managers understand the importance of balancing organization and technology. They understand how the effective combination of the two creates an agile, profitable company. A look at a few of the profiles of the company, shown in Figure 3.8, demonstrates how it is able to sustain its leadership position in the industry.

The strategic profile reveals some of the reasons for the successes of Sprint PCS. It is important to remember that the whole organization is in strategic balance with its environment. Notice how the CEO's emphasis on change, creativity, and risk-taking is perfectly matched for the environment. At the same time, its aggressive technology strategy is strongly supported by the other two.

LEADING IN MAJOR ENVIRONMENTAL SHIFTS

Rob McCoy is famous among industry-watchers for his dynamic leadership and his success at empowering people to achieve excellence. When I began working on this book, I called McCoy's office (then at GTE) and he agreed to visit and discuss his philosophy of management. It turns out that McCoy is a level 5 leader, and he's also someone who can take the principles he practices to different product and market segments and make them work.

CEO Attributes

Factor	1	2	3	4	5
Attitude Toward Change	Reject	Resist	Slow Adaptation	Drive Change	Aggressively Drive Change
Attitude Toward Creativity and Risk	No Value	De-Value	Necessary Evil	Drive Creativity	Aggressively Promote
Attitude Toward Subordinates	Expect Performance	Expect Efficiency	Meet Objectives	Respect and Value	Encourage as Team Member

Culture

Factor	1	2	3	4	5
Values	Defend the Status Quo	Support the Status Quo	Maintain the Status Quo	Challenge the Status Quo	Create the Future
Value of Employees	Little	Minimal	Moderate	High	Very High
Rewards and Incentives	Historic Performance	Accuracy and Efficiency	Productivity	Solutions Development	Creativity

Product Technology Applications

Factor	1	2	3	4	5
Technology Applications (Product)	None	Limited	Moderate	High	Very High
Technology Philosophy	None	Last In	Adapt with Competition	Seek Early Adaptation	First Mover

FIGURE 3.8. Sprint PCS: CEO, Culture, and Product Technology Profiles. Adapted from H. Igor Ansoff's Strategic Diagnosis procedures. Used with permission.

Rob McCoy cut his teeth in the telecommunications industry. Until 1996, that industry was highly regulated, with a lot of monopolistic markets. When the opportunity to move to new markets such as long distance service arose, companies like

GTE found that they had to move from familiar, regulated markets to unregulated markets. Additionally, they had to find managers who could make that move in the face of high levels of unfamiliar competition. Rob McCoy was the man chosen to create GTE Long Distance.

McCoy knew that the new market would involve creating an entirely different type of organization. During those formative months, McCoy was accused of stealing many of GTE's "brightest and best" people for the new venture. ("Guilty as charged," responds McCoy.) He also hired only 40 percent of his new team from within GTE. He carefully chose people that would provide the right balance of skills within the new company. "It did not take them long to figure out we were not going to be an old typical telco competitor," says McCoy.

One of the things that McCoy and a group of associates did that positioned the company for deregulation was to begin building a world-class sales organization. "Ten years before all this happened, we realized that we needed an entirely different type of sales organization. We created the national accounts team. What we did was lay the foundation for the move into long distance. We also realized that as we built that organization, we had to keep it separate from the rest of the organization or its culture and values would deteriorate. It would lose its adaptability," McCoy recalls. McCoy is proud of what that sales organization did. In 1998, that team was selected as the Supplier of the Year by JC Penny. "That's because they're one of the best sales teams in the industry," McCoy says.

Rob McCoy also worked hard to create a highly flexible, adaptable team. Like a lot of the other extremely successful executives cited in this book, he moved his executive team to the center of the building, rather than giving them the window offices. He set the example by having his office in a cubicle in the middle of his team. McCoy laughs when he describes the "prairie dogging" that he and the team members engaged in.

(In case you haven't run into the expression, it refers to a common practice in open office spaces divided by low cubicle walls, where people stand up to talk to each other. Prairie dogs are burrowing rodents [rather like ground squirrels] that live in large groups sharing a tangle of tunnels with many holes to the outside, and they continually pop their heads out of the holes to look around.)

The executive team also wanted to make sure that the new team had a lot of cross-functional links, so the formal organization involved a lot of such teams. When asked about the keys for making a move from a highly predictable environment to an unregulated, highly turbulent environment, Rob McCoy lists four elements:

1. Separate the entrepreneurial efforts from the rest of the firm. (In the case of GTE, that meant that the new organization did not share any of its functions with the old organization. He made it a point to keep the organizations separate.)
2. Focus the new business segment on matching the new environment, and let the old business area stay focused on maximizing profits.
3. Remember that new business environments demand entirely new competitive profiles. You just can't take something that worked well before and expect it to work in a different, more competitive environment.
4. Drive entrepreneurial behavior from the top.

McCoy believes in what he calls "positive paranoia." That means that the CEO must constantly expect the team to focus on the future and must stay alert for potential discontinuities that could harm the organization. That also gives the firm an opportunity to profit from change by being the first mover in responding to market shifts.

When GTE Long Distance was formed, the company had numerous goals for year one. It should be no surprise to discover that the new organization created by Rob McCoy exceeded all of its goals. By December 1996, it had 825,000 customers. That was 75,000 above the goal. By the end of the first year of operation it had gotten its millionth customer, almost 30 percent above the first-year goal. Additionally, the firm had hoped to get certified to do business in 29 states during the first year—and actually got certified in all 50 by the end of the year.

As noted earlier, level 5 leaders like Rob McCoy will be effective regardless of what type of industry they are in. In August 2000, Rob McCoy was appointed president of TXU Energy Services, Inc. In addition to pursuing the deregulated power market, the new company is expected to enter a number of diverse markets, including technology markets. Rob McCoy should do quite well in leading such an organization.

SUCCESSFUL LEADERS

Most of the executives and companies featured in this chapter were technology companies. It is important to understand that whether or not a manager is managing in a technology-focused arena, the basic principles of success are the same. Managers who take a holistic, systems thinking approach to the environment will understand the critical role of technology in the new economy. They will also understand the critical need to balance all parts of the organization—not just the technological aspects—with the emerging environment.

Here is the most important point in this chapter: Although the featured executives probably do have extremely high levels of intuitive skills when it comes to balancing organization with environment, that is not necessary for success. Strategic balance can be developed as a management skill. It is a way of thinking that can be learned.

Business Policy Theory (budgeting and analysis)	Ansoff's Theories (turbulence and balance)	Traditional Strategy (mission and competency)
Moderate success and low levels of contributions	Significant success and high levels of contributions	Moderate success and low levels of contributions

FIGURE 3.9. Changing Mental Models and Success.

A PERSONAL NOTE

In the early 1990s I had the opportunity to visit San Diego and have dinner with Dr. Ansoff. During the dinner he told a story about a phone call and subsequent visit he had received from the dean of a business school where he had once served.

Ansoff and the administrator eventually went out to dinner together. At the dinner, the administrator began to discuss the reason for his visit. It seems that he had done a study of the history of the university's school of business, measuring the level of success of different cohorts of students and the level of endowments that the university had received from each group. The lower part of Figure 3.9 shows what he had found.

Prior to Dr. Ansoff's arrival, the school's graduates had done well, but few had reached the senior executive level. They also donated limited amounts to the university. During the five years that Dr. Ansoff was at the school, that pattern changed. Those graduates appeared to have reached much higher levels in corporate America—and subsequently made major contributions to the school. After Dr. Ansoff left, the pattern returned to what it had been before he joined the university.

The administrator finally got to his question: "Can you tell me how you recruited such exceptional students, when those before and after you could not?" Dr. Ansoff chuckled as he told me the story, sketching the history of the university's program that I've shown in the upper part of Figure 3.9. He said he told the administrator, "The success of the students had little to do with how they were recruited. . . . We didn't change recruiting. What we changed is what they were taught."

As the figure shows, before and after Dr. Ansoff's tenure with the university, the school taught what might be called linear approaches to organizational strategy. During Dr. Ansoff's tenure, the students learned an approach that is more nonlinear (basically, strategic balance).

Yes, there are some exceptional CEOs in the United States today. Generally, they manage in almost the same way. They all challenge organizations to discover the future and to think out of the box. They all use words like *balance, communication,* and *empowerment.* They all tend to behave in much the same way and to value the same qualities. The most important thing is this: Managers do not need to be born with the same skills . . . they can learn them!

CHAPTER 4

THE ICONOCLASTIC ORGANIZATION

A FEW YEARS AGO, THE WATCHWORD FOR MANAGEMENT WAS "lead, follow, or get out of the way!" That idea also applies to companies entering the 21st century. In e-chaos, first movers win and followers usually lose.

Figure 4.1 returns to the Triad of Success to point out how environments characterized by chaotic change may affect the basics of leadership, learning, and agility for an organization. The speed of communication and action within the firm must increase as the outside pace increases. Additionally, the way that people think must change if the firm is to respond to the new uncertain, discontinuous environment.

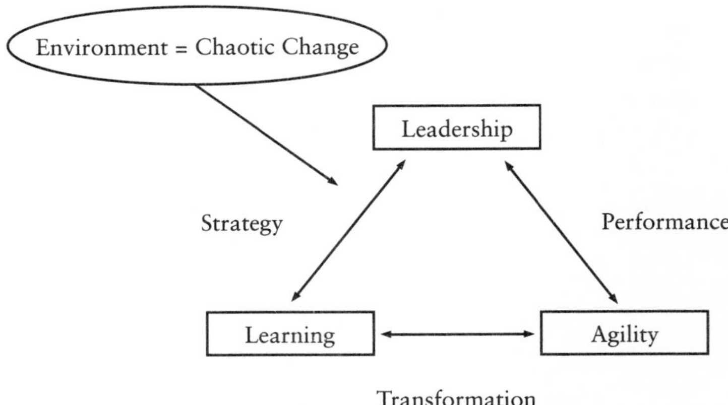

FIGURE 4.1. The Impact of Chaos on the Firm.

As noted earlier, agility comes in two flavors: reactive and proactive. But agility always has to do with speed. The faster the firm responds to discontinuous events, the lower the impact such events can have on profit. It is always important for a firm to have agility that is balanced with the environment. In e-chaos, it is critical.

Many writers address issues related to agility. For example, Henry Mintzberg focuses on what I like to call "incrementalism"—that is, he believes that it is not possible to plan for an uncertain future, so he suggests that the best way to do strategy is to respond to events incrementally after they occur.[1] Incrementalism is a form of organizational agility, but incremental responses to events must be at lighting speed if organizations are to thrive. It's easy to move a hair too slowly and fall by the wayside. And that tells only part of the story.

In chaotic environments an organization must have both reactive and proactive agility. Proactive agility involves more than being the first mover, it involves being the first *learner.* If all a firm has is reactive agility (regardless of how fast), it will always lose against firms that have both reactive and proactive agility. Success takes both.

Management in the new economy has everything to do with managing agility. To drive sustained performance, both the proactive speed of the organization and its reactive speed must be carefully matched to the speed of the environment. As pointed out in Chapter Two, it does no good to overprofile a firm and be more aggressive than the environment demands, because that costs more in money and resources than the firm needs to spend to maximize its profit—and also serves to heat up the environment unnecessarily. At the same time, it's just as unsafe to live in the past and stick with techniques just because they used to work. The companies featured in Chapter Three did well because they lived in the future. They began moving toward their anticipated target (just as Arthur Ashe did at the tennis clinic I described in Chapter Two) long before the events or circumstances they foresaw had an opportunity to affect the firm. Dave House changed the structure and culture of Bay Networks when he took over so the company could have higher levels of reactive agility. Texas Instruments began changing its culture and product portfolios years before the actual impact of digital technology hit the environment. Both companies were proactively agile.

Proactive agility means getting to the future first and then acting on the information obtained. I like to describe proactive agility as *iconoclastic*—a term that conveys the idea of challenging tradition. It really is necessary to break the current way of thinking about a business segment so that the firm can learn what the future is really going to be like.

Dave House encourages iconoclastic behavior in his organization. So does Carly Fiorino of Hewlett-Packard. So does Herb Kelleher of Southwest Airlines, and Jack Welch of GE. The list is extensive.

The problem is, iconoclastic behavior goes against much of the management theory that has developed in the past century. For a long time, the corporate world focused on command-and-control compliance reminiscent of early-20th-century military doctrine. Even today, people are rarely rewarded for going against the grain in companies. They are often fired or ignored when they behave in an iconoclastic manner. But the bottom line remains: To be successful in the emerging e-chaos environment, companies (and their leaders) must learn how to foster iconoclastic behavior. If they do not, their firms may cease to exist.

LEARNING TO WIN

Companies that do well on a long-term basis differ from those that do badly. In studying companies that deteriorate slowly and those that thrive, it becomes clear that the companies that go through long, steady deterioration tend to be the ones that focus on historic competencies. Those that enjoy sustained growth and performance are just the opposite, eagerly challenging the past and the present. They become concerned if they are not constantly finding new markets, new products, and even new types of businesses to enter. They are consumed with finding products that will keep them at the top.

Read almost any management book today and its author will tell you to focus on a firm's historic competitive advantage and core competencies if you want to lead the firm to profitability. At the heart of the idea behind core competencies and competitive advantage is the presupposition that the external environment is linear, or repetitive. What that means is that most management theories today are based on the idea that while the environment will change, the basic constructs of the firm—its core competencies and competitive advantage—will not need to change.

In the light of reality, this idea seems to fade. Companies that are successful are those that develop the ability to think and act in ways that consistently challenge the status quo, including such sacred areas as the firm's "core business" or its unique competitive advantage. It is those iconoclastic organizations that will challenge and win in the emerging infotech environment.

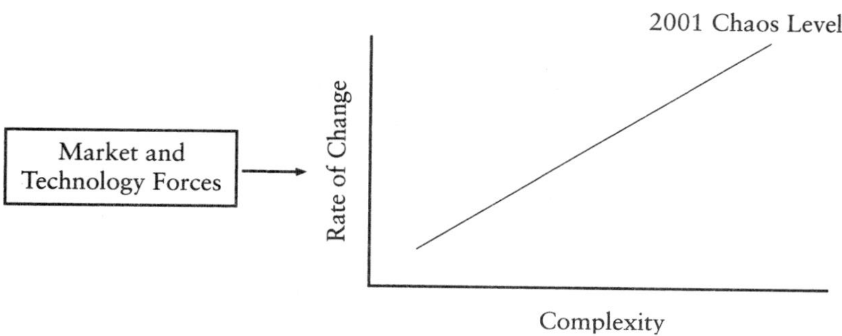

FIGURE 4.2. Complexity in the New Economy.

As Figure 4.2 suggests, the rate of change and the level of complexity had become quite high by the year 2001. As one of the two key components of the rate of change, global technology diffusion entered a near-vertical climb in the mid-1990s and was still going strong. As a result, both market forces (the other driver of the rate of change) and the other eight forces (which drive complexity) have continued to create an environment characterized by unprecedented change and complexity.

Richard D'Aveni does a wonderful job of recognizing the new nature of change and competition of the 1990s.[2] One of D'Aveni's propositions is that firms must learn how to purposefully make *discontinuous* (iconoclastic) moves. That is, since market and technology forces often result in a momentary advantage for a competitor, organizations must be able to create their own discontinuities in the market for the purpose of creating their own advantage.

At the heart of D'Aveni's ideas is the proposition that with time, companies lose their ability to think and act discontinuously, that is, "out of the box." There is reason to believe that is true. In fact, as an organization ages its core behavior usually changes from entrepreneurial to incremental ("after the fact") responses to discontinuous events.[3] Figure 4.3 portrays the phenomenon quite well—as an organization grows older, entrepreneurial behavior

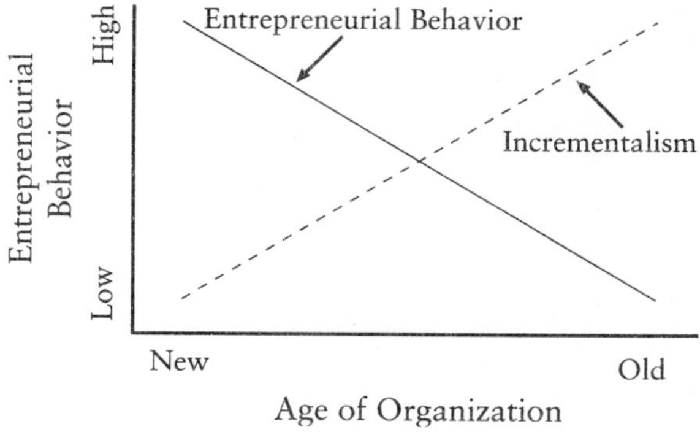

FIGURE 4.3. Age of Organization and Entrepreneurial Behavior.

will almost always decrease while bureaucracy with its attendant incrementalism increases at the same pace, drastically undercutting agility.

Incrementalism, as previously discussed, involves focusing on the present and making after-the-fact responses to events. The idea behind incrementalism is "wait until something happens, then respond." By way of contrast, entrepreneurial behavior is concerned with discovery and creativity. It is future focused. No organization can survive without the capacity for incrementalism, of course—it is a necessary coping behavior because any course of action needs to be refined in the light of actual events. However, unless it is paired with entrepreneurial behavior, it becomes a formula for failure.

TONI & GUY: ON THE LEADING EDGE OF CHANGE

One of the most interesting outcomes in the new economy has to do with who is winning. When early signs of e-chaos began to appear, many suggested that the old brick-and-mortar companies could be in trouble. While a few of the pure Internet companies have done well, it appears that the real winners are the brick-and-mortar companies that have adapted their businesses to the new technology-driven environment.

Page Brady is a 23-year-old hair stylist with Toni & Guy. She is not just any young woman and certainly she is not just any stylist. She is a member of a team that is committed to challenging tradition. At her ripe young age, she has been given opportunity and responsibility that is normally reserved for those who are much older at other organizations. Page has worked her way up to the position of staff trainer and art director for the organization. She is representative of many of the people who come to Toni & Guy and are encouraged by the leadership to discover just how gifted they really are. This 23-year-old spends much of her time in different parts of the United States or Canada preaching the Toni & Guy gospel of excellence and innovation. Who is she training? Often she trains Toni & Guy's competitors. Who in the world would be willing to train their competitors?

"We believe that we're a company that succeeds because we constantly break the mold," says Bruno Mascolo, the firm's founder and CEO. "I've always felt that our industry had a less than desirable reputation and that needed to be changed. We send people like Page around the world to share our secrets so that we can all become better as an industry." Some might say Mascolo's strategy is more than iconoclastic—it's downright crazy. Not so, says Mascolo. In fact, it benefits the industry as well as Toni & Guy.

The history of the company reveals that Bruno Mascolo failed on his first attempt to bring his innovative ideas from England to the United States. But he still wanted to build a company that was radically different. He had a vision of a company built upon innovation, excellence, people, and speed. He believed that such a company had global potential. His brothers had invested in his company the first time he tried, and he says that he was embarrassed by his failure. But "I never lost sight of that dream," he adds. "So when I got ready to try again, I did it on my own. I sold everything I had . . . my home, my cars, everything and came back to the U.S. to make it happen."

And happen it has. In a few short years, the company has developed revenues of $95 million in the United States and $200 million globally. Its growth rate over the last five years has averaged 39 percent. How does a company maintain those levels of growth? An analysis of Toni & Guy reveals that the company does it by balancing culture, innovation, and leadership. A commitment to excellence serves as the foundation for all that the company does.

As with most companies that experience sustained growth, Toni & Guy has a culture that strongly supports its people. "We understand that we have to build and maintain a people-oriented culture and values if we are to maintain our ability to be innovative," says Mascolo. "At the same time, our standards are extremely high." He goes on to explain that everyone hired at Toni & Guy must go through the Toni & Guy "university," regardless of previous training or experience. That's where employees get Mascolo's unique perspective on the business. It's the same training that the company offers others in the industry.

Bruno Mascolo often says of the Toni & Guy approach, "We catch people before they fall." The company has extremely high standards of excellence that could discourage a new employee. But Mascolo believes that if the company is to maintain its ability to innovate and lead the market, extremely high levels of trust and encouragement must be fostered.

Strategic balance in e-chaos involves the effective balance of people and technology. In a brick-and-mortar world—it's hard to do hair styling without a place for the customers to visit—Toni & Guy's leadership understands the impact that technology can have on their business. Certainly, as Figure 4.4 shows, they realize the importance of using technology in managing global operations. The company has committed to maximizing

Factor	1	2	3	4	5
Technology Strategy	Very Slow Adaptation	Slow Adaptation	Stay with Competition	Leading Edge not Bleeding Edge	Consistent First Mover
Redundancy	Unnecessary	Unimportant	Important	Serious	Critical

FIGURE 4.4. Toni & Guy's Internal Technology Applications. Adapted from H. Igor Ansoff's Strategic Diagnosis procedures. Used with permission.

the use of its GAN (global area network) so as to manage the efficiency as well as the required speed of supporting its operation.

A few years ago, Bruno Mascolo recognized a problem on the horizon. He realized that the styling industry was beginning to change at an extremely fast rate. "By 1999," says Mascolo, "we were seeing our styling change every 12 months. That meant that we needed to become even more aggressive in recognizing trends and then getting new training out to our organization."

In early 1999, Toni & Guy set out to create a technology backbone, in addition to its operating systems, that would support extremely high levels of organizational learning. The company added the latest in videoconferencing technology so that the management team could have better access to one another. But its management realized that they also had to have some way to rapidly diffuse information out to all their locations, worldwide. Mascolo hired a leading-edge technology manager from a Big Six consulting firm and told him to create a state-of-the-art system for remote learning.

Despite the realization that the World Wide Web would undergo significant change in the 2000–2004 time period, the company decided to commit to moving its university to the Web. When the project is complete at the end of 2001 (about the time the broadband capabilities of the U.S. should begin to expand significantly), the company will be able to use its technology network to deliver "just in time" training around the world. That means that the firm will be able to match the "one year cycle" (turbulence) of products with a high-speed, technology-based learning system.

Toni & Guy is a company that reveals how more traditional companies can thrive in the new economy and become highly agile, learning organizations. The willingness to challenge old ways and to integrate a firm into the new technology-driven economy can result in phenomenal success in e-chaos.

THE BIG BANG

Scientists have long talked about "the big bang" that got the universe started. Big bang events occur in business settings. They are events that "break the frame" and radically change the rules of the game. A big bang event may be the discovery of a new technology or a new business model. In the new economy, success depends on an organization's ability to create not only an occasional big bang but also a continuum of "little bangs" or profit opportunities.

Microsoft is an example of a company that engages in this type of behavior. Microsoft's big bang event was the development of Windows software. Rather than sit on this historic success, Microsoft created an internal culture that drove the development of numerous little bang events. The opportunity to milk the profits of the big bang event plus the continuing dynamics of little bang events makes Microsoft a firm that is in constant flux. It might be more accurate to call this phenomenon *dynamic renewal.* Figure 4.5 illustrates how Microsoft creates numerous products over time to keep itself at the forefront in its industry. This is the key to the ability of the firm to continually renew itself.

The strategic profile of Microsoft shown in Figure 4.6 demonstrates how the company continues to do well. Because of the CEO, the management, the culture, and the level of innovation, Microsoft is able to be a consistent first mover. Bill Gates and his cohorts tend to think iconoclastically. That is,

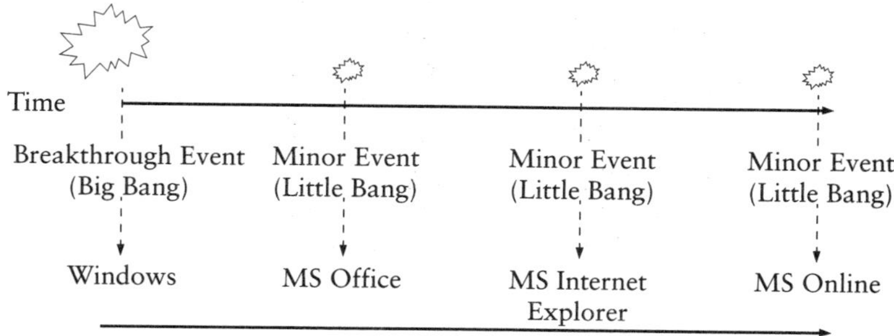

FIGURE 4.5. Microsoft: An Example of Dynamic Renewal.

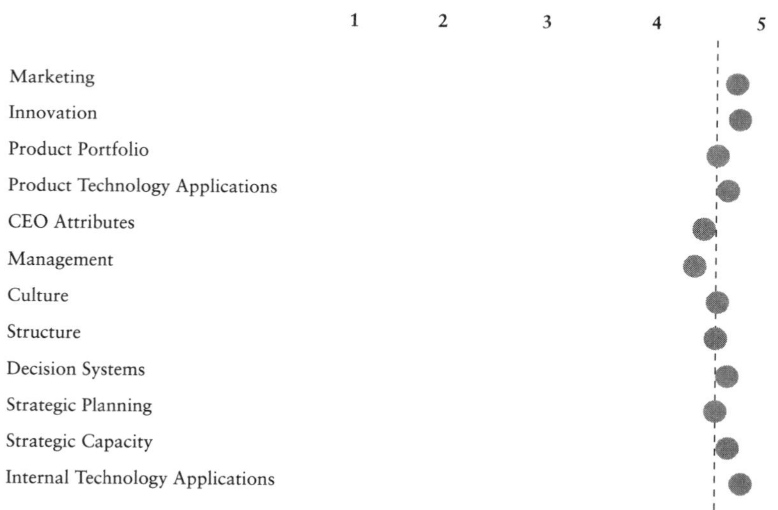

FIGURE 4.6. Profile of Microsoft Corporation.
Adapted from H. Igor Ansoff's Strategic Diagnosis procedures.
Used with permission.

they are willing to go wherever they see opportunity, not just where they think they have a competitive advantage.

Because Microsoft is designed to learn, its people are able to make iconoclastic leaps to opportunities that they see. They are not blinded by a mission-imposed mental model that limits them to some historic success area. Instead, Microsoft leveraged its big bang event of creating Windows so as to continually create little bang opportunities that fund even more growth and opportunity for the firm.

In a television interview on one of the major networks, someone asked Bill Gates what he worried about the most. "The Next Bill Gates," he replied. He often describes himself as "paranoid." Regardless, he understands that maintaining the balance of his firm with the environment is extremely important. He also realizes that Microsoft's willingness to challenge the past and the present is its key to discovering the future.

INCREMENTALISM VERSUS ICONOCLASTIC BEHAVIOR

Companies that experience a big bang event do not always continue their entrepreneurial behavior. Xerox Corporation introduced xerography to the world over 30 years ago. The patent gave Xerox a virtual monopoly on the copying business for 20 years. Unlike Microsoft, Xerox failed to continue the behavior that had earlier led to its big bang event. In fact, in the late 1970s when Xerox's patent ran out, many people thought the company was in serious trouble.

In the 1980s Xerox was able to introduce a corporate-wide total quality management program. The effect was positive, but TQM did not produce the type of change or entrepreneurial behavior that could transform the firm back into a global leader. The Xerox story is perhaps the best illustration of how and why companies fail to repeat big or little bang events. Xerox's total focus on its historic product families significantly restricted its ability to reinvent itself. In spite of almost 20 years of effort to create a new Xerox, by 2000 the basic problem of Xerox's inability to foster dynamic product renewal had not changed.

In considering Xerox and other companies that experience similar problems, a common thread emerges. These companies are unable to challenge historic thinking and historic success paradigms. It turns out that such challenges must be intentionally driven into an organization if it is to self-renew, and that organizations must purposefully engage in continuous renewal if they are to enjoy sustained success. Organizations that foster an attitude of renewal tend to both adapt well and profit from uncertainties.

From a business standpoint, the real conflict is between continuous improvement and continuous (or dynamic) *renewal.* Continuous improvement is extremely comfortable for organizations. It avoids radical change and keeps the firm in a familiar product family. Simply put, continuous improvement feels good because it does not force anyone to think in unfamiliar terms. Continuous renewal is iconoclastic in nature. The firm's leadership must constantly challenge traditional business assumptions and be willing to live in unfamiliar territory.

WAL-MART: JUST ANOTHER RETAILER?

A student in a strategy class recently said, "What I'm hearing is that companies should no longer think in terms of their historic core competencies. Doesn't the success of Wal-Mart conflict with that idea?" Actually, no, it does not conflict with the idea.

Sam Walton built his first Wal-Mart in Rogers, Arkansas, in 1963. At the heart of his concept was the idea of eliminating the wholesaler. The traditional value chain in the retailing industry had always evolved around the wholesaler. What Sam Walton did to create a big bang event in retailing was to eliminate one of the largest costs to the customer, the wholesaler. This was a significant change in the retailing industry.

To understand the implications of direct buying, consider the plight of a typical office supplies retailer in the 1970s. A standard name brand stapler had a list price of $29. The office supply retailer bought the stapler from the wholesaler at approximately $14.50 and usually resold the stapler for around $21. The wholesaler, buying in large lots, was often paying less than $3 for the stapler. The discount retailer that bought in large quantity was able to buy the stapler for $3 and sell it to

Innovation (Aggressiveness)

Factor	**1**	**2**	**3**	**4**	**5**
R&D Spending	Low	Moderately Low	Competitive	Moderately High	Highly Aggressive
Product Life Cycles-Plan	Very Long	Long	Moderate	Short	Very Short
Customer Focus	Respond To Demands	Meet Demand	Stay Close to Customer	Anticipate Needs	Anticipate Unrealized Needs

FIGURE 4.7. Wal-Mart's Innovation Aggressiveness.
Adapted from H. Igor Ansoff's Strategic Diagnosis procedures.
Used with permission.

the consumer for $6, and still make a substantial margin. The office supply retailer couldn't compete with the discounters, and during the 1970s all but about 4,000 of the 12,000 office supply firms in the United States went out of business.

Sam Walton created a big bang event. By the year 2000, there were over 2,000 Wal-Mart stores in the United States with sales of over $55 billion. The Wal-Mart big bang event was so traumatic that every time a Wal-Mart store opened in a market, numerous traditional retailers were forced out of business. Consider the high level of innovation of Wal-Mart profiled in Figure 4.7.

But Sam Walton and Wal-Mart did not allow the firm to rest on its historic success formula. Between 1963 and 2000, the Wal-Mart competitive model changed many times. The company vertically integrated from the customer all the way back to the primary manufacturer. The final step in the process was to cut out the manufacturers' representatives, some of whom had served Wal-Mart for decades.

One writer suggests that the key to understanding Wal-Mart's success is to understand Wal-Mart's ability to align itself with the environment.[4] Nothing could be further from the

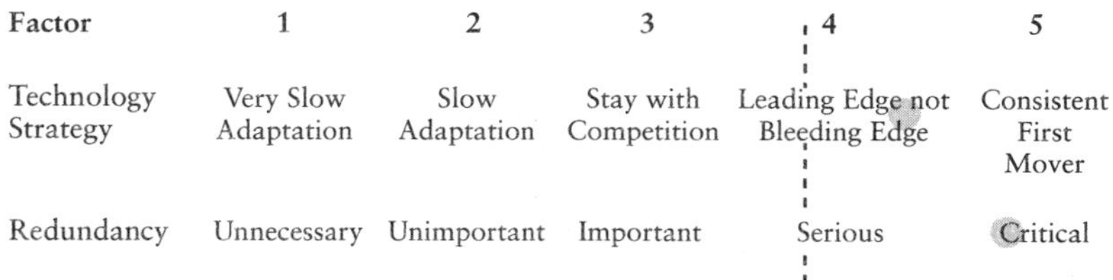

Factor	1	2	3	4	5
Technology Strategy	Very Slow Adaptation	Slow Adaptation	Stay with Competition	Leading Edge not Bleeding Edge	Consistent First Mover
Redundancy	Unnecessary	Unimportant	Important	Serious	Critical

FIGURE 4.8. Wal-Mart's Technology Applications.
Adapted from H. Igor Ansoff's Strategic Diagnosis procedures.
Used with permission.

truth. An investigation of Wal-Mart's history certainly reveals that the company is highly reactive. However, the most important attribute of Wal-Mart has been the organizational ability to create a series of little bang events to sustain profitability. As I've noted, Wal-Mart was a first mover in creating a true vertically integrated retail organization. Later, it created its own transportation division. Still later, it created a highly successful warehousing mechanism that enabled it to keep every store supplied on a daily basis. By 1995, Wal-Mart's commitment to innovation resulted in the creation of a wide area network that provided very high-speed transfer of in-store information.[5] As Figure 4.8 shows, Wal-Mart's technology applications are extremely well balanced with the environment.

Wal-Mart has never been willing to rest on what the firm used to be. It has maintained high levels of innovative capabilities throughout the years. That has translated into leading its industry instead of following. The creation of internal technology support systems to drive the efficiency and speed of the organization is just one illustration of those abilities.

With few exceptions, companies that go to the top and stay at the top are companies that foster entrepreneurial attitudes and behaviors. They are companies that continually seek to be the first movers. Rather than repeating historic success behaviors, they tend to concentrate on the future and its complexities as well as its possible discontinuities. Jim Collins, coauthor of *Built to Last,* expressed the idea as follows: "You focus not on what you do but on what you could do."[6]

Research supports the idea that a mental model, or how a leader thinks about the present and the future, has everything to do with the ability of the organization to continually renew itself.[7] Further research shows that if an organization is to maintain an attitude of entrepreneurship, this attitude must be carefully planned and supported.[8]

THE ICONOCLASTIC ADVANTAGE

In an age of e-chaos, competitive success must relate to the ability of a firm to think and act in an iconoclastic manner—not to its ability, however great, to focus on sustainable historic competencies. Organizations that create both big bang and little bang events are those that challenge tradition. They are led by and populated by people who are unwilling to accept existing competitive limits and view their raison d'être as the discovery of new and better ways to live and do business.

IBM's pioneering work in mainframe computer technologies is an example of iconoclastic behavior. Early in its existence, the firm was willing to move from its historic arena of mechanical business machines into electronic computing. However, at some point the company lost that willingness to think and act iconoclastically. Once IBM became internally focused, its entrepreneurial efforts ceased. It took a succession of CEOs plus the loss of billions of dollars for IBM to get back to its iconoclastic roots. By the year 2000, Lou Gerstner had driven IBM to reinvent itself. The evidence that IBM had changed its basic character was twofold—the company was again involved in the rapid development of new, potentially breakthrough types of products, and it had returned to profitability. That return to profitability was not driven by any back-to-basics or historic competencies approach, it was driven by creativity and the discovery of new market opportunities. Under Gerstner's leadership, the firm became a primary player in the digital revolution.

Intel's historic success has come from what the firm's former chairman calls his personal paranoia. Andy Grove has been known to describe himself as paranoid about the competition. As a result, he drove Intel to maintain its ability to consistently be the first mover. The same has been true of Hewlett-Packard. The firm is a global leader in a number of key product areas because of its commitment to maintain a first-mover position in its industry.

Iconoclastic behavior is not usually an accident. With the exception of a few rare events in history, iconoclastic events have been the result of an unceasing commitment to discover new and better ways of doing things. The question might be asked: If an attitude of iconoclastic behavior is so important to a firm, why don't we see evidence that organizations are attempting to foster such behavior?

WHY ORGANIZATIONS (PEOPLE) RESIST ICONOCLASTIC EFFORT

Chapter Seven focuses on the issue of change in more depth, but it is important at this point to go over some of the issues related to human perception and actions designed to support profitable responses to emerging environments.

The first problem is the impact of change itself. The process of changing is both disruptive and unprofitable in and of itself.[9] Organizational change disrupts organizational flow. As a result, it may have a negative impact on performance, and it might therefore seem prudent to avoid change at all costs. Second, when confronted with complex change in the environment, organizations try to simplify the various aspects of the change into smaller, more understandable ideas.

What this means is that organizations tend to act like people (since organizations are made up of people) and resist the idea of complexity. It would follow that at the same time,

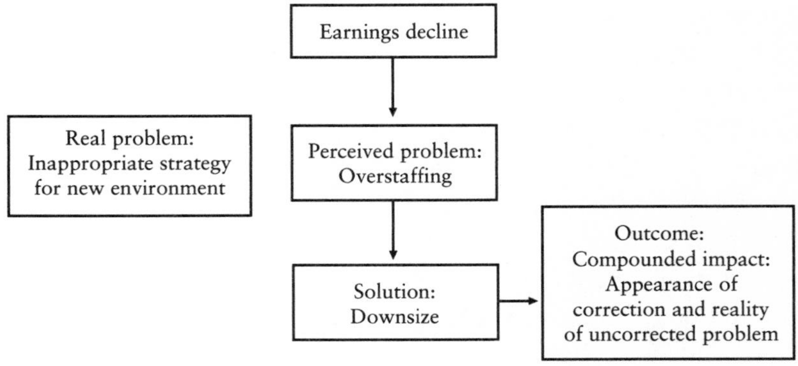

FIGURE 4.9. Failing to Differentiate Between Symptoms and Problems.

organizations encountering complex challenges would then seek out simplistic explanations and simplistic solutions to the complex challenges. This is often translated into inappropriate solutions or the rejection of any solutions at all.

In the mid-1990s—when profits plummeted for many companies—management resorted to downsizing as the solution of choice. In reality, the downsizing initiatives were a Band-Aid at best. Figure 4.9 shows the way many firms respond to problems by missing the actual cause of their troubles.

The firms were appearing to correct the problem since their downsizing boosted short-term results enough to make it look as though the problem had been solved. In reality, the failure to correct the organizational mismatch with the environment resulted in increased negative impact on future earnings. Even the popular press picked up on research suggesting that "downsizing rarely results in increased performance."[10]

UNDERSTANDING ROOT CAUSES AND PERFORMANCE-ORIENTED SOLUTIONS

Market change and technology change, as I've noted on several occasions, drive the rate of change in the environment. The failure to internally address the changing rate of change results in decreased performance in the organization. At the same time, changes in the remaining eight forces drive substantial changes in the complexity of the external environment. Logically, neither downsizing nor any other singular fad can solve the problem of increased rates of change or complexity—but the problem can be solved. Here's how the correct identification of problems can lead to effective solutions:

Root Problem	*Solution*
Increasing rate of change	Process reengineering Highly flexible structure Technology applications
Increasing market change	Increased marketing aggressiveness Enhanced decision systems Increased levels of innovation
Increasing Complexity	Strategic intelligence Open, learning organization New organizational structures (flexible) Leadership (focused on innovation and creativity; empowering) Nonlinear planning New rewards systems

These are just a few of the ways that an organization needs to use to address changes in either the rate of environmental change or the level of environmental complexity. Notice that each solution is specifically addressed to one root problem.

Sustainable iconoclastic advantage is based in such thinking. That is, iconoclastic organizations continually discover the future because they plan on doing just that. Iconoclastic organizations do not just wake up in the morning and decide to do something different that day. What really happens is that they first understand that the future will require a different approach because they understand that the future will be different. Since iconoclastic organizations focus on learning, they make internal changes based not on a new fad approach to managing but on their understanding of the emerging rules of the game (as driven by the rate of change and the complexity level of the environment).

As the rate of change increases and the complexity changes, the need for entrepreneurial behavior increases substantially. Also, as organizations age, their predisposition toward entrepreneurial behavior decreases. Simply put, as an organization ages, its ability to learn (and therefore engage in iconoclastic behavior) decreases. At the same time, if the rate of change and complexity is increasing, the need for entrepreneurial (iconoclastic) behavior is increasing.

Therefore, it is reasonable to conclude that organizations need to be led by people who understand the need to foster entrepreneurial behavior. Organizational learning, which is driven by entrepreneurial behavior, allows the organization to engage in logical change driven by impending environmental change. To competitors, such change may appear illogical, since it is iconoclastic in nature. To the learning organization, however, it makes perfectly good sense.

THE ICONOCLASTIC ORGANIZATION

By its very nature, the e-chaos of the new economy produces an environment that is unpredictable and uncertain. That means that the rules of the game will shift frequently. If an organization is to keep pace with the shifts in the environment, its leadership must foster activity and thinking suitable for that type of environment. It should be no surprise to discover that companies that foster iconoclastic thinking and behavior are those that are winning in the new millennium. It is companies such as Microsoft, Toni & Guy, Hewlett-Packard, Intel, and others like them that will continue to thrive in e-chaos. They will thrive because they are designed to thrive in such environments.

These are not organizations that just decide to do something different to keep the competition unbalanced. They are organizations that are designed to learn about the future environment. Once they learn, they can rely on people who understand the need to transform the organization with speed and efficiency. They understand the importance of using all the tools of the organization to accomplish those goals. These are companies and people that live the iconoclastic principle.

CHAPTER 5

THE FOUR-PHASE CYCLE

CHANGE CAN BE AN ORGANIZATION'S FRIEND OR ITS ENEMY. The choice belongs to the company itself. A number of factors determine which it will be. It's useful to revisit the Triad of Success, as in Figure 5.1, to see how every aspect of the organization is influenced by external cycles of change. Leadership, learning, and agility all play an increasingly important role as cycles of change shorten.

Organizations are by their very nature designed to operate at specific levels of complexity and speed. The type of leadership, the way the organization learns, and the level of agility determine its ability to deal with both the complexity

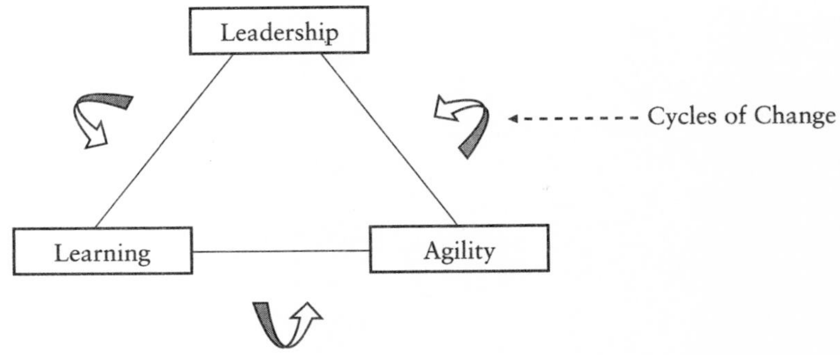

FIGURE 5.1. Cycles of Change and the Triad of Success.

and the rate of change of the environment. As the 10 forces that control environmental speed and complexity change, organizations must likewise mirror environmental change or they will suffer. Business strategists have long understood the relationship between an organization and its environment. The problem is, few have attempted to develop effective ways of dealing with mismatches as they appear.

The reality of environmental change, or e-chaos, and the problems that businesses have in dealing with it is generally an accepted fact.[1] Over the years, theorists have concluded that most companies appear to go through predictable cycles as a result of changes in the external environment and their own development, just like products. One of the most exhaustive writings on this topic is *Corporate Lifecycles* by Ichak Adizes.[2] These are the four characteristic phases:

- Explosion
- Stagnation
- Crisis
- Renewal

In this chapter, two realities about the phases that organizations go through will become apparent:

1. It is not necessary for organizations to go through the four-phase cycle.
2. The ability of a company's management to mirror environmental change by maintaining strategic balance between the environment and the organization is the key to achieving sustained success (and avoiding stagnation and crisis).

THE FOUR-PHASE CYCLE

Companies come to exist, or experience an explosive growth phase, because they are simply in the "right place at the right time." Some propose that it is not possible to do that on purpose, that in reality "accidental management" is at the foundation of success.[3] That is, they assert that all learning is "after the fact."[4] In my experience, however, although it is true that sometimes someone does stumble on a great opportunity by accident, that is generally not the case. It is certainly not true at companies that continue to innovate. Those companies keep discovering new opportunities because they plan to do so. They are committed to discovery. Generally, entrepreneurs and dynamically renewing companies see future opportunities before others do and consequently become first movers.

A look at the four-phase cycle of organizations will be helpful in understanding what happens to companies when they encounter environmental change. More important, it will show how to avoid the downward spiral associated with the cycles of change.

When cycles of change speed up, it becomes obvious that organizations must change to meet them. In Figure 5.2, "miles per hour" represents the speed of change in the environment and the speed of the company's reaction to it. It is painfully clear that an organization designed for a 60 mph environment will have problems dealing with a 75 mph environment. When the level of complexity and speed increases to 100 mph, the

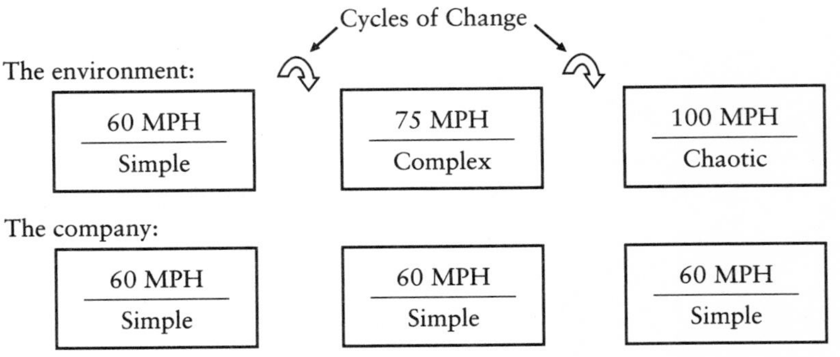

FIGURE 5.2. Organizational and Environmental Speed.

mismatch of the organization to the environment becomes increasingly critical.

As the environment goes through each cycle of change, the organization faces larger and larger gaps between its ability to cope and the increasing speed and complexity of the environment. If the environment is running at 75 mph and the organization at 60 mph, the two are 15 "miles" apart after the first cycle, 30 after the second, and so on until the organization is hopelessly lost. The inability to mirror (that is, the lack of the internal abilities to operate at the higher environmental speeds and deal with the higher levels of complexity) results in the deterioration of an organization's ability to make money. The company enters a stage of strategic imbalance when this occurs.

The ladder of performance makes it easy to lay out the problem and begin working on solutions. Although an organization may be perfectly profiled at a given time, if the environment is continually changing, the firm will begin to fail if it does not change to mirror the environment. A look at the profile of Xerox shown in Figure 5.3 will clearly show the sources of the company's troubles.

In 1990 Xerox had faced environmental turbulence only slightly above level 3. In 1995 this turbulence reached level 3.75 and by 2000 it was at level 4.5 (Chapter Two goes into detail on

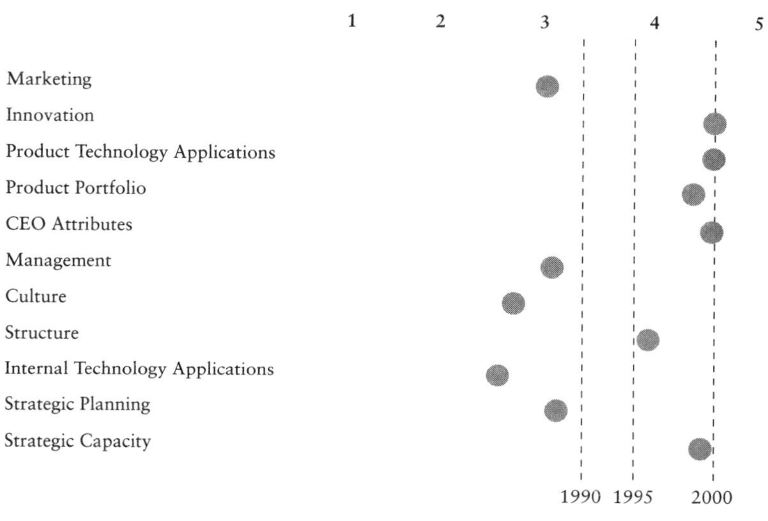

Xerox Gaps

Attribute	Gap	Profit Impact
Marketing	-1.5	Critical
Management	-1.5	Critical
Culture	-1.6	Critical
Technology Applications	-1.6	Critical
Strategic Planning	-1.4	Serious

FIGURE 5.3. Xerox 2000: A Strategic Profile.
Adapted from H. Igor Ansoff's Strategic Diagnosis procedures.
Used with permission.

the ladder of performance" charts.) Notice also that parts of the firm remained unchanged during the ten-year period from 1990 to 2000. Much of the firm was designed for moderately fast change and moderate levels of complexity. When that organization hit the fast and complex environment of 2000, the company was simply no match for the environment. The numerous "critical impact" gaps reveal just how severe the mismatch was.

In essence, during the five-year period between 1995 and 2000, the environment began to go through increasingly faster cycles of change while the organization began to deteriorate. This type of deterioration is not unusual in companies that find themselves in strategic imbalance. Such firms tend to focus more and more on internal issues such as power or politics and ignore the increasingly difficult external issues such as changing customer requirements. That reality of Xerox's profile is revealed in a statement by a Xerox employee: "We're frozen at this point. Our senior vice president is unwilling to do anything for fear of making a mistake. Instead of aggressively seeking change we're running away from it." *I return to Xerox later in this chapter for a more complete analysis of the company's problems.*

The most important issue a company must deal with is *cycles of change*—environmental changes that produce significant changes in the rules of the game. The management of a company is responsible for profiling the organization. That is, the executive team determines the nature of the marketing (aggressiveness), the culture, structure, and so on. It stands to reason that the profile of the company will position it either as one that self-renews or as one that rejects renewal. Companies that are not designed to self-renew go through the four-phase cycle shown in Figure 5.4. The figure illustrates what happens to firms that do not change with their environment. With each cycle of change, the increasing mismatch increases the organization's likelihood of going under.

When the rules of the game change, the rules of management and success change. That means that whatever the company was, or whatever it used to do, will have to go through a similar shift if the organization is to be able to thrive under the new rules of the game.

In low-turbulence environments, cycles of environmental change are long, and internal change is therefore infrequent. As the turbulence goes up, the cycles occur more rapidly. The nature of high-turbulence environments, especially those charac-

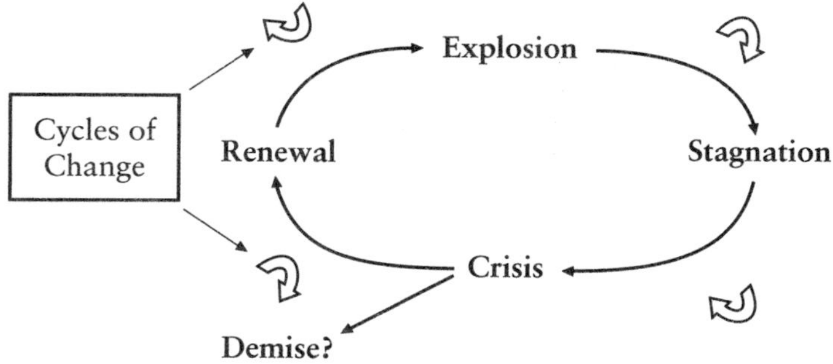

FIGURE 5.4. The Four-Phase Organizational Life Cycle.

terized by e-chaos, is that companies are faced with continual cycles of frame-breaking change. These days, the cycles of change in e-chaos are coming at an unprecedented speed.

That is why a lot of the traditional fixes for organizations fail in e-chaos. If the root problem is the organization's inability to deal with complex, supersonic cycles of change, a simplistic fix such as "get back to basics" will not help. In fact, it will increase the negative impact on the firm. Consider what happens to many organizations as they go through each of the four phases.

The Explosion Phase

The explosion phase is typically found toward the beginning of the life of an organization, shortly after the entrepreneur develops a dream or an idea that is different from existing products on the market and begins to make it a reality. Successful companies (that is, the ones that don't join the 90 percent of small business start-ups that fail in the first 60 months), usually begin with a period characterized by some successes, some failures, and a lot of challenges. If the entrepreneur has both a good idea and the management expertise to take it to fruition, the company has a chance to avoid the pitfalls and begin to grow faster and faster. At some point, the company may grow large enough that it can go public. For most companies, these are great times.

The explosion phase is the result of learning. An entrepreneur, unhindered by the constraints of a large corporate bureaucracy, can think and act out of the box. The explosion phase is a big bang event for most companies.

It should be noted that the explosion phase is not limited to small, entrepreneurial companies. By understanding the success triad (some executives understand it intuitively) it is possible to reengage a company and take it back to its entrepreneurial roots. As earlier pointed out, the ability to continually renew stems from the organization's ability to produce successive little bangs of innovation (new product opportunities).

The explosion phase is a great time to be in an organization. It's exhilarating and often just plain fun. Companies in the explosive stage are apt to be in extremely good strategic balance. There is usually little bureaucracy at the beginning. Policies are developed "on the run" as they are needed. There is little time for self-importance during this phase. The organization works as a team and there is usually little emphasis on title or position. The focus tends to center on "getting the job done."

As time passes, the organization begins to develop a more formal structure. More rigidity develops because of the problems related to managing larger groups of people. Policies are necessary for practical as well as legal reasons. There is just one problem: The company begins to focus on internal stability and continued growth in revenues while the external environment continues to develop—perhaps undergoing one or more full cycles of change. Generally, the rules of the game have already started to shift by the time the company reaches the end of the explosion phase. As the end of the explosion phase approaches, the organization is usually getting signals from the environment that change has occurred.

Often those signals reach the bottom line of the company in the form of decreased earnings and profit margins. A decline in the *gross profit margin of a firm* (that is, its gross profit, or gross revenues minus cost of sales, divided by gross revenues) is a clear indication that the firm is entering a more turbulent environment. *In other words, a decrease in the gross profit margin generally signals an increased level of competition in the market.*

At the end of the explosion phase, revenues may continue to grow at historical levels. However, environmental dynamics begin to affect the entire firm. Profit margins may begin to deteriorate for key product lines. Competitor firms may be entering their own explosion phase. The firm is forced to compete much more vigorously than it did before. Usually, these signals create little response within the company.[5]

Companies that emulate the success triad rarely enter serious levels of stagnation. While other organizations are consumed with internal problems, triad firms are growing. That is because they have continued to manage their learning, transformation, and performance.[6]

Companies with strategic balance have not lost their entrepreneurial focus. Certainly, they continue to work on performance issues, but not to the detriment of organizational learning and transformation.

The Stagnation Phase

As a company enters the stagnation phase, its leadership becomes increasingly aware of its deteriorating condition, yet does little to alter the firm's profile in response to environmental changes.[7] Instead, stagnating organizations tend to respond by creating larger bureaucracies. Rather than enhancing the flexibility and responsiveness of the organization, this often leads to increasingly inhibited adaptation.[8]

Companies that are well into the stagnation phase often begin a search for solutions to their problems. Many choose TQM (total quality management), or process reengineering. The solutions run the gamut from "getting back to core business" to open book management. These are usually very simplistic solutions. The problem the organization has is complexity as well as increased levels of environmental rates of change, and no one answer will ever deal with that.

In a lot of cases, business strategy has taken a back seat during the explosion phase as well as the early part of the stagnation phase. In addition to that, it is rare for senior managers to understand the real importance of maintaining strategic balance. It's during this time that a lot of executives decide that their company needs a really good strategic plan. So what do they do? They spend a lot of money on a consultant to help them identify what they used to do well (core competencies) and a mission statement that keeps them in the box. Jay Mendell was right: *apodictic* (linear, or historically based) planning models often lead to organizational disaster.[9]

As the end of the stagnation phase draws near, the organizational bureaucracy begins to grow even larger. The structure is usually hierarchical, and such steep structures tend to significantly inhibit flexibility. The culture of the firm also begins to degenerate during this time. Cultural values tend to turn toward risk-avoidance, and creativity reaches new lows for the organization.

During this phase the firm experiences another hit on its competitive abilities. It bleeds intellectual capital as its most gifted people begin to bail out. The deterioration of the culture and the proliferation of the hierarchy encourage the most capable and creative people to find work elsewhere.

The Crisis Phase

By the time the firm enters the crisis phase, the external environment has been through whole cycles of change while the firm has changed little. In spite of program after much-touted program, the competitive profile of the firm is still aligned for a former environment. It is at this point that major initiatives are

Factor	1	2	3	4	5
Technology Strategy	Very Slow Adaptation	Slow Adaptation	Stay with Competition	Leading Edge not Bleeding Edge	Consistent First Mover
Redundancy	Unnecessary	Unimportant	Important	Serious	Critical

FIGURE 5.5. Oxford's Internal Technology Mismatch. Adapted from H. Igor Ansoff's Strategic Diagnosis procedures. Used with permission.

undertaken to correct the problems. The first tool management seizes on is usually downsizing.

Downsizing is a public declaration that an organization's strategy has failed. As noted before, firms that go through downsizing initiatives rarely experience increased financial performance. Nonetheless, the opportunity vacuum created by the failure to use effective strategy may force management to cut costs (downsize) so as to get time to revitalize the firm.

By this time, most of the brighter and more creative people have left the firm. The drain on intellectual capital decreases the organization's ability to engage in entrepreneurial activities, even if it wanted to. This leads to an increasingly narrow focus on the internal aspects of the firm instead of outward, where opportunity resides.

The story of Oxford Healthcare Plans back in Chapter Two is a striking example of how fast a company can go from stagnation into crisis. As a refresher, Figure 5.5 shows how far Oxford's internal technology applications were out of sync with its environment.

In most areas, Oxford was well matched to its environment. It had somewhat inadequate levels of strategy, culture, management, and CEO attributes, which slowed it down in responding to its main problem, the failure to maintain strategic balance between the changes in the environment and its internal computer applications—and it nearly died as a result. The point is this: The failure to match any aspect of the firm with the changes in the environment can have disastrous consequences.

The Renewal Phase

Companies that survive the crisis phase go into renewal. Such companies are loaded with problems. In most cases, they have had to terminate the CEO and much of the executive team. Additionally—as noted earlier—they have lost many of their best and brightest people (their intellectual capital), who left the firm because they were frustrated with being ignored when they tried to tell the old management team how to correct the firm's problems. A lot of things have to be fixed if a firm is going to effectively renew itself. That is why people like Dave House (described in Chapter Three) include things like culture, structure, and products as the foundation of their turn-around strategy. They know that renewal involves the creation of an entirely new organization, not just better products.

A lot of times executives involved in renewing an organization will talk about re-creating an entrepreneurial spirit in the firm. That makes a lot of sense, since it was entrepreneurial behavior that pushed the company into the explosion phase in the first place. It stands to reason that it will take entrepreneurial behavior to get it back on track. Renewal involves transformation. It is difficult because managers are operating on two fronts. On one hand, they are putting out the fires left over from the crisis phase while simultaneously trying to get the operation back on track. On the other hand, they are trying to change the basic nature of the firm from one extreme (seriously imbalanced) to another (balanced). If the firm is effectively transformed, then it will again enter the explosion phase. And it will stay there unless the firm's management fails to maintain the company's balance with the environment.

Product Portfolios and the Four Phases of Organizations

It is usually the product area that serves as an indicator that companies are in one of the four phases. New companies in the explosion phase will tend to have a majority of their products in stages 1 and 2 of the product life cycle (shown in Figure 2.8)—that is, introduction or growth, rather than stages 3 and 4 (maturity and decline). This is obvious since learning is what produces new product opportunities. Where there is no learning, there are no product opportunities. Where there is learning, new products proliferate.

Companies that are strategically balanced will have products in every stage. As a company moves into the stagnation phase it will have insufficient stage 1 and 2 products. By the crisis phase, the firm will often have few if any products in these stages. That simply reflects the reality that as companies are allowed to grow stagnant they stop learning and innovating.

Companies in the stagnation phase will usually have a majority of their products in stage 3, with a few in stage 4. And they will have very few products in stages 1 and 2. Companies in stagnation also tend to innovate within existing technologies and product lines instead of outside. They tend to embrace "continuous improvement" instead of the dynamic renewal of their product portfolio. It might be best to describe their innovation as linear instead of nonlinear. That is, their innovation efforts are focused on existing products, with little or no effort to find potential breakthrough opportunities. The strategic imbalance of the organization keeps the firm from discovering the products needed for future success.

Crisis phase companies will stand out due to the absence of products in stages 1 and 2, and the presence of few if any products in stage 3. The sales force of such companies is usually fairly well beat up from trying to sell past-prime products against more nimble and innovative competitors.

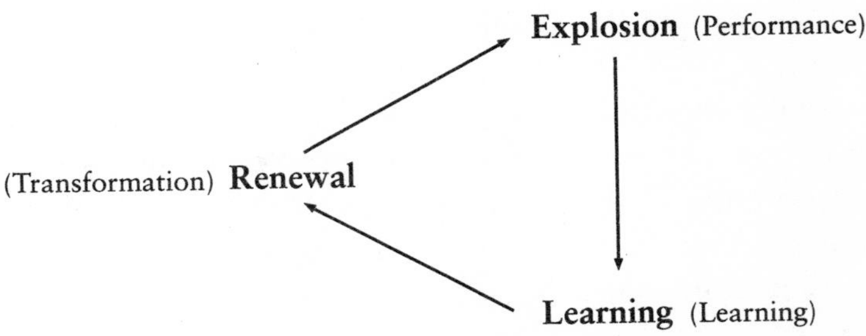

FIGURE 5.6. The Three-Phase Cycle of a Strategically Balanced Organization.

But the problem is much more serious than just the failure to create new products. In almost every case, crisis phase companies are unable to behave iconoclastically. That is because so much of the focus is inside the company instead of on the outside environment. Crisis phase companies also lack agility. More often than not, they have that "deer in the headlights" look.

Avoiding the Four-Phase Cycle

No company will ever be able to avoid some minor downturns. Economies deteriorate, markets go through frame-breaking shifts, and customer preferences change unexpectedly. The fact remains, however, that if a company maintains its match with the competitive environment, it will not be subject to the same kinds of problems that its less alert competitors endure. Companies that maintain their profile avoid the four-phase cycle and are in a constant state of dynamic renewal of the type shown in Figure 5.6.

STRATEGIC BALANCE AND CYCLES OF CHANGE

Strategic balance allows a company to persist in a state of dynamic renewal. Robert Waterman suggests that there are two types of organizational change:[10]

1. Dynamic imbalance, leading to renewal
2. Crisis-driven

He also supports the hypothesis that companies that are continually renewing achieve that ability because of organizational leadership. Other research supports Waterman. It indicates that there is a correlation between a firm's success and having a senior executive who drives innovation. The correlation is conversely strong for firms that experience failure and have senior executives that do not see the need to drive dynamic innovation.[11]

It is clear that dynamic renewal must be fostered at the executive level or it does not occur. Research suggests that unless otherwise directed, learning tends to be in terms of historic parameters, and not in those related to the existing or emerging paradigm.[12] Again, it should be noted that the self-organizing view of management fails the test. Left alone, organizations will tend to self-destruct. Still other research affirms the positive side of leadership and cultural values, stating that organizations that foster an attitude of renewal tend to adapt smoothly and profit from uncertainties.[13]

THE THREE TYPES OF FIRMS

One other dimension needs to be considered in the discussion about the four-phase cycle: the asset base (which is usually related to the age) of a firm. Assets provide staying power. Firms with limited assets tend to disappear quickly.

This observation leads to a useful recognition of three types of firms. As noted earlier, an organization's ability to anticipate future environmental change and to respond to emerging environmental discontinuities is the result of a purposeful design process on the part of management. In other words, organizations thrive or fail because they are designed to behave in a specific way, so it would seem that there are just two types of firms, nonadaptive (imbalanced) or adaptive (balanced). That is true in a way—but there are also two types of nonadaptive firms, based on their age and asset base. For the manager, understanding the differences between the two is important because one has more of a cushion than the other and thus more time to make improvements.

The three types of firms are identified as follows:

Type I (Nonadaptive). Organizations with massive asset bases that lack strategic imbalance.

Type II (Nonadaptive). Organizations that lack strategic balance and also have limited assets.

Type III (Adaptive). Organizations that maintain strategic balance.

A look at the characteristics of each type in Figure 5.7 reveals the importance of understanding which type an organization is. The chart simply reflects the common characteristics of each of the three types of companies. Only the Type III adaptive organizations are really likely to survive on a long-term basis. In looking at the characteristics of Type I and II organizations, the limitations on leadership, learning, and agility become obvious.

Type I and Type II Organizations

The only difference between a Type I firm and a Type II firm is the size of the asset base (which is generally a function of age). This is a critical difference, as it governs the amount of time a firm has to recover from stagnation or crisis. Type II firms have little time because—unlike IBM in the early 1980s—they do not have billions of dollars in assets that they can liquidate to enable them to reprofile themselves. Thus the sense of urgency for a Type II firm must be very high early in the process of organizational renewal or the firm will not survive.

Type I and Type II firms are in strategic imbalance. They have few if any learning or agility skills. Two factors can accel-

Strategic Imbalance Type I	Strategic Imbalance Type II	Strategically Balanced Type III
Historically focused	Historically focused	Future focused
Internal focus	Internal focus	External focus
Old firm; large asset base	Young firm; small asset base	May be young or old
Nonadaptive	Nonadaptive	Adaptive
Usually in stagnation or crisis phase	Usually in stagnation or crisis phase	Continually in renewal or explosion phase
Often have narrow, focused product family	Often have narrow, focused product family	Often have diverse, sometimes unrelated product families
Market laggards	Market laggards	Consistent first movers

FIGURE 5.7. The Three Types of Organizations.

erate the demise of companies that are in strategic imbalance. First, their asset size can restrict their ability to cover losses resulting from the imbalance. Second, since both Type I and Type II firms are in strategic imbalance, their demise will be accelerated if the level of change and complexity of the environment goes up.

There are a number of excellent examples of each type of firm. Xerox will serve well as a typical Type I firm. In 1978, the firm was approaching the crisis stage, but its asset base enabled it to survive. Incremental change fostered by TQM programs has allowed Xerox to continue in business, but it still looks like a Type I firm as it remains limited in its adaptiveness and focus.

IBM Corporation was clearly a Type I firm in the early 1990s. Lou Gerstner's leadership of the firm moved it back to its entrepreneurial roots, and thus IBM became a Type III firm later in the 1990s.

Type II firms by definition do not make it to the Fortune 500. Most people are familiar with organizations that meet the criteria. They experience the explosion phase as a result of an entrepreneurial effort, only to quickly disappear from the marketplace when they stop innovating.

Type III Adaptive Organizations

Type III firms maintain their strategic balance by continually learning about the future and transforming the firm into what it must become. Any number of firms meet the Type III criteria: consider TMP Worldwide, Hewlett-Packard, IBM, and Intel. All these firms share a commitment to live in the future as well as the present. They are committed to maintaining a first-mover advantage in all that they do. Entrepreneurial risk-taking and open cultures characterize them and enable them to proactively anticipate the future as well as respond rapidly to discontinuous change in their environment.

Strategic balance creates highly adaptive organizations. Strategic balance is the result of both intuitive understanding of the complex drivers of organizational success as well as the commitment to winning. But then . . . there are some people that just do not ever get it. A company's managers can view themselves either as victims or as winners. It is a matter of choice. The key to organizational survival and success is the commitment of the firm's leadership to maintain its adaptive capabilities. This requires an obsession with getting to the future first as well as maintaining high levels of organizational adaptiveness.

That's Never Happened Before

Some companies are surprised by change. Others profit from it. As the new economy continues to increase the rate of change and the complexity of the competitive environment, people will continue to say "that's never happened before." Likewise, some companies are designed for change, and others are not. It is important to remember that every company that exists is capable of successfully operating at a specific level of complexity and rate of change. Some companies will encounter stagnation, enter the crisis phase, and ultimately cease to exist. Others will encounter the same environments and profit from the challenges of uncertainty and change. It is possible to determine which firms will rise and which will fall by finding out the type of firm each one is.

XEROX: AN INSIDER'S VIEW

As shown back in Figure 5.3, by the year 2000 Xerox had largely converted itself from an old-line copying company to a leading-edge developer of digital applications. After years of struggling to regain its lead in the reproduction market, the firm had finally created a portfolio of products that looked likely to allow it to re-create much of the success it had enjoyed in the 1970s. But by late 2000, that success had not yet begun to crystallize.

On October 10, 2000, the *Wall Street Journal* featured a story about how Xerox was in a "liquidity crisis." The article went on to cite comments by some experts regarding the possibility that Xerox would have to declare Chapter 11 bankruptcy. How in the world does a company with a great portfolio of products find itself in such a mess?

"Thoman did some great things for Xerox," former Xerox executive Ernie Riddle told me, "But along the way there were some major mistakes made. At least that's what it looks like to me as an outsider." Richard Thoman was recruited from IBM in 1998, where he had worked with Lou Gerstner. Thoman was seen as a financial guru, but the jury was still out regarding his ability to translate his information into profit.

"I'd give them an 'A' for their concept and an 'F' for execution," says Riddle. "I think that Xerox has done a brilliant job in moving from the analog world into the digital world." Xerox has been through three tsunamis of change in a few short years:

- The imaging industry rapidly changed from an analog business into a digital business.
- There was a major convergence between all forms of imaging (copying, printing, and so on) producing one morphous business area.
- The products became software-centric. That is, the moving of all of the imaging applications onto the LAN created a product that rapidly became subject to software applications and integration.

The years of TQM implementation at Xerox had worked to create an open, adaptive culture. Leadership styles had become supportive and empowering. When Thoman joined the company, there was a general understanding across Xerox that the massive changes that had swept the industry would require fast responses on the part of the company. Thoman's team took immediate steps to address the extreme changes in the marketplace. They realized that the staff needed to make the change from being excellent salespeople to being excellent solutions people. The competitive and technological changes in the market changed the nature of the product drastically. The new solutions-based product involved not only functionality (imaging or whatever) but also the networks and software that delivered the functionality.

The new organization involved the shuffling of Xerox's sales professionals, changes in technology systems, elimination of support staffing, and changing the commission structure as well as the way commissions were handled. Unfortunately, the new approach was riddled with problems. First, the technology systems were not in place to support the new approach. Sales personnel, according to one source, were spending more time figuring out how to place customer orders and computing their commissions than they were with the client. Second, rather than approach the change with a collaborative attitude, top management instituted the changes without adequate input (or buy-in) from the marketing team. As a result, a chasm broke open between the marketing team and the management of the organization. The trust level plunged significantly.

All this occurred during a time in which the company continued to create new products. Additionally, Xerox was active in the acquisition of companies that had high levels of technology savvy, such as Tektronics. Its managers were doing a lot of things well. They just failed to execute.

By October 2000, the company was predicting losses for its third quarter and trying to deal with the rumors that the company was in trouble. The problems can be summarized as follows:

1. The near-elimination of the sales administration and support staff damaged the firm's ability to adequately serve its customers.
2. The in-house technology wasn't up to the job of replacing the former sales administration team—automated systems could theoretically do much of the job, but such systems didn't exist.
3. The division between the marketing team and senior leadership as a result of the changes created serious problems in both revenues and customer relationships.
4. The firm was unable to execute the new market strategies that it was targeting.

The Xerox product strategy was apparently well founded and placed the firm in a good competitive position. Figure 5.8 returns to the Triad of Success to illustrate Xerox's problems in executing its strategy.

The firm apparently did an excellent job of learning and creating an appropriate product portfolio that had high levels of attractiveness. The failure to create adequate support systems

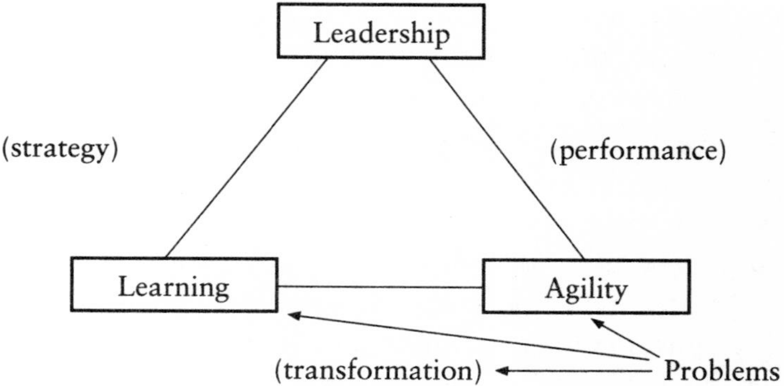

FIGURE 5.8. A Broad View of Xerox's Problems in 2000.

(both human and technology), combined with the damage done to the marketing team, stopped the company in its tracks. Its leadership failed to transform the organization, and that then led to an inability to perform. Not only did Xerox lack the agility (speed) it needed, it created serious barriers to the transformation of the organization. The resulting organization did not fit the system in which it was operating. A second look at the Xerox profile (back in Figure 5.3) will illustrate the impact of the firm's problems in leadership, learning, and agility. Note how marketing aggressiveness was one of the company's major problems in 2000.

The strategic profile allows the comparison of the emerging environment and the current organization. Obviously, the further off the firm is from the desired profile (the vertical dotted turbulence line), the higher the impact on profitability. Xerox, according to those interviewed, had five serious barriers to performance:

- Marketing had deteriorated.
- Organizational management had deteriorated.
- Culture had deteriorated.

- Internal technology applications were not suited for the organizational strategy.
- Strategy was inadequate for the environment the firm was moving into.

Notice that the new CEO, Anne Mulcahy, has the right leadership characteristics to lead the organization into renewal. It is important to note that the firm's innovation has let it anticipate the technology changes of the market, but at the same time, the firm has failed to create appropriate internal technology applications to effectively support the marketing effort. The gaps in leadership and marketing are simply the result inadequate strategy in transforming the firm.

Figure 5.3 points up the strategic imbalance of the organization. In the case of Xerox, this failure to create strategic balance in the organization has taken it from the stagnation phase to the crisis phase. At the same time, all this has occurred while the firm has been creating a new and exciting product portfolio.

WINNING IS A CHOICE

Type I and Type II companies are destined to enter the stagnation phase. Due to their nonadaptive profile, they will generally go on to the crisis phase. Some Type I firms are able to enter the renewal phase by going through a radical redesign of the firm. For Type II firms, which are lighter in assets, survival is much more difficult. Firms that achieve a Type III profile have the opportunity to take the leadership role in their industry for a sustained period of time. Becoming a Type III firm or sustaining a Type III profile requires a management team that understands how to manage the right things.

Companies that win are those that choose to win. They understand two things clearly: First, change is an opportunity to enhance profitability. Second, winning requires the leadership of the organization to manage a complex set of characteristics. Companies like Hewlett-Packard, Cisco, Southwest Airlines, and Intel demonstrate that it is possible to achieve sustained growth and profitability by maintaining the strategic balance of the organization. Companies that fail to maintain strategic balance go into the four-phase cycle of change . . . and only some of them survive it.

CHAPTER 6

THE TRADITIONAL MODEL, AND WHY IT DOESN'T WORK

WHY STOP TO TALK ABOUT THINGS THAT DO NOT WORK? WHY worry about a strategic approach that is flawed at best, especially in light of the obvious need to abandon the approach? If core competencies, mission, and competitive advantage are not the proper way to create value, why in the world spend time learning about them?

The answers to those questions are important. First, the traditional strategic model focused on historic core competencies and competitive advantage is still the basis for strategy courses at almost all universities. It is also still used at most companies—though not in most of the ones that are thriving in the new economy—and the language of strategy is still based on that model. In any case, understanding of the traditional model is essential to understanding its problems so as to avoid the pitfalls related to its use.

CORE COMPETENCIES, COMPETITIVE ADVANTAGE, AND STRATEGY

The history of strategic planning is tied to the development of overall management theory. However, unlike many of the theories related to the management of people, a lot of the current ideas about organizational strategy are lacking in relevant foundation.

That reality has not deterred academicians as well as business practitioners from selecting currently popular theories as the basis for their view of strategic planning. The truth is that little if any time has been spent in discussing the philosophy and logic that underlies most planning approaches.

Another reality is that the leaders of companies that do extremely well simply do not use the popular approach. In most cases, if they do use it, they then ignore the firm's strategic plan in favor of an informal or unwritten plan based on their intuitive understanding of the complex environment. In personal interviews, many if not most senior executives will affirm their lack of confidence in current planning approaches.

In either case, it takes little discussion in the business arena to understand that successful organizations take a radically nontraditional approach to strategy. Those same executives will often use the words "core competencies, mission, and competitive advantage" in conjunction with their strategic planning, while in practice denying their validity. Consider the following statements as a starting point for the discussion:

> *The most striking feature of business life at the turn of this millennium is the rapid, often unanticipated rise of new winners. Across a wide range of industries, we see these*

new businesses seizing on one or more of the forces roiling through world markets and riding them to leadership. Among others, these forces include rapid technological obsolescence, increased complexity, high volatility, rapidly changing industry settings and value drivers, lowered political barriers, disintermediation, open product offerings, the emergence of new market spaces and positive-return markets (including network markets), and the shift from resource-based competition to information-based competition. This increased turbulence and unpredictability seem likely to continue indefinitely, and even intensify, making change into the only steady state.

In such an environment, conventional approaches to strategy development and implementation lose traction. Traditional, orderly strategic planning, monitoring and control simply cannot accommodate the greater uncertainty and complexity, *and firms cannot seize new opportunities quickly enough—as several onetime leaders in their markets have learned, often too late.*

—Strategic Management Society: Call for Papers, 2000 Conference

If self-confirming beliefs (core competencies and competitive advantage) are held (as a basis for developing organizational strategy), an entire industry may become unnecessarily stuck in a low-profit equilibrium. . . . In such situations, managers may unwittingly destroy a significant portion of potential firm value.

—*When Competencies Are Not Core: Self-Confirming Theories and the Destruction of Firm Value,* by Michael D. Ryall, University of Rochester

These quotes reveal the deteriorating confidence that many academicians have in current strategic planning approaches. Notice that rather than branding these approaches as somewhat harmless, both sources apparently believe that current strategic approaches may not only damage a firm's value but may ultimately destroy the firm. That is why the topic of organizational strategy is so critical. It involves the very survival of the firm. Consider the following headlines:

MANY FIRMS FLYING BY SEAT OF PANTS[1]

NAVIGATORS WITHOUT A MAP OR COMPASS[2]

These headlines appeared in major publications in 1993. Both articles went on to say that most companies really do not have effective plans for the future. For those that do plan for the future, it is truly rare for their strategic plan to be anything more than a budget or a plan that is an extension of what they have done in the past.

That doesn't mean that companies don't do a strategic plan. Each year, most continue to use an age-old tradition of considering core competencies, recognizing their competitive advantage, and then developing their mission statement out of that process. With few exceptions, those firms use what I like to call "the traditional strategic model" or the "competency-based model."

The traditional model, although still used by academic theorists and corporate strategists alike, is failing companies. Nonetheless, it's worth repeating that even though this approach often isn't an effective way to develop strategy, managers do need to understand it because of the way it permeates business life—and because only a full understanding will reveal the reasons for its failure.

Current management and strategy still largely rely on "equilibrium systems" theories developed in the 1800s.[3] Generally, equilibrium theory is based on the idea of rationality or linearity. It assumes predictable cause-and-effect relationships. That is, if one competitor does one thing, another would rationally respond with a specific type of action, and so on.

Eric Beinhocker suggests that the introduction of technology has changed the landscape so much that rationality is eliminated from the environment as a general rule.[4] In its place, he suggests, are discontinuous environments with new winners and old firms that are unexpectedly failing. He further suggests that mental models based on equilibrium theory should be replaced with ones based on the idea of "complex adaptive systems." Beinhocker's views track very closely with the 10 forces model I've presented in this book.

Mental models, or *paradigms* as Thomas Kuhn called them, provide the structure and foundation for the way people perceive and process information.[5] Some people already tend to think in nonlinear, complex models, or to use a blending of the simple and the complex. Most, however, still prefer the simple, linear model that worked so well for the past two centuries, and thus find the traditional approach to organizational strategy very congenial. The antidote for this pleasant paralysis is called "systems thinking." Once you have the tools to think about complex e-chaos environments without getting lost in them, they're much easier to deal with. It becomes possible to design for success.

SYSTEMS THINKING: SOMETHING THAT DOES WORK

Peter Senge is best known for introducing the idea of systems thinking to the business community. Behind Senge's work is the conflict between thinking in a linear, simple manner or in a nonlinear, complex manner. The term *systems thinking* has a number of definitions, but I prefer the one developed by Ron Davison:

> Systems Thinking. *1. A sensitivity to patterns, wholes, process flow, environments, and interactions. 2. The perception of, or attempt to articulate and model, the system dynamics that define and constrain systems. 3. Pondering the mysterious connections between events and issues.*

4. *A rigorous, yet holistic way of describing the world.*
5. *A change in thinking.*[6]

There are other excellent definitions that help further explain the concept. Barry Richmond suggests that systems thinking is "making reliable inferences about behavior by developing an increasingly deep understanding of underlying structure."[7] Katz and Kahn suggest that systems thinking involves "problems of relationships, of structures, and of interdependence."[8]

Systems thinking, in essence, is an attempt to metaphorically represent the world as it is or as it will be. If the world is assumed to be a macro system, then organizations are subsystems of that system. As subsystems, competing organizations, government, consumers, and such are all interrelated parts of the macro system. Therefore, systems thinking is a way of representing and analyzing the relationships of the parts to each other as well as of any part (say, a firm) to the whole. Systems thinking attempts to move from a mental model focused on scattered individual entities to a model that regards all individual entities as parts of larger systems, which are themselves parts of still larger systems, and so on.

Systems thinking involves seeing the whole instead of a part of the whole. It involves the intuitive understanding of the complexity and rate of change of the emerging environment. It is a critical aspect of the new concept of management. Once a realistic mental model of management is adopted, that necessarily leads managers to understand their raison d'être in an entirely new context. The temptation to "manage to the quarter" is balanced by the real need to continually engage in the creation of future opportunity for the enterprise. Systems thinking reveals the need to abandon historic, linear (and simplistic) mental models as the basis for thinking about the future in favor of complexity-based models that derive profit potential from learning about the future.

Why Systems Thinking Matters

- Systems thinking is an attempt to match an individual's mental model with the external environment.
- The way people perceive their environment determines the way they will respond to it.
- Managers who accurately understand the environment (complexity and speed) are more effective than those who do not.

The business literature is crowded with ideas that were supposed to be the "perfect solution" for businesses. Most, if not all, have failed to deliver what they promised. The continuum of perfect solutions may be explained by using a systems thinking model. In much the same way that the proverbial blind men described the elephant in five different (yet accurate) ways reflecting the part of the elephant they could touch but missed the nature of the beast entirely, solutions that fail to recognize the systems aspects of competition will ultimately fail the organization.

Thinking of elephants, a lot of management "experts" claim success on the same basis as the self-appointed sentry in this instructive tale:

> *A tourist in San Francisco once walked up to a hippie who was standing on a street corner and snapping his fingers, and asked him why he was making that noise. "To keep the elephants away," replied the hippie. "That's ridiculous," the stranger snapped. "There's not an elephant within three thousand miles of here!" "You see," retorted the hippie, "it's working! It's working!"*

This is the type of thinking that has brought us numerous books on strategy. Even Henry Mintzberg's *The Rise and Fall of Strategic Planning* fell victim to this fallacy.[9] Ironically, Mintzberg's proposition was that he had explained why every other strategic approach had failed but his own. Unlike a Wagnerian opera, which builds to a wonderful dramatic close, Mintzberg reaches a solution that leaves the reader with the same myopic focus that he criticizes in others' writing. Just like the hippie in San Francisco, Mintzberg proposes that since strategy *seems* to emerge companies should in like manner develop their strategy.[10] But it is by no means true that the simple existence of a condition indicates the operation of a specific cause, and it is entirely possible for effective strategies to be developed deliberately rather than by waiting for them to emerge. The next session discusses a parallel case from the world of research.

GLOBAL MODELING

Regardless of their field, researchers are taught that effective research begins with the development of a global model of the area to be studied. For example, consider the question of the impact advertising has on revenue.

Say a firm decides to double the advertising budget during a specific calendar year and measure the relationship between increased advertising and sales. It sounds like a straightforward question, but how trustworthy is the data if the sales department reduces the product price by 50 percent during the study. Assuming unit sales volume rose, was it because of the advertising or the price? If gross sales revenue did not rise, was it because the advertising failed or because the price drop was too large? It doesn't take much analysis to conclude that the research would be invalid because of the uncontrolled variables. This same problem would exist if a competitor doubled the size of its direct sales force during the study.

The systems thinker will look at the preceding illustration with an immediate "aha!" and see that the question as asked has no possible answer. That is why the systems thinker will also look with suspicion at any business doctrine that funda-

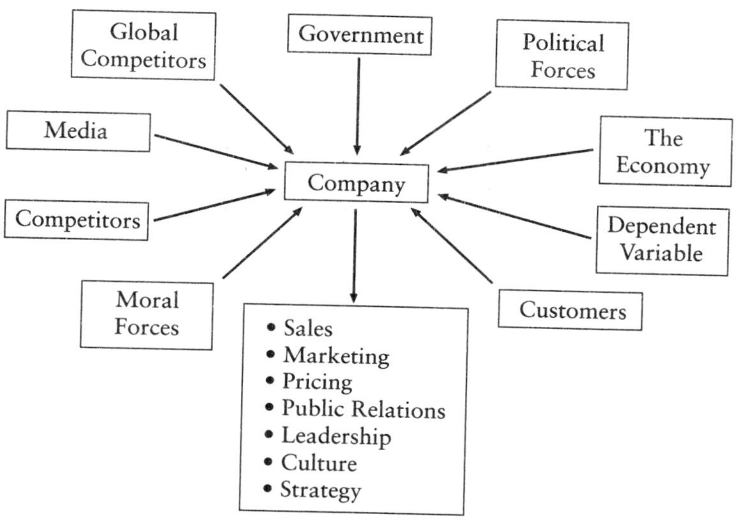

FIGURE 6.1. A Global Model Illustration (Systems Thinking).

mentally rejects systems in favor of a single perfect solution. Figure 6.1 helps explain the conflict between simplistic management approaches and the reality of complex environments.

Global models recognize the existence of variables. Dependent variables are those factors that apparently depend on others for performance (just as revenues depend on items like advertising). Independent variables are factors like advertising, public relations, marketing, and so on, which can affect dependent variables. Global models attempt to recognize the major variables and their impact on outcomes such as organizational performance. Using a global model means that instead of just managing product quality or some other singular aspect of the firm, the manager must be concerned with all the external variables that affect organizational performance as well as with the internal variables that do likewise. The 10 forces model presented in this book is designed to provide a systems thinking foundation for analyzing the environment.

SO WHAT DOESN'T WORK?

Systems thinking provides a context from which a number of current management practices can be evaluated. Take the traditional strategic model, an approach characterized by ideas like mission, competitive advantage, and core competencies. Some refer to this approach as the Porter Framework, named after Michael Porter of the Harvard Business School.[11]

The traditional strategic model builds on the work of David Ricardo, a British economist of the early 1800s who developed a number of ideas about competition.[12] One of those, which I call his Theory of Comparative Advantage, involves the idea of a distinctive competence. What Ricardo hypothesized was that organizations each have different competencies that give them an advantage over others. He also suggested that each competence was unique to an organization and could not be easily duplicated by a competitor.

Ricardo believed that if an organization focused on its own area of unique competence and avoided areas where others had a unique competence, it would maximize its performance. Out of Ricardo's work came other theories that supported his idea. Ultimately, the concept evolved into the concept of competitive advantage, as espoused by Michael Porter[13] and others. Figure 6.2 illustrates the importance this theory places on identifying a company's distinctive competence so as to secure its own share of the pie—and on avoiding areas where other firms have distinctive competencies and can compete overwhelmingly.

Basically, the idea underlying the Ricardo-Porter mental model is *stay in the box*. If a company is to maximize its performance, they propose, it must focus on staying in the box where the organization has a distinctive advantage. Equally important, they say, is to avoid getting out of the box into the area where others would have distinctive competencies. This is accomplished by using a mission statement.

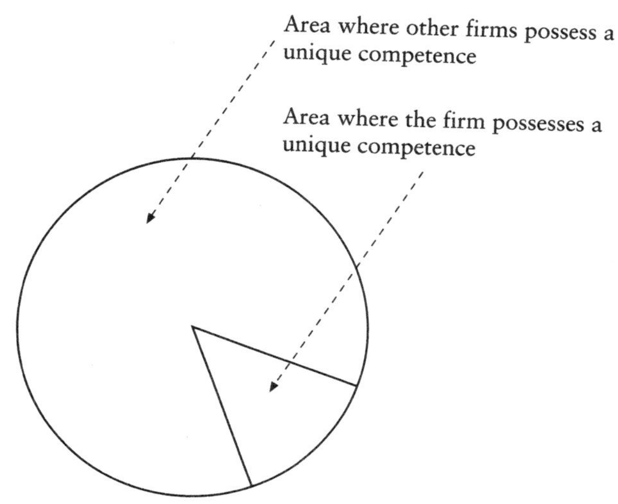

FIGURE 6.2. Distinctive Competencies and Organizational Mission.

Developing Strategy the Traditional Way

The development of the firm's mission statement is not the first step in the planning process. The planning process begins with the use of two other tools: Michael Porter's Five Forces and the SWOT analysis.

Porter's Five Forces model is an industry analysis tool.[14] It is the first step in developing an understanding of an organization's industry structure. The Five Forces model is an attempt to study the various forces a company must consider in analyzing an industry. Its purpose is to get a comprehensive view of the environment prior to developing the company's mission and strategies.

Michael Porter's Five Forces include:

1. Rivalry (or competition)
2. Threats from buyers

3. Threats from sellers
4. Threats of substitutes
5. Entry and exit barriers[15]

Once the planner has developed an understanding of the industry structure, the next task is to lay the foundation for the firm's mission. That is done with what is called *SWOT analysis*. SWOT stands for Strengths, Weaknesses, Opportunities, and Threats. Some would suggest doing SWOT analysis after developing the firm's mission. However, in a true Ricardian approach (focusing on distinct competencies), SWOT analysis is the step in the process in which the firm would develop an understanding of its distinct competencies. SWOT involves two types of scanning: internal scanning for strengths and weaknesses, and external scanning for opportunities and threats. Figure 6.3 provides a visual summary of SWOT analysis.

Internal scanning is the process by which the firm identifies its unique competencies and areas where it has inadequate competencies (and competitors have unique competencies). Out of this analysis, the company is able to develop its mission statement. External scanning provides input related to competitive segments that will provide opportunity and also identifies specific threats. By understanding the firm's unique competencies and assessing them related to threats, planners develop input for guiding the firm's strategy. The same is true for opportunities.

The traditional model is designed to be like a pilot's checklist. Once the industry analysis and the SWOT analysis are complete, the firm has input for its mission as well as its strategies. Its planners then begin systematically going through each step of the model. The mission statement of the organization must control each step. The mission statement serves as the umbrella under which all the actions and strategies of the company must stay. Otherwise, it would be moving into areas in

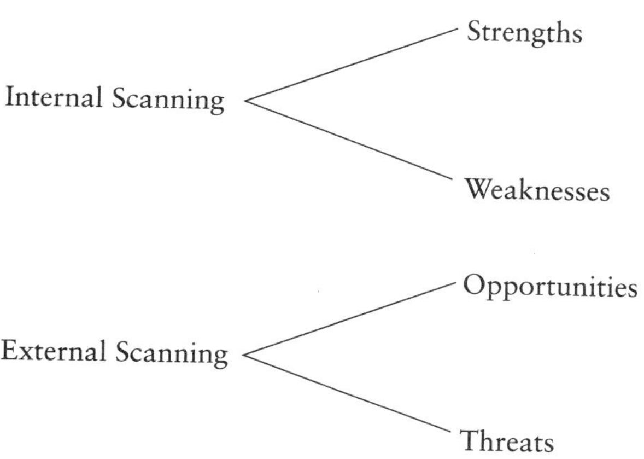

FIGURE 6.3. Environmental Scanning Using SWOT.

which competitors have unique competencies. The traditional strategy process is normally employed on an annual basis. Figure 6.4 is a checklist for the process. Like a pilot's checklist, it gives a step-by-step approach to the job. It is designed to focus all of the assets of an organization on its unique areas of distinctive competence.

The mission—usually developed at the senior executive level of the organization—is generally a *qualitative* statement about the company. The next step involves translating the qualitative strategy of the firm into quantitative statements or objectives. Objectives are designed to set goals that fulfill the mission, and usually involve things like sales objectives, profit objectives, internal rate of return, and so on. That process is also usually done at the senior executive level of the firm.

Next the management team begins converting the objectives into specific strategies. Strategies are the battle plan for the firm. This process usually involves the senior executive team and SBU (strategic business unit) managers. SBUs are distinct divisions of

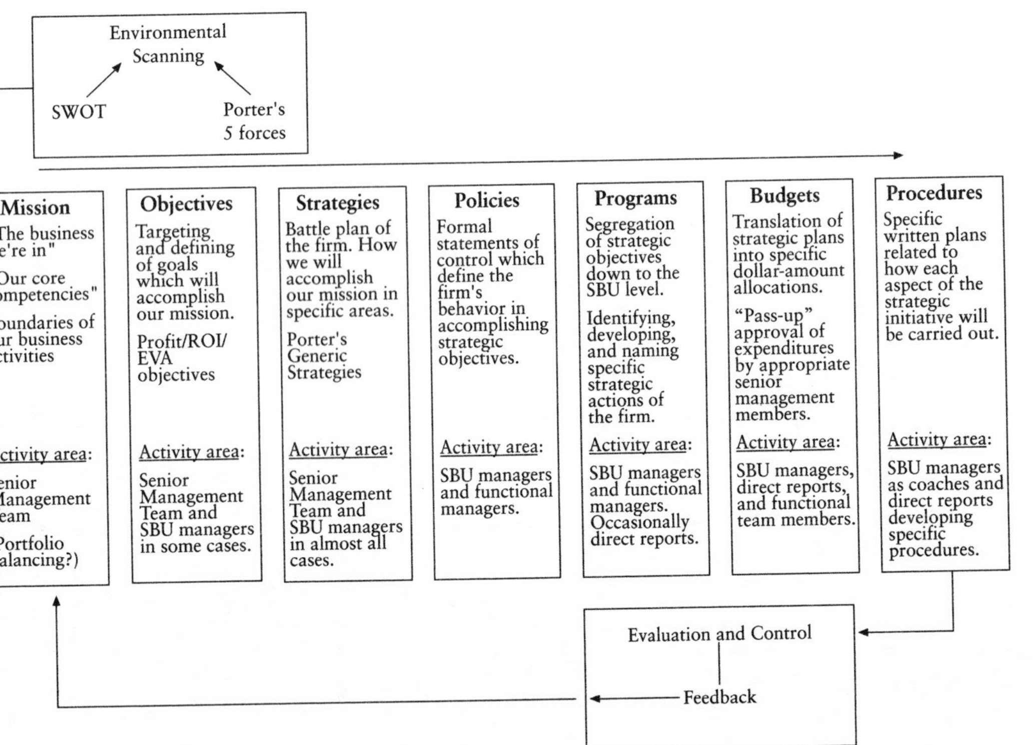

FIGURE 6.4. The Traditional Approach to Organizational Strategy.

a company such as product areas or geographic areas. During this stage of plan development, the team employs Porter's Generic Strategies.[16] His idea was that the strategist first had to choose whether the product was going to be marketed to a broad market or to a narrow, or niche, market. Then the decision regarding price/value had to be made. The product value decision involved either pricing the product as a high differentiation product (such as a Rolls Royce automobile) or a low differentiation product (such as a Volkwagen).

Porter proposed that products needed to be generically positioned if profit was to be maximized. That meant that the product market (narrow or broad) and differentiation strategy (high or low) had to be carefully determined. In a 1998 film released by the Harvard Business School, he cited the following examples of companies that used his generic strategies in determining differentiation (quality and price) and market (broad or narrow).

- American Airlines: High Differentiation/Broad Market
- Cray Research: High Differentiation/Narrow Market
- Ivory Soap: Low Differentiation/Broad Market
- La Quinta Inns: Low Differentiation/Narrow Market

According to Porter, if a firm failed to properly position its products, reduced profits would be the result. Additionally, positioning the product in the middle (no distinct positioning strategy) would result in low profits.

Next, policies are developed—normally at the SBU level and usually in conjunction with functional managers. Policies are formal statements of control that define the firm's behavior in accomplishing objectives. A good example of a policy is IBM's requirement (in the 1980s) that all investments have a 20 percent internal rate of return. When turbulence in the PC environment went up during that time, the market would no longer tolerate such high levels of profit. IBM's policy (which it was unwilling to change) virtually eliminated it from the market at that time.

Programs are generally SBU specific, taking mission-objectives-strategy-policy and converting those concepts into real activity-based objectives for the SBU. Once programs are established, budgets are developed. Budgets ideally involve the effective allocation of funds in accordance with the mission-driven objectives of the firm. In reality, internal politics often changes those allocations.

Finally, the entire process is summed up in the development of procedures. Procedures might involve sales policies or advertising allocations. Procedures are the way that the entire process ideally winds its way down to each individual in the firm. Once the strategic plan is developed, feedback systems are created to communicate the level of success or failure of the execution of the plan.

It Sounds Great, Doesn't It?

The idea that a company could identify its unique competencies and understand its competitive advantage just plain feels good. It feels good for a number of reasons. First, the process involves affirming the value of what the firm is and what it used to be, which is bound to be reassuring to the people in the firm now. For those still fond of linear thinking, it seems both natural and right. And it's familiar—and most human beings feel better when they can avoid change, which is apt to be a major source of discomfort.

In addition, the process involves goals, and there is good reason to believe that goal-setting enhances performance. The approach also allows for the development of BHAGs (Big Hairy Audacious Goals), which some see as a characteristic of excellent organizations. So what's the problem? Why not follow the old maxim: "If it feels good . . . do it"?

It May Feel Good . . . But It Can Lead to Disaster

When the airlines began the upgrade from piston aircraft to jets, they encountered unexpected problems. It seemed that the change was extremely difficult for a number of pilots. Jets differed from piston aircraft in many ways. In a piston aircraft, for example, a pilot who needed to abort a landing could hit the throttles and immediately begin climbing. Not so in a jet. The water-injected engines used in the early jets had a seven-second delay between throttle opening and response—and seven seconds is a long, long time in a plane roaring toward the ground. Additionally, the jets had different landing approach characteristics. That is, they had different sink rates. A number of pilots just could not make the transition—they could not change their mental models from one way of thinking to another.

Basically, the pilots who could not make the transition were unable to change their mental models as to how they viewed speed and complexity of the aircraft. The result was that they were continually doing the wrong thing in the context of the flying environment they had entered. That is analogous to the problem faced by people who attempt to use traditional, linear mental models in the new e-chaos environment. Figure 6.5 charts the differences between the two approaches.

The figure reveals numerous problems with the traditional approach to strategy. The first is the self-confirming nature of that approach. It starts with the assumption that what the firm is today (an accumulation of past decisions) is the appropriate foundation for the firm's future. Jay Barney, a professor and writer in the field of strategy, has suggested that the model be adapted to what he calls a "resource view" of the firm.[17]

There is no apparent global rule of the game that requires the world to continue needing or demanding whatever the firm has done, or does today. There is no apparent link between the resources a successful firm has today and the resources that will

	The Traditional Model	The Ladder of Performance
Mental Model	Simple	Complex
Planning Context	Present	Future
Strategic Balance	Not considered	Critical
Assumptions of Future	Linear extrapolation of historic experience	Predicts levels of change and complexity, not specific conditions
Economic Foundation	Equilibrium theory	Complex adaptive systems
Validity	May cause firm to operate below optimum; in some cases, may lead to organizational failure.	Companies in strategic balance significantly out-perform those in imbalance

FIGURE 6.5. A Comparison of Traditional and Strategic Balance Approaches.

produce a profit in the future. A systems thinking view that looks from the future back may well reveal that whatever the firm is and whatever it does now will be irrelevant in the future.

Resources and core competencies are relevant only if they match the emerging future environment. Companies that do well have the ability to forget what they do or once did and look toward the future to define what they must become. Firms always possess two types of resources:

Assets: Resources that can be liquidated and converted into other resources.

Intellectual Capital: People and the knowledge that they possess.

Dynamically adaptive organizations understand that they must be willing to sell any asset if it means adapting to the future for the purpose of profit maximization. That means that any attachment to what the firm does or what its assets produce can stand in the way of its ability to renew itself. Renewal has everything to do with survival.

Dynamically adaptive organizations also understand that as environmental demands change, the nature of their intellectual capital must change. That can be accomplished in two ways:

New People: Hire people who possess the knowledge needed for the new environment.

New Knowledge: Train existing personnel to give them the knowledge and skill base that the new environment will demand.

Resources are assets that must be viewed in an adaptive context. The world's best buggy whip manufacturer in 1905 needed to be totally different by 1920. The ability to transform the firm entailed the ability to transform assets (liquidate and reinvest) and to retrain or hire personnel capable of competing in an entirely new market segment. The world is no different today. The name of the game is adaptation, not continuation.

The conclusion that the reality of e-chaos leads to is simple: It's a brand new world that demands entirely new ways of thinking and managing. The new competitive world is characterized by difference, not sameness. It is characterized by high levels of complexity and speed. The slow, incremental nature of the traditional strategic model renders it useless in e-chaos.

What About Other Approaches?

SWOT analysis has many of the same problems as the traditional strategic model in the context of complexity and speed, not to mention time frame. The real issue is not what the company does well in the context of today. The company's weaknesses in the current context are equally irrelevant. Certainly, it would be great if whatever the company does today will be needed in the future, but that cannot be assumed. The real issue is: What does the company need to do in the future to be successful? SWOT analysis not only fails to answer that question, it misleads managers into thinking that understanding the present condition of the company will make them successful in the future.

Porter's Five Forces model is equally flawed. Notice that it focuses on the present environment. Further, it is highly simplistic in nature. Compare the Five Forces model with the environmental and innovation turbulence approach introduced in Chapter Two, which is reproduced in Figure 6.6. The latter is significantly more complex and revealing, and would be much more useful in preparing future strategies for a firm.

When combined with a 10 forces analysis, which involves a much more holistic look at the environment, the predictive power of the turbulence tools is substantial. At the same time, a SWOT/Five Forces analysis provides little if any insight into complex challenges an organization may face in the future.

Porter's Generic Strategies have similar problems. As turbulence indexes rise above level 3, change accelerates. Vertical integration or industry consolidation becomes highly probable. Additionally, the ability to apply any of Porter's generic strategies goes out the window. A look at the product life cycle—shown in Figure 6.7 for computer chips—serves as an excellent example of that reality.

When a new computer chip is released, the first mover has a very short time in which to charge a high price. Within months, the product becomes commodity priced. Generic strategies, rather than helping a firm understand how to position its products, can be extremely damaging because the long-term view they promote is so far out of sync with the real world.

Future Marketing Turbulence

Market Behavior (Competitors)	1	2	3	4	5
Sales Aggressiveness	Low		Competitive		Highly Aggressive
Marketing Aggressiveness (Advertising and PR)	Low		Moderate		Very High
Market Strategy	Serve Customers		Grow Market		Expand Share
Industry Capacity vs. Demand	Excess Demand		Equilibrium		Capacity Significantly Exceeds Demand

Future Innovation Turbulence

Innovation Behavior (Competitors)	1	2	3	4	5
Innovation Aggressiveness	Low		Competitive		Highly Aggressive
Technological Change	Slow		Moderate		Extremely Fast
Innovation Strategy	Follower		Product Improvement		Product Innovation
Customer Strategy	Meet Needs		Stay Close to Customer		Anticipate Unrealized Needs
Product Life Cycles	Long		Moderate		Very Short

FIGURE 6.6. Using Marketing and Innovation Turbulence to Determine Future Environmental Turbulence.
Adapted from H. Igor Ansoff's Strategic Diagnosis procedures. Used with permission.

EDS: RETHINKING THE WORLD

When Ross Perot started EDS (Electronic Data Systems) in his garage with $1,000 over 40 years ago, he had a business idea that hit at an ideal point on a demand curve. As shown in Figure 6.8, a *demand curve* looks a lot like a product life cycle curve, except it has to do with the demand for a specific

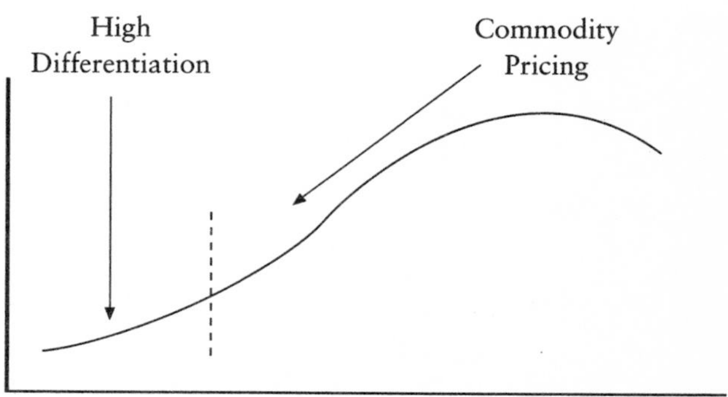

FIGURE 6.7. The Change from Differentiation to Commodity Pricing in Turbulent Environments.

product or service. Companies that are fortunate to get in early on the demand curve of a product usually grow explosively, and EDS is a striking example of this phenomenon.

Whether Perot was brilliant or just lucky, no one knows. In fact, it doesn't matter, because Ross Perot and a lot of his employees got to experience one of the most exciting changes in the history of civilization: the early growth of the computer age.

EDS entered a global market that was driven to convert from people to technology in much the same way that IBM Corporation was the first mover in the mainframe computer industry when firms were searching for ways to replace people with technology (and shorten processing times and costs). Even though the global demand for this conversion continued to grow at phenomenal rates in the mid-1990s, EDS got into trouble then because its core competencies no longer carried the firm. By 1997, EDS was experiencing serious problems despite the exploding global market for computer-related products. The underlying causes of EDS's decline are tied to the traditional strategic model.

Over the years from the late 1980s to the late 1990s, the systems integration business began to change as shown in Fig-

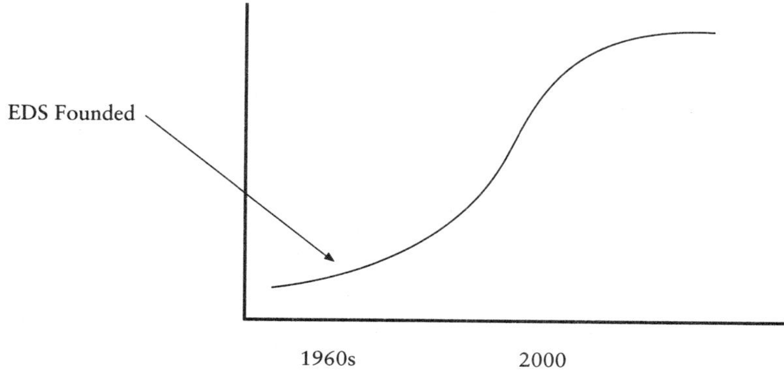

FIGURE 6.8. The Demand for Process Conversion from People to Technology.

ure 6.9. New competitors entered the market. Some old competitors like IBM recovered and came back hungry and eager. During the late 1980s, EDS was recognized as being one of the most formidable powers in the industry. During the 1990s, the firm began to have serious problems. In 1999, EDS fired its CEO and chairman and hired Richard Brown instead.

Ross Perot left EDS in 1988 after the sale of EDS to General Motors. Les Alberthal took his place and managed the company through its spin-off into a separately held public company. Figure 6.10 traces the company's approach to the various areas under the two CEOs. Notice that when Perot was chairman, the environmental turbulence was around level 3.3, indicating that the level of competitiveness and rate of change was moderate. During the mid-1990s, the turbulence began to change, increasing to level 3.8, indicating that the environment was highly competitive and rapidly changing.

When Ross Perot left the firm, EDS leadership began working with a number of consultants in the area of management. As a result, during that 10-year period, there was an increasing emphasis on the traditional strategic model. A lot of attention

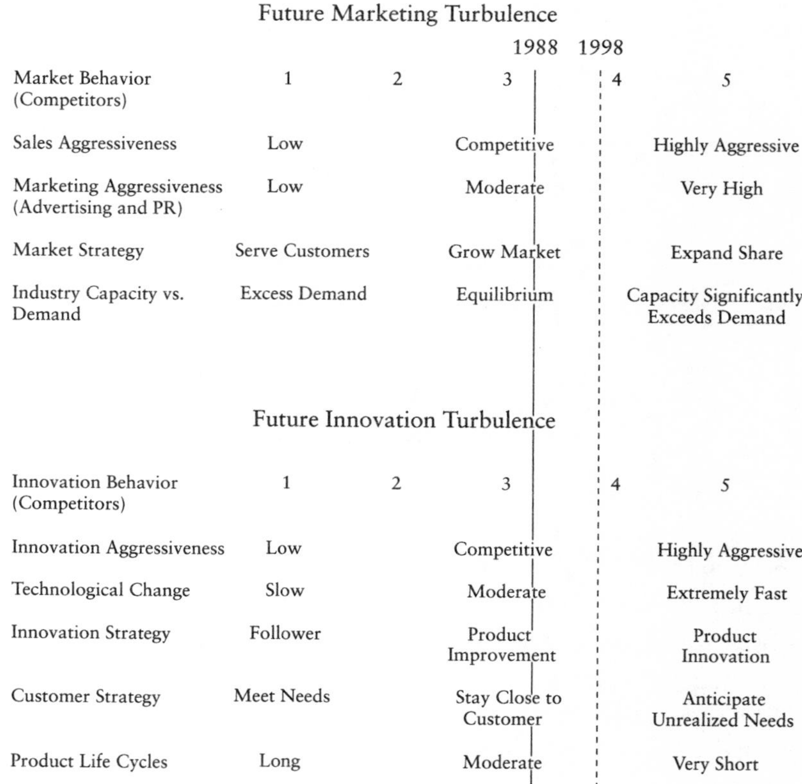

FIGURE 6.9. EDS's Increasing Turbulence: 1988–1998. Adapted from H. Igor Ansoff's Strategic Diagnosis procedures. Used with permission.

went into the firm's historic core competencies—and very little to the need to create an entirely different organization with the agility to operate in the new environment. As a result, the firm entered a time of relative deterioration. As Figure 6.10 shows, the firm changed little under the leadership of Alberthal; what did change was the environment. As a result of the changes in the environment, by 1997 the firm had numerous gaps (as indi-

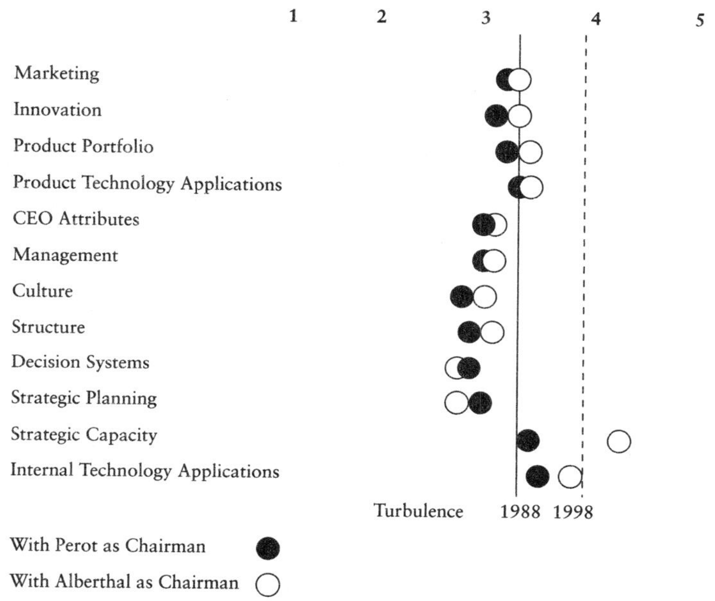

FIGURE 6.10. The Impact of Turbulence on EDS Performance: 1988–1998. Adapted from H. Igor Ansoff's Strategic Diagnosis procedures. Used with permission.

cated) in excess of –1.0. Generally, the firm had reached a fairly serious stage of strategic imbalance by that time. In 1997, the firm lost 40 percent of its market value and experienced the single largest one-day decline in its stock price in its history.

EDS and other firms like it enter times of stagnation and crisis because the mental models underlying the corporate strategy do not reflect the rate of change and complexity of the environment. The decision to focus on historic competencies during periods of extreme change only accelerates the deterioration of the firm's condition in comparison with the environment. Generic strategies, Five Forces analysis, and SWOT are all flawed in the same manner. If the competitive world was simple and repetitive (linear), they might work. In fact, they probably would at least appear to work since the rate of change would be slow enough that the firm could incrementally respond to environmental change. *(Chapter Seven features an interesting update on the EDS story.)*

The failure to use a management system that matches the speed and complexity of the firm to the environment can lead to disaster. That usually means that the firm often gets into the competition with "too little too late." In e-chaos environments, cycles of change occur with a fairly high frequency. That means that the four-phase cycle of organizations (shown back in Figure 5.4) accelerates as well. In other words, in more rapidly changing environments it takes less and less time for an organization in strategic imbalance to fail.

THE WALLACE COMPANY

The traditional model, with its emphasis on confirming historic competencies, results in the creation of a nonlearning organization. Such firms tend to reject signals from the environment (and the bottom line) that something is wrong. The Wallace Company, a small provider of oil field equipment, offers a vivid illustration of the dangers of linear thinking.

In 1990, the Wallace Company became the first small service company to win the prestigious Malcolm Baldrige National Quality Award—surely one of the most exciting achievements in the life of any company. The Baldrige Award is comprehensive when it comes to assessing a company, applying principles of Total Quality Management to the mission of the firm and all of its processes. It measures the ability of the firm to focus on its customers.

Imagine the shock of many when the Wallace Company went into Chapter 11 bankruptcy less than 24 months after winning the Baldrige Award. The company stayed in bankruptcy for a while, and was finally acquired by Wilson Industries, Inc.

Critics suggested that the Baldrige Award might have led to many of the problems that the Wallace Company encountered. They cited the massive amount of time required to go through the process to compete for the award, not to mention the amount of time it took to change the company so it could compete for the award. They also talked about the problems that occurred after the award was won. Executives of the winning company are expected to evangelize other companies on the benefits of process improvement and quality.

But the Baldrige competition was also good for the Wallace Company. In increasingly difficult times for oil-related businesses, the Wallace company was able to decrease debt substantially. Additionally, it achieved numerous performance and process improvements in the course of preparing for the competition.[18]

John Wallace, the former chief executive of the firm, did make one statement that might help understand what had happened: "I was slow to react to economic conditions."[19] On the surface it is clear that while the Wallace Company was competing for the Baldrige Award, the environment was going through increasingly rapid cycles of change. To be fair to the Wallace Company, it did reduce its bank debt during this time by almost 80 percent, to $5 million. The triggering event of the bankruptcy was the bank calling the Wallace Company's loan.

At the same time, the Wallace Company story illustrates the problems associated with equilibrium-based, linear thinking. A change in complexity and the rate of change in the environment changes the rules of the game. Internal efficiencies such as reduced cycle times, increased customer focus, or enhanced quality have little effect on the changing rules of the external environment. To survive, a firm must change its entire profile to match the new rules of the game.

A manager from an aerospace company recently asked, "When are these people going to figure out that Total Quality Management deals with about 10 percent of the solution? Why do they ignore the other 90 percent?"

Quality is the table stakes to get into the game. You have to have it. But when it's paired with historically based, linear planning, it does little more than help a firm go bankrupt a little more efficiently.

THINGS THAT DON'T WORK

There are a lot of great management tools in existence today. Total quality management is one of them. Process reengineering is another excellent management tool. However, TQM has an 80 percent failure rate and process reengineering is said to have a 70 percent failure rate at companies. Does that mean that these are bad tools? Absolutely not—it means that a company that lacks the holistic or system view of itself and its environment cannot use those tools effectively. TQM is not strategy. It can't do everything, even though a number of companies have tried to make TQM the whole show. Process reengineering can't do it all, either. Both are simply tools that can be used to improve a company's performance if they are used correctly. Using them as part of a traditional strategic planning process is probably going to fail. Using them to resolve specific performance issues in conjunction with a system that focuses on achieving strategic balance will usually be successful.

Managers in the 21st century will be unable to achieve success if they continually chase different fads. They will be unsuccessful if they do not understand how to manage an organization in relation to the speed and complexity of the competitive environment. The good news: Leaders who understand how to create strategic balance in organizations will be able to create magic for their companies. It's just that simple!

CHAPTER 7

MANAGING CHANGE IN A SUPERSONIC ENVIRONMENT

New economy environments are characterized by rapid, complex change. Of all of the problems that plague organizations, managing change appears to be the most widespread. Environments involving high levels of technological change can create extremely high levels of uncertainty, and the people in an organization who can see the change coming rarely have the power to adapt the organization to meet it. The result is internal conflict on top of organizational crisis.

Creating a learning organization is not enough. The challenge is managing the learning into the organization in the form of transformation, because learning without transformation is useless. Nonetheless, it is possible to manage organizational change effectively. This chapter discusses six keys for managing change:

1. Change or diffusion always occurs in a predictable way.
2. Different personality types have characteristic points in the process at which they adopt change, and this is consistent in every cycle of change.
3. Appropriate leadership and structure can combine to facilitate the rapid diffusion of change through an organization.
4. Managing the various learning personalities can create an effective learning organization and reduce the impact of change-resistant personalities.
5. Implementation strategies are the key to effective transformation.
6. Having an appropriate organizational culture is extremely important in fostering effective change and organizational learning.

E-chaos creates other problems for organizations. Speed becomes critical to success. The ability to tap many minds to solve problems—instead of just a few, as is traditional in most management systems—is extremely important. The complexity resulting from e-chaos further complicates the challenges that organizational leadership has to deal with. Basically, the result of technological change is the need for new ways to deal with change.

Change and organizational learning are inseparably linked. Change creates a new competitive environment and organizational learning seeks to recognize and understand that change. Ultimately, organizational learning should eliminate the negatives of environmental change and convert them into opportunity for profit.

Change, organizational learning, and strategic balance are also tightly linked. Many factors can affect organizational learning (which subsequently affects strategic balance), but organizational culture is among the most important. I have investigated the impact of culture on organizational learning in a number of companies, and this chapter is designed to share my understanding of how change diffuses into organizations and to provide a logical process for managing change.

CHANGE AND ORGANIZATIONAL LEARNING

Organizational learning, despite the volumes written about it, is elusive at best. True learning organizations tend to be led by "change obsessed" executives. Effective learning involves mining intellectual capital, which can only be accomplished in a truly empowered organization. Finally, by effectively linking the various personalities of change together, it is possible to create a learning-driven organization.

"We're running out of orders for our current generation of products," one senior analyst told me, "and we have no hope of new contract opportunities for our next generation of products until the year 2007." He went on to explain the battles his team had been having with some of the leadership of this international organization. "They don't understand," he continued, "We have a massive infrastructure to support between now and then . . . and we don't have a prayer without going into some entirely new business areas. We have the people and the ideas to pull it off . . . they just keep saying no."

The executive response to the idea of trying new product areas is almost always the same: "Our mission statement says we're in the [whatever] business, that settles it." How is it that a firm that can be a world leader in high-technology products at the same time cannot apply the same leadership principles to renewing itself? That is a difficult question to answer. Once understood, it not only explains why firms have problems with change, it also provides some insight on how to resolve the problem. Russell Ackoff believes that the problem involves the unwillingness of senior leaders to give up power.[1] He also suggests that the organization has the people to lead change, they are just not at the top of the organization.

The inability to manage change well often leads companies to downsize, creating an atmosphere of failure and despair, according to Richard Barlett of Mary Kay Cosmetics.[2] The result, he believes, is the loss of the company's most important asset: its intellectual capital. Many mistakenly believe that the intellectual capital of a firm is concentrated at the top. In reality, the reverse is true. That is why the unwillingness of those at the top to release power translates to the ultimate loss of the company's future. It loses those who have the knowledge of the future that is critical to the survival of the firm.

THRIVING IN A TSUNAMI OF CHANGE

The conventional wisdom regarding change has been that it normally takes at least seven years to affect meaningful improvements in an organization. While that may have been the case for most organizations, the leadership that took charge of the spin-off and reinvention of Pizza Hut, Kentucky Fried Chicken, and Taco Bell refused to be limited by historic norms. (The three restaurant chains are combined under the umbrella of Tricon Global Restaurants, Inc.)

I decided to focus upon Pizza Hut in taking a look at an organization that was challenged with the implementation of massive change. In my opinion, the Pizza Hut story demonstrates how frame-breaking change can be driven into an organization in a short period of time. While the Pizza Hut people admit that they are not yet where they want to be, it is my opinion that they have demonstrated how an organizational redesign can be accomplished in a short time frame, and further, what it takes to create an aggressive, adaptive, competitive organization.

On October 7, 1997, PepsiCo completed the spin-off of Pizza Hut and its other two restaurant companies under the name of

Tricon Global Restaurants, Inc., leaving them to face a number of challenges. They had great cost control—always a strong point for a restaurant that manages to achieve it—but the environment had changed so rapidly during PepsiCo's ownership that they were drastically out of sync with customer demand. Additionally, pressure to meet PepsiCo's financial goals undermined product quality, which allowed numerous rivals to gain business.

David Novak and his executive team had already begun making changes in the Pepsico restaurants. When Novak became president of the new spin-off company, one of the first things he did was bring in Mike Rawlings, a former president of a major advertising agency, to head up Pizza Hut.

Prior to the spin-off, Novak and Rawlings spent a great deal of time in planning the changes that would be implemented to enhance the competitiveness of the new company. They realized that the new company needed to shift their focus from a packaged goods mentality to a service mentality. The turbulent environment that existed at the time of spin-off was characterized by rapidly changing consumer tastes and lifestyles.

The spin-off day became the day that the Tricon team was going to lay the foundation for performance. They knew that success had to start in the restaurants. Turnover was a problem, not only for the company-owned stores but for the franchises as well. As with all franchise organizations, the new companies had a lot of areas where relationships with franchisees needed improvement. The end result was the equivalent of an all-out military assault. The strategy was very carefully designed to move the company to a position of industry leadership within a few short years. In developing their strategy for the new Tricon, the senior management team obviously focused on the need for creativity, products, and speed.

The spin-off day dawned with a new declaration as to what the organization was to become. Every Restaurant General Manager in Tricon received a copy of the new company's "Founding Truths," a document that defined the behaviors that were going to lead the company to excellence in the next millennium.

Managers' titles were changed to "coach" to convey the new culture of the firm. Extensive work was done to make sure that the culture of the firm was transformed. The new company had to be open, risk-rewarding, and a great place to work if the corporate objectives were to be achieved. To ensure success, all the managers were asked to sign off on the Founding Truths.

The Founding Truths

1. People capability first . . . satisfied customers and profitability will follow.
2. Respond to the voice of the customer . . . not just listen.
3. The RGM (Restaurant General Manager) is our number 1 leader . . . not senior management.
4. Run each restaurant like it's our only one.
5. Recognition shows you care. . . . People leave when you don't.
6. Great operations and marketing innovation drive sales. ... No finger pointing.
7. Operation discipline through process and standards ... consistency, not "program of the month."
8. Franchisees are vital assets ... operate as one system, not two.
9. Quality in everything we do ... especially the food.

A SLICE OF SUCCESS AT PIZZA HUT

Pizza Hut's senior management team carefully coached all their managers in moving from a command-and-control approach to a "coaching style of leadership" designed to tap into the general human desire to be appreciated for a job well done. Some resisted, but Pizza Hut's team would not be deterred from creating their vision of an entirely new, people-focused company.

With time, trust in the new organizational leadership began to build as did the performance of the restaurants. By proactively demonstrating the value that the firm's leadership placed on its people, the organization began to take on a new look—that of a creative, dynamic winner.

Are You a Cheese Head?

As part of the Pizza Hut commitment to excellence, president Mike Rawlings created the Big Cheese award. Did you ever see the triangular hats—like a big piece of Swiss cheese—that fans at Green Bay Packers games like to wear? That's what the Big Cheese award looks like. The award is only given to a few selected people each year, those who demonstrate the excellence that Pizza Hut has selected as its standard. It may be given to someone in a restaurant or any other person in the company. The award can only be given by the president of the firm and must be signed by the president. Being a Big Cheese is a big deal at Pizza Hut. One manager describes being at an event where a coworker was given the Big Cheese award. As the new Big Cheese went forward to accept the award, tears began rolling down his face.

Staying on a Fast Track

The new leadership culture of Pizza Hut has served it well. In 1999, the firm beat out Southwest Airlines as the "top company to work for" among companies around Dallas, Texas. The first 36 months of operations reveals the benefits of stressing creativity and innovation, creating the right type of culture, and developing appropriate leadership style. Consider the results after the first three years of operation:

- Same Store Sales Growth has increased 16 percent.
- Same Store Restaurant Margins are up 28 percent.
- Operating profits have more than doubled.

The casual observer might assume that Pizza Hut management might be able to turn on the cruise control and rest for a while now. Not at all, according to insiders at the company.

Focusing on Long-Term Value Creation

Pizza Hut has achieved many of its major goals. It has created a new culture and leadership mentality. It has streamlined operations, as demonstrated by continuing success at controlling costs. Further, the continual stream of new product concepts is evidence that the company is now a creative, innovative organization. That just leaves the technology objective.

The management team realized that they had to fix the restaurants first. They did that by creating an entirely new company. They also realized that the new economy is one of complex, high-speed change, and that the efficient use of technology would be critical to their long-term success. "We're simply not there yet," one executive told me. "We're seeing some changes in the market that are going to radically change the food business. We realize that we need to continually upgrade our internal technology applications—those that affect our internal processes, but we are going to have to go much further than that. We realize that technology is going to play a major part in the product area of our business in the future. The challenge is getting a handle on just how those changes will occur."

The Technology Challenge

The 21st century involves a number of new challenges, even for an organization such as Pizza Hut that has already begun to change its internal performance. At the heart of those challenges is technology—again, even for pizza. Late in 2000, I led a group of graduate students in a study of pizza consumers, in an effort to develop an understanding of trends in the pizza segment of what is called the "home meal replacement" market. Here is what the study revealed. *(This was a study with a limited sample of 250 people in one region of the United States. Please view the results with that in mind. The study compared Pizza Hut, Papa John's, Domino's, and Pizza Inn.)*

- Pizza Hut's pizza was rated the highest of all of the pizzas in taste and quality by a significant majority of the respondents.
- The respondents overwhelmingly preferred cooked, delivered hot pizza over supermarket (uncooked) pizza or delivered fresh (uncooked) pizza.
- A significant number of the respondents who wanted their pizza delivered indicated that their choice of pizza was determined by how close the pizza store was to their house. (A speed issue.)
- The bottom line:

  Taste and quality are less important than speed of delivery.

  It's all about speed: When consumers are ready to eat, they want their meal as quickly as possible.

Pizza Hut's management realizes that product-related technology applications may be the key to this competitive challenge. The study found that most pizza orders came in by telephone. Cell phone orders were second and Internet ordering was third.

Pizza Hut's competitors understand the new reality of competition in the 21st century. For example, Domino's (the largest home delivery pizza company in Great Britain) has paired up with AOL UK (AOL's British subsidiary). In July 2000, the two announced that every pizza delivered by Domino's would come with a packet of AOL UK software. In conjunction with the promotion, Domino's will begin running special online promotions for AOL customers. Most important, the AOL/Domino's program gives AOL customers the opportunity to order a

Domino's pizza online—with a guarantee that it will arrive within 40 minutes after it is ordered.[3]

The Domino's European strategy does not stop with AOL. Over the past few years, the company was the first to develop a relationship with SKY, a digital television network that features interactive services, including online ordering. Additionally, Domino's has developed relationships with wireless phone distributors, who now program Domino's Web site into new cell phones before the customers ever leave the store. Domino's has taken the same strategy to the cable television business.[4]

Domino's has brought this aggressive technology strategy to the United States. In 2000, Domino's began installing a system called QuikOrder in its stores. QuikOrder is an online service that has the reliability of telephone service built into it. Through QuikOrder, Domino's will guarantee that all orders will be delivered within 30 minutes. Domino's expects that 50 percent of all orders will come in online by the year 2006.[5]

A look at the Domino's technology applications strategy as presented in Figure 7.1 reveals the challenge that Pizza Hut faces. Notice the high level of innovation and technology aggressiveness that characterizes Domino's.

Notice also that Domino's innovation aggressiveness is extremely high. The good news for Pizza Hut is that its own profile matches very nicely with Domino's in that area. The challenge, as the profile reveals, is to Pizza Hut's ability to upgrade technology applications in the product area.

Profiting from Change

Pizza Hut is an organization that thrives on change. It has developed a combination of systems and people that fosters high levels of learning. Out of this learning, its managers are able to drive continuous transformation. Pizza Hut is truly an organization that will do well in the new millennium. How well it does will depend upon its ability to infuse technology into its product.

Product Technology Applications

Factor	1	2	3	4	5
Technology Applications (Product)	None	Limited	Moderate	High	Very High
Technology Philosophy	None	Last In	Adapt with Competition	Seek Early Adaptation	First Mover

Innovation (Aggressiveness)

Factor	1	2	3	4	5
R&D Spending	Low	Moderately Low	Competitive	Moderately High	Highly Aggressive
Product Life Cycles-Plan	Very Long	Long	Moderate	Short	Very Short
Customer Focus	Respond To Demands	Meet Demand	Stay Close to Customer	Anticipate Needs	Anticipate Unrealized Needs

FIGURE 7.1. Domino's Innovation and Product Technology Applications. Adapted from H. Igor Ansoff's Strategic Diagnosis procedures. Used with permission.

Organizational learning is often presented as a solution to all a company's problems—but in reality it's just one aspect of what might be called the learning and implementation process. That process involves a number of important steps:

1. Learning about the future; understanding the systems implications of the future macro system.
2. Linking organizational learning effectively with organizational power.
3. Developing transformational strategies and feedback systems to ensure transformation.
4. Implementing the learning.

Pizza Hut's management understood that radical change was needed to make the company a real winner in the new millennium. They also understood that they had a lot of the right ingredients for success, but they didn't have the ability as an organization to manage change. They faced two challenges. First, they had to change the strategic profile of the firm and make it competitive. Second, they had to create a way to maintain the firm's strategic balance on an ongoing basis. They needed both a short-term and a long-term solution.

Since change and diffusion of change through an organization is predictable, it is possible to design an organization to embrace change. Once that's understood, the ability to carve success out of e-chaos becomes much more understandable.

MANAGING CHANGE

A few years ago, I had the opportunity to address a group of division presidents of a large bank. Prior to the speech, the assistant to the chairman of the board asked for copies of the overheads that would be used. The night before the presentation the assistant called with this frantic message: "You can't give that speech!" "Why not?" I asked in some puzzlement. The assistant went on to explain that the bank had just spent a lot of money on one of the larger consulting firms to teach it how to change. "What we discovered was that you were going to tell us to do exactly the *opposite* of what they had said to do."

It seems that the bank had been told to do two things to manage change. First, it was told to form teams. (That's often the first recommendation consultants come up with—regardless of the problem.) Second, it was told to put one of its change agents on each team. Based on extensive research, I can say confidently that this approach would most certainly destroy the bank's ability to drive change. I'll get back to this story in a bit, but first I need to digress into psychology and introduce the "Five Personalities of Change" to explain my conclusion.

E. M. Rogers—who should be recognized for his contribution to the management of change—is the one who first discovered that there are five personalities in the change process:[6]

- Pathfinders
- Listeners
- Organizers
- Followers
- Patriots

People rarely test out as pure representatives of a type. Almost everyone has a combination of tendencies, but one will be predominant. In any given situation, people settle into one or another of these roles as though born to them.

By analyzing over 1,500 studies about how change occurs, Rogers found that it is an extremely predictable process. He also concluded that each of the personality types he identified is somewhat fixed. That is, people who act in accordance with each type really cannot be taught to behave differently than they already do when facing change, especially discontinuous change. Rogers discovered in all the studies that the process of change fit the normal curve. He also discovered that the percentages of each type of "change personality" were basically the same in each study. This work resonates with my own, and I believe that Rogers has identified the basis of organizational learning in a way that makes it possible to understand how change is defeated as part of a natural process—and how to use the same process to drive change and renewal. It all starts with the Five Personalities of Change.[7] Figure 7.2 shows how change diffuses through an organization. Those familiar with statistics will recognize that the process fits the bell-shaped curve, a characteristic distribution pattern that indicates the operation of many random variables balancing each other in a stable and predictable fashion.

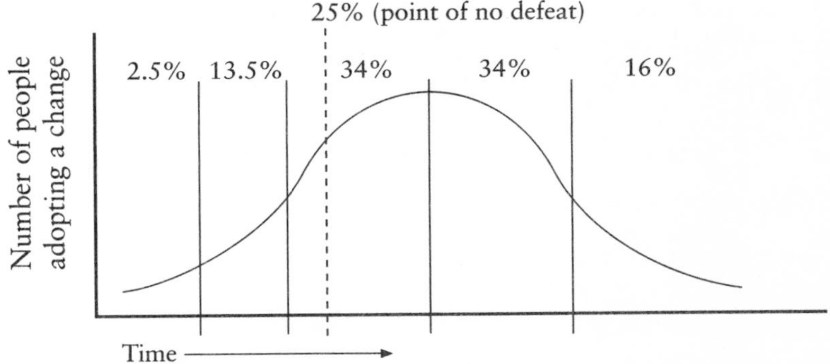

FIGURE 7.2. The Diffusion of Change into Societal and Organizational Structures.

Change normally diffuses through a societal structure or an organization in a highly predictable manner. In essence, that means that the predictability of the process lends itself well to change management. Change always starts with the pathfinder personalities (who amount to 2.5 percent of any population) and diffuses through each successive group in order. (More on the groups in a moment.)

Another important aspect of change is what I like to call the "point of no defeat." The researchers on diffusion concluded that somewhere between 10 percent and 25 percent diffusion into the organization, a change takes on a life of its own. Generally, if a change reaches 25 percent diffusion into the organization, it cannot be stopped. Thus, 25 percent diffusion into the organization becomes the "point of no defeat." It is that percentage that those managing change initiatives must keep in mind. It is essential to have a change strategy that targets 25 percent adoption by the organization, because then it becomes a done deal. Change will then cycle through the firm normally and its momentum will carry it throughout the organization. It turns out that the key to driving effective organizational learning is the linking of the first three key personalities of change. Absent those linkages, it will be difficult to deal with chaotic futures.

At a technology research lab in Ottawa, Canada, the staff decided to investigate just how critical the links between the personalities were in driving change. The senior lab manager did post mortem assessments of two recent projects—one a gigantic success and the other a horrible failure. The conclusion: "What we discovered was that we accidentally had the personalities correctly aligned for the successful initiative. Our mistake on the failed project became equally obvious. We had all of the wrong personalities in all of the wrong places."

The following pages involve a detailed look at each of the personalities of change.

Pathfinders

The pathfinders are the first people to see change coming. They are usually 2.5 percent of the population. Rarely are they found at the top of a mature organization, but often they can be recognized as founders of organizations. Steve Jobs (Apple Computer) and Jimmy Treybig (Tandem Computer) represent pathfinder personalities who had the basic instincts to see what others could not see (a characteristic of the pathfinder personality alone among the five types).

Pathfinders tend to be multi-network personalities. That is, they often cycle through numbers of learning-type organizations. One person referred to the pathfinder as "someone who daily bounced off the ionosphere." Pathfinders struggle in company settings because they cannot get others to see the facts. A simple story illustrates the problems pathfinders tend to have in organizations.

> *It was a typical hot summer evening in Dallas, and a young man sat with his sweetheart's family on the patio, trying to nerve himself to ask her parents for her hand. Somehow, he got the only chair that looked directly into the kitchen—and what he saw there made his mind go blank.*

> *Unknown to the suitor, his sweetheart's little brother had a problem with sleepwalking. On this particular evening, the little brother needed to use the rest room. The only problem was he sleepwalked his way to the kitchen, where he proceeded to use the trash can instead.*
>
> *"What the heck do you teach your kids at this place?" blurted the suitor, much to the surprise of his company. Since he was the only one who could see into the kitchen, they had no idea of what he was talking about. It took a lot of explaining, and finally a lot of laughing, before he got down to the reason he was there. They still joke that the only reason they took him in was to keep it in the family—but they tell the tale often enough that he knows it's not so.*

When it comes to change, pathfinders are the only people who can "see into the kitchen." As a result, not only do they become frustrated when they try to communicate change, the people around them also become quite frustrated. Even when there is overwhelming evidence that what the pathfinder is saying is true, the other personalities often reject the information.

It is often the pathfinders who are the only systems thinkers in the organization. For whatever reason, this seems to be the only personality type that can truly see around corners hidden from the rest of the group, and this leads to an ability to see issues from a systems standpoint. After years of study, researchers have come to call the pathfinder personality the "gatekeeper to the future."

Pathfinders often find themselves unwelcome in an organization. Ultimately, they often give up trying to tell their managers about the future or new opportunities they have discovered, and they leave the firm to form their own. It is this process that gives birth to clusters like the one shown in Figure 7.3. There are varying opinions as to what causes *clusters,* or groups of similar companies to form in a general area, but in the end the characteristic behavior of the Five Personalities of

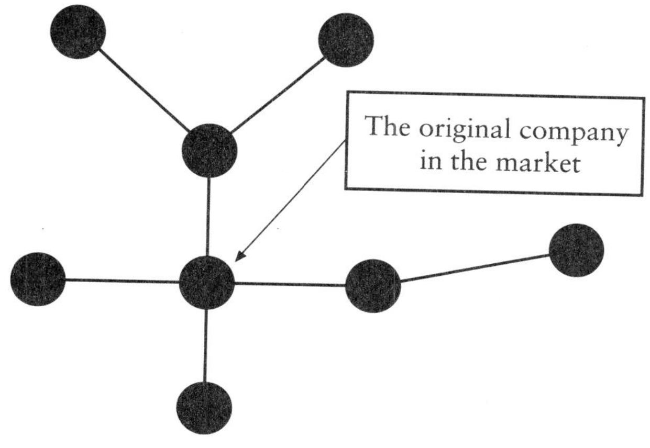

FIGURE 7.3. Clusters of Competitors.

Change reveals the reason—pathfinders see paths but can't persuade other personality types in the firm to take them, so they walk off on their own and assemble new organizations.

Around almost every major firm it is possible to find firms that all have one thing in common: They are made up of former employees (almost all of them pathfinders) who left because they could not get their former employer's leadership to listen to their ideas and information. In a number of cases, these offshoot firms are multibillion-dollar companies. What happened? The former employers let their "gatekeepers to the future" walk out the door.

Listeners

Listeners—about 13.5 percent of the population—are the only ones who will listen to the pathfinder personality. They are typically single-network personalities; when they look out into the future, they see nothing. Nonetheless, they tend to have exceptionally high organizational credibility. Often they are referred to as "champions" or "resident experts." They will listen to the pathfinder, and since they also have organizational credibility, they are able to carry the learning about the future to others in the organization.

Organizers

The third group of people involved in organizational learning are the organizers, including the next 34 percent of the population. It is from this group that senior executives of mature organizations are often drawn. They typify the obsessive compulsive personality types. They are resistant to change, which puts them at odds with the organizational learners, the pathfinders. They often view a pathfinder as insubordinate since they are trying to keep things stable while the pathfinder is trying to communicate the need for change.

It is not unusual for organizers to find ways to get rid of pathfinders. They resent the instability represented by the information that the pathfinder seems to continually bring in. Things turn positive, however, when the listener personality is interjected into the process. The organizer is quite willing to listen to the listener (even when acting as a messenger from the pathfinder). While pathfinders tend to communicate with abruptness, listeners are able to craft the message with patience and ultimately gain acceptance from the organizer. Once the listeners win over enough organizers to get past the "point of no defeat," the change initiative is on its way to success.

Followers

Followers—who make up the next 34 percent—are extremely resistant to change. They are single-network personalities and view those who bring in new ideas as being disruptive at best. Followers reject any idea of change with disgust.

At the same time, followers tend to be very tenacious. They make great salespeople. They rarely give up. The only problem is, they hate change and the people who bring it.

As noted earlier, people rarely test out as pure representatives of any one type. I did meet a flat-line follower once, however, at a senior management seminar for an international firm. The individual had a short, military-type haircut, and had the physique to indicate that he was very much into physical fitness. When we talked about his assessment, the conversation went like this:

> *"You are a tenacious person who hates change. You can take a lot of rejection and you don't get discouraged easily."*
>
> *"That's right!"*
>
> *"Your profile indicates that you would be great in sales, maybe leading a sales team."*
>
> *"That's right. In fact, I manage the sales force for an entire international region."*
>
> *"To maximize your capabilities, you need to find some links with the pathfinder personalities. You also need to have a listener on your staff that you force yourself to listen to. Additionally, you really need a subordinate who is a strong organizer personality . . . and you need to find a way to link all of these people together."*
>
> *"That's right—I've got that. My boss is the listener personality, and we finally discovered that we are a great team. He is excellent at seeing the issues I just can't recognize. I also found an excellent assistant who can manage the pants off of anybody. That keeps me out in the field where I belong. I've got one of the top divisions in our company."*

This man had the humility to understand what he was good at . . . and what he was not good at. His solution to his own shortcomings was to find others who could do what he could not do. Remember Ackoff's comments about managers being unwilling to let go of their power? What this encounter provided was an illustration of the benefits of understanding how everyone, regardless of position in the firm or personality type, can make a positive contribution to the success of the organization. It also demonstrated the importance of linking each of the personalities effectively.

Patriots

Sometimes the patriots (the last 16 percent) are called "diehards" because when it comes to change, they never seem to stop resisting. I must confess to a tendency to refer to them as "charter members of the Flat Earth Society" because they are usually still resisting one change when the next change down the pike is entering the organization with the pathfinders.

If followers are resistant to change, patriots have suicidal resistance to change. Patriots hate pathfinders. They will fire them if they have the opportunity. They view the pathfinder as organizationally unfaithful.

It is not unusual to find a lot of patriots in the most tenured employee groups. For while they hate change, they also are very patriotic to their firm. They will often refuse to leave a company when it gets into trouble and will often work for no salary to save it. Patriots make excellent safety inspectors as well as salespeople. They never give up.

A PRACTICAL LOOK AT THE FIVE PERSONALITIES

It is a temptation for those who study Maslow's "hierarchy of needs" to view themselves as the "self-actualized" actors.[8] In fact, it is rare to find anyone who does not think they are self-actualized after studying Maslow. The same is true for the five personalities. Those who encounter the concept always like to think of themselves as pathfinders—but the reality is still that only 2.5 percent of the population fits that description. So the key to using the concept is to understand which of the five really applies so as to know how to use its strengths for the good of the organization.

In the course of administering more than 1,000 "personalities of change" tests over a six-year period, I noted a number of interesting tendencies. First, it really is rare for an individual to test 100 percent as any one of the personalities. Even testing as high as 90 percent (responses) in a specific personality area is relatively rare. Generally, the assessment will indicate primary tendencies as well as secondary tendencies. Engineering types are apt to test out as 60 percent pathfinder and 40 percent organizer, or vice versa. It makes sense that technical people would have these natural tendencies. By the very nature of their discipline, they must be inquisitive (pathfinder), but the rigor of their training is such that a high level of organizer skills is necessary just to complete the academic program required for the field. It should come as no surprise that organizer personalities often have obsessive compulsive traits. They tend to be highly motivated and somewhat perfectionistic.

In the case of the engineers who test as 60 percent organizer (and 40 percent pathfinder), the indications are that they need to be in some area of technical management such as a research laboratory. In the case of the 40 percent organizer/60 percent pathfinder types, they are better suited to highly demanding sole contributor positions, and in some cases make fairly good managers. They are apt to be very good managers of organizations in highly turbulent environments because they tend to have great intuition.

When someone tests extremely high in one category, pay very careful attention to that person. In one case, a college junior checked almost 100 percent of her answers in the organizer category. Did her behavior correspond to her test? After less than 90 days as a student worker in the college of business of a university, she was basically running the place. While she was "shaping up" the administrative side of the university, she was involved as an officer of a number of university organizations. As if that was not enough, she ran for and won the office of class president.

People who are predominately "listener" personalities make great number two people for senior executives. They are able to gain the confidence of the executive while at the same time making great peacemakers for the organization.

On very rare occasions, an individual will test with equal percentages in all five areas. Despite their scarcity, it is important to understand where these people do well in an organization. Such individuals really fit the saying "jack of all trades and master of none." They never develop a passion for "just" marketing or "just" accounting. I often suggest that they find organizational roles that involve problem solving. They are great people for the complaint resolution department of a company. They are also great at doing a lot of things at one time.

The important thing to remember about the personalities of change is their role in organizational learning and change management. Each unique personality brings valuable skills to the table. A manager's job is to make sure that each is put in a position to do the most good.

Lon Roberts, author of *Process Reengineering* (one of the best books about process management), suggests that when firms began encountering 70 percent failure rates with process reengineering initiatives, they discovered that it was the high-resistance personalities that were at the root of the problem.[9] By segregating them out of change initiatives in the early stages (prior to 25 percent adoption), the firms were often able to change the 70 percent failure rate to a 70 percent success rate.

Learning about the future is the foundation of the future success of an organization. Understanding the five personalities and how to link them together to maximize organizational learning is the starting point for becoming a dynamic, renewing organization.

BACK TO THE BANK

Earlier in this chapter, I mentioned preparing a speech that ran afoul of the recommendations a consulting group had given a

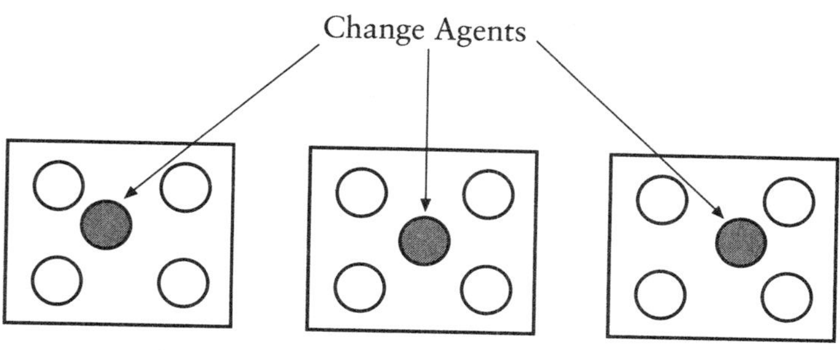

FIGURE 7.4. Change Agents on Teams.

major bank. The consulting firm had suggested that the bank identify its "change agents" and put one on each of several change teams as in Figure 7.4.

Obviously, this action would not help the organization in seeing and responding to change because isolating each change agent on a team of moderately to highly change-resistant personalities would make the change agents completely ineffective. In fact, that structure would guarantee that the change agents (pathfinders) would not be effective.

There is also research about teams that provides some excellent insight as to how to create more change-positive organizations. Numerous studies reveal that teams do increase the willingness of a group to take risk (which offers a good way of understanding when teams can be beneficial). Figure 7.5 shows how a change team such as a strategic intelligence team can be organized to maximize organizational learning and adaptation to environmental change.

To make sure that the pathfinders are allowed to maximize learning, the team should be made up largely of that personality type, along with some listeners. A few organizers also need to be on the team, but it is important that they always be kept to a minority to assure the group's willingness to consider change issues with a minimum of bias.

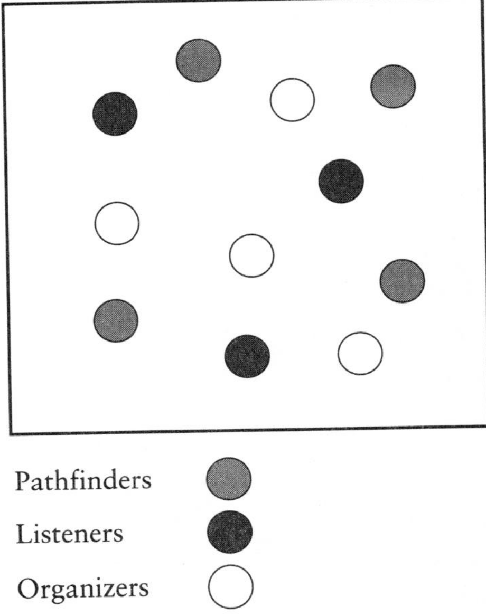

FIGURE 7.5. An Effective Strategic Intelligence Team.

LINKING ORGANIZATIONAL LEARNING EFFECTIVELY WITH ORGANIZATIONAL POWER

Peter Drucker suggests that the CEO is not the key to driving organizational change.[10] More recent research by Michael Tushman and others suggests that the opposite is true.[11] Tushman and Ackoff tend to agree that it is the senior executive of the firm who must be the key driver of innovation and entrepreneurship if it is to happen. The problem is, How do you manage the conflict between the change resistance of the typical organizer-CEO personality and the need for that same individual to be the leader of change in the organization?

The answer is twofold: linkage and accountability. First, the firm's intelligence team (the strategy group, the competitive intelligence group, or whatever) should be composed of a good blending of pathfinders and listeners, with a few organizers. The intelligence team should *never* report to a subordinate executive, but should have a direct reporting relationship to the CEO of the firm. In turn, the CEO must understand that the intelligence team *must* have the long-term protection of the power of the CEO's office (regardless of who the CEO is). While this is difficult, it is not nearly as difficult as the other aspect of this process.

The CEO must also agree to be accountable to the data. In other words, the CEO must recognize that, being high on the organizer personality scale, he or she is instinctively going to want to reject most of the information provided by the intelligence team. So the CEO must agree to become accountable to an outside group. (The data would be sent to the CEO and to the accountability group at the same time.) The accountability group, usually made up of board members, outside consultants, and other external resources, would then enable the CEO to take a more in-depth look at the information. When the CEO is accountable to the information, internal issues recede in importance. If the CEO becomes an effective learner, then the information can be driven into the organization with the necessary power to achieve organizational renewal.

I use the term *change matrix* to describe the organizational form described. Much like a matrix structure, the change matrix organization would include members from each functional and product area of the firm. The "matrix" aspect would involve the reality that they serve in both areas, as well as on the change matrix team. Ideally, the change matrix team would be where strategic intelligence would be gathered and processed. The change matrix team is critical to the organizational learning process.

DEVELOPING TRANSFORMATIONAL STRATEGIES AND FEEDBACK SYSTEMS

One of the most important lessons learned in recent years about organizational transformation has come from the area of

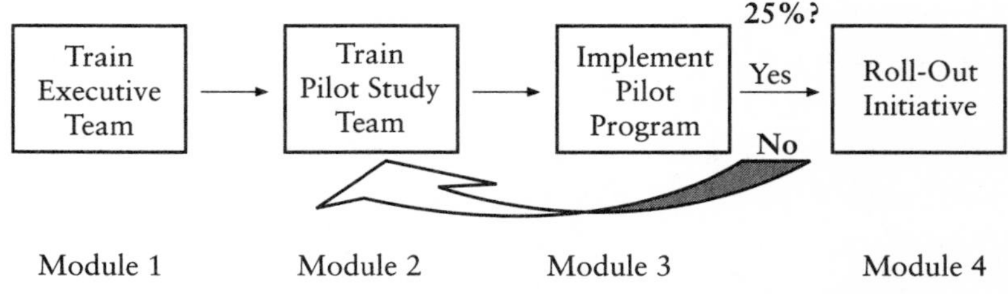

FIGURE 7.6. Modular Implementation.

implementation. It's always tempting to make a grand announcement of what the firm will become. Unfortunately, such an announcement often creates excessive resistance—just because it involves change. Increasing success in transformation has come from *modular change strategies.*

There are two keys to developing modular change initiatives: the high-resistance personalities must be segregated early in the process, and the change must be introduced in planned segments. A typical transformational plan for an organization might look like the one in Figure 7.6.

Experience has shown, as Lon Roberts and others have pointed out, that this approach can significantly enhance the success of change initiatives. As suggested, the project must be designed from the front end with the objective of achieving 25 percent adoption within the organization.

The transformational initiative must be accompanied by an effective feedback system to guarantee adoption, or what can be referred to as "system accountability." The ability to develop system accountability measurements across the firm is quite important. Since few firms have such accountability assessments, the challenge is to find ways to develop them.

Systems Thinking + System Accountability = Strategic Balance

Learning organizations are not just created with a directive from on high. There must be accountability systems in place to ensure that transformation occurs as a result of learning. In some companies, core values help establish and maintain the learning community. In others, the culture is integral in sustaining learning. Additionally, the attributes of the CEO are critical in this area.

In some companies, a 360-degree assessment is used to evaluate managers. The idea is to make sure that high levels of empowerment are maintained in an organization. System accountability involves more than what most such assessments provide. Transactional assessment instruments are best suited to this task. (See *The Significance Principle* by Les Carter and Jim Underwood for an explanation of transactional issues. In essence, the key is not to measure people's opinion of managers; it is measuring managers' treatment of others that is important.)[12]

How people are treated can be directly related to success in specific environments. It has often been said: "What you measure is what you get." The same is true from a system accountability standpoint. If the firm does not have system accountability for organizational transformation from top to bottom, transformation will be difficult to achieve.

Implementation of Learning

Systems thinking about the future provides guidelines for new paradigms for success or failure. Developing transformational plans paired with system accountability metrics leads to the obvious: System-fit organizations. To put it another way: System fit is what provides the profit of the firm.

EDS: THE REST OF THE STORY

When Richard Brown took over as chairman of EDS in 1998, he faced numerous challenges. The company had fallen behind in a number of areas. The strategic profile was in even more serious imbalance than in 1997 because of drastic shifts in the

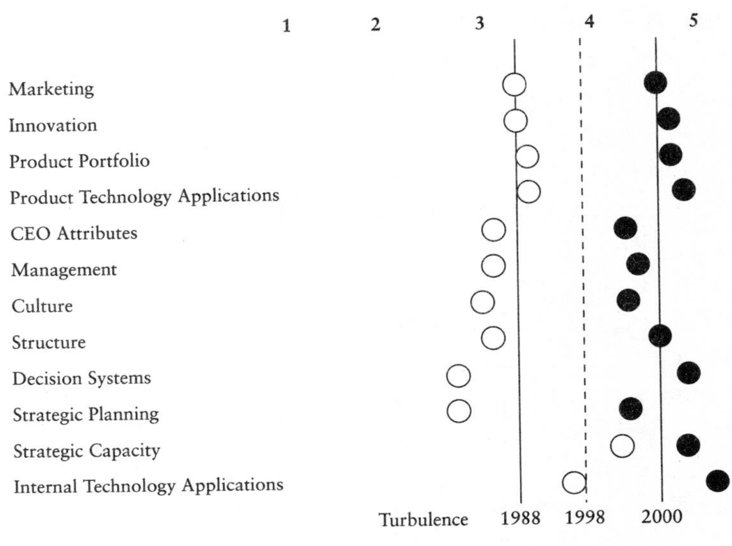

FIGURE 7.7. EDS Profile: Before and After Richard Brown's Takeover. Adapted from H. Igor Ansoff's Strategic Diagnosis procedures. Used with permission.

competitive environment. Turbulence had gone from 3.8 to 4.5. Nonetheless, the firm began to prosper almost at once. An analysis of the changes in the strategic profile of EDS under Brown's leadership, as shown in Figure 7.7, reveals the reasons for the change in the firm's condition.

Richard Brown made drastic changes in EDS's management structure almost at once. He took a hard-line attitude about getting the company back on track and regaining its leadership position in the industry. He spent a lot of time focusing on the future revenue pipeline.

He also created a unique learning organization. In many ways, he functions as the chief learning officer of the firm. Figure 7.8 shows how he does it.

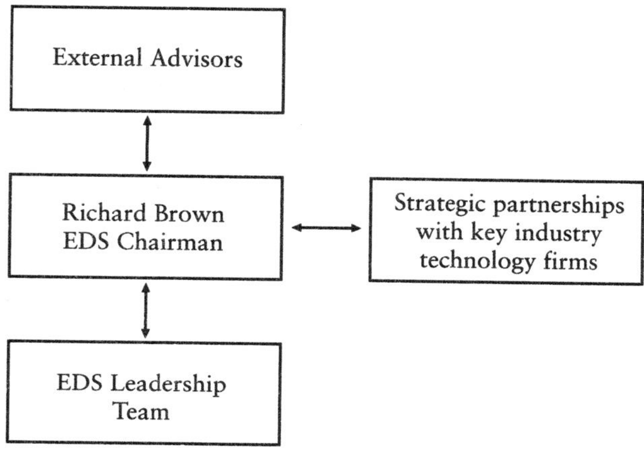

FIGURE 7.8. Richard Brown's Approach to Creating a Learning Organization.

Each group in the figure plays a critical role in driving learning and change at EDS. Since Brown does not view himself as a technology expert, he has set up an ingenious system for anticipating change and using it as a basis for continually transforming EDS.

- Richard Brown has a small group of individuals that he uses as advisers. In some ways, they serve as a think tank for him.
- EDS now maintains extremely close relationships with the leading technology companies in the world, such as Cisco Systems. Since EDS develops the applications to run on emerging technologies, its staff are able to anticipate where their products need to be positioned so as to maximize future performance.
- The executive team under Richard Brown is expected to do two things:

    1. Engage in creating new market opportunities for EDS by accessing the intellectual capital of their organizations.

2. Take the knowledge generated by Brown's intelligence team (and their own) and use it to continually transform the organization.

Richard Brown has changed EDS. As Figure 7.7 shows, he has drastically changed the strategic profile of the company from one of serious imbalance in 1998 to one of strategic balance in 2000. As a result, the firm is again asserting its global leadership in the market.

CONCLUSION: CHANGE AND E-CHAOS

Once an organization has learned about the future, the battle has just begun. The real challenge is transformation. E-chaos environments demand that change must be managed so that transformation is fast and effective. The other reality of e-chaos is that rapid, discontinuous change is the norm, not the exception.

The concepts in this chapter are perhaps the most difficult for many people, especially senior managers, to deal with. They involve turning historic processes upside down. They involve trusting subordinates to drive change. Most important, they redefine the senior executive's role from one of operational caretaker to one of entrepreneurial change-leader. And they identify the importance of everyone in the organization. They establish that intellectual capital resides in the entire organization and that intellectual capital is the future of the firm.

All too often, organizational leaders become obsessed with making the quarterly numbers. They often do this by sacrificing culture, quarter after quarter, until the company culture becomes one of abrasive control. Change is a two-edged sword. It can be an organization's worst enemy. At the same time, it can present the firm with unlimited opportunity. The only difference between the two is the organization's ability to learn and then use that new knowledge to lead transformation. The effective management of change means that intellectual capital becomes transformation, which ultimately becomes profit.

CHAPTER 8

PRODUCT MANAGEMENT AND COMPLEX ENVIRONMENTS

ORGANIZATIONS TEND TO HAVE FAMILIES OF PRODUCTS—product portfolios that can reveal much about their health and their future. Hewlett-Packard, for example, has a family of printers, and a family of computers, and so on. Texas Instruments has its well-known family of digital products, including digital signal processors and digital light processors, and many other product families. Within each family of products are individual products. Each of those products is in a specific stage of its life cycle and each one has its own profit outlook. Each has a number of extremely critical aspects, and unless all those aspects are considered, the future health of an organization is likely to suffer.

Texas Instruments is a company with a particularly rich history. The firm has worked in such diverse fields as geology, defense, computers, and semiconductors, to name just a few. Between 1985 and 1993, under the leadership of Jerry Junkins, the senior executive team of the company became increasingly involved in understanding the firm's product portfolio. This wasn't a pleasant process. They concluded that they really had no products with high future attractiveness—that is, the future profit and growth potential of every product family they looked at was disappointing.

Texas Instruments is and always has been a company with extremely high levels of intellectual capital. It has historically hired the brightest and best technical people around. As a result, the executive teams that develop out of this pool of technical intellects are a powerful resource. The company has always used this pool of executives to develop its strategy.

Their study of the future led the TI team to conclude that substantial changes were needed if the firm was to grow as they wanted it to. The team also developed some deep insights as to the future of digital technology. Under Junkins, the team began the task of reinventing Texas Instruments in 1993. As they came to understand the massive changes that the digital revolution could bring, they concluded that the future of TI could be much better than its past, and that was saying a lot. The company radically restructured its senior strategy and leadership team so as to develop a consistent strategy for taking advantage of the changes coming in the new digital world. According to George Consolver, TI's director of strategy process, TI's strategists saw some specific opportunities:

- Digitization was going to create a common language for telecommunications, computers, and wireless applications.
- The convergence effect brought about by the digitization of these three arenas would be enormous—digitization was going to change the world.

- There would also be massive opportunities in applications like voice mail, where digitization would allow personalization as well as connectivity.

"We saw that we had the opportunity to lead in a number of highly attractive markets," says Consolver. "Keep in mind the fact that in 1991 DSP technology was a minuscule part of our business." DSPs, or digital signal processors, allow for the digitization of analog voice signals, thus opening the door of opportunity to a number of areas. These include digitizing voice mail messages and automatically forwarding them to the recipient via e-mail. Basically, the invention of DSPs has totally changed the way people can stay connected.

In the spring of 1996, the company suffered a devastating loss that could have ruined its plan to take the leadership role in the new digital economy. Jerry Junkins unexpectedly passed away while on a business trip in Europe. Because of the strategy that the firm had in place at that time, however, its new leaders were able to aggressively move forward to take advantage of the opportunities that Junkins and the leadership team had predicted years before.

By the third quarter of 1996, the new leadership team was rapidly repositioning the company to compete in the new high-growth markets. The firm sold off its defense group for $3.7 billion. According to Consolver, it was a difficult move for the company to make. The defense group had a history of consistent profits, but it just did not have the attractiveness that the firm's leadership saw in the new markets. The leadership team also divested a number of other divisions.

The reallocation of the firm's product portfolio allowed TI to make serious inroads into the digital revolution by the end of 1996. The leadership team also understood the other opportunities that would be presented in the software solutions area as a result of the digital revolution and made investments in those areas.

"When we started looking forward in the early '90s and realized what the world was going to become, we had to face some organizational issues," says Bill Mitchell, former vice chairman of the firm. "We did not have the culture to support the rapid changes that we saw coming. We made the decision to proactively change our culture at that time." This turned out to be the right move.

By 2000, TI had what George Consolver describes as a "new risk-taking, speed culture." The history of companies rooted in the defense industry is to overtest. That results in decreased time-to-market cycles, as well as lost opportunities in e-chaos. "We're interested in seeing our people take risks to make sure we find opportunity first," says Consolver. "We believe that people who are trying to sustain a winning tradition are going to experience occasional failures if they're doing their job. The pendulum has swung away from the old TQM attitude of 'do it right the first time' to Gifford Pinchot's attitude that 'faster learning beats better planning.'"

TI has also worked hard to create a highly flexible organization. As new opportunities are presented, virtual groups are formed as others go away. The organization continually reinvents itself as new opportunities demand.

George Consolver credits TI's leadership team with establishing the company's ability to stay ahead of the curve. He calls them "street smart." He suggests that they stay that way because they are constantly engaged with the competitive environment. "Our people are rarely here," he says. "They spend most of their time traveling and learning about products, technologies, or opportunities. That's one of the main reasons we are continual first movers."

In summing up the philosophy of Texas Instruments, George Consolver made two statements that aptly describe the new role approach that drives the firm.

- The ideal market position is to be the one who creates the change.
- Always strive to be the one who writes the new "rules of the game."

It is that attitude that allows Texas Instruments to maintain its product leadership in the new digital world. It is a philosophy that results in a continual ability to create highly attractive product portfolios, and is the reason that the firm will continue to thrive in the e-chaos of the 21st century. TI deliberately applied a systems thinking approach to its product portfolio decisions, and that is something any company can choose to do.

BEING SIX MONTHS LATE MEANS YOU LOSE

More often than not, organizational resources are allocated as a result of internal political issues instead of emerging challenges and demands of the future environment. Systems thinking necessitates a new and comprehensive approach to deciding how assets will be employed for both existing and new products.

Companies in strategic imbalance usually have fairly low levels of innovation. It is not uncommon in such companies for senior executives to sacrifice the future to maximize short-term profits. Ultimately, in most cases, the strategic imbalance of the organization is most obvious in the company's product portfolio. In such cases, most of the firm's products will be in the mature phase of the product life cycle.

THE ACID TEST OF A FIRM'S HEALTH

Product portfolio balancing, the way the firm allocates funds to existing and new products, becomes even more critical as the turbulence of the environment increases. The use of single portfolio tools, such as IRR (internal rate of return), must be replaced with a comprehensive system of assessment tools. This new system should give the organization a more realistic understanding of where its investment dollars need to be placed for the benefit of the dynamic renewal of the firm.

There is perhaps no better test of an organization's health than to look at its product portfolio. Much like a financial acid test, which compares liquid assets and current liabilities to indicate the immediate financial health of a company, product portfolio analysis provides numerous indicators of organizational health—and not just for the short term. The product portfolio of a firm reveals the organization's present, near future, and far future health.

PRODUCT PORTFOLIO: THE KEY TO SUCCESS

Ideally, product portfolio balancing is the way companies make investment decisions in products. It is the process of deciding which products to divest, which products to maintain, and which products to invest in more heavily.

The stock market of the 1990s was awesome. Yet, with few exceptions, no wise investor was willing to put everything into just one stock during that period. Some stocks increased over 1,000 percent, others increased only 25 percent, and still others went down. Securities professionals understand that long-term investment success has mostly to do with an investor's ability to have a balanced portfolio.

That is, investors need a balance between the higher-risk, high-growth stocks and the lower-return, slow-growth stocks. Most investment advisers suggest that a combination of stocks, some in old brick-and-mortar industries and some in the new economy sectors, is best. The same idea is analogous to a company's product portfolio. Observe the changes that TI executives made to prepare the company for the new digital economy.

Texas Instruments and the Challenge of E-Chaos

An analysis of the Texas Instruments situation as shown in Figure 8.1 is extremely revealing. TI's leadership team realized that they were going to have to become an entirely different company (in the terms used here, they needed a new strategic profile) if they were to be successful in the digital economy that

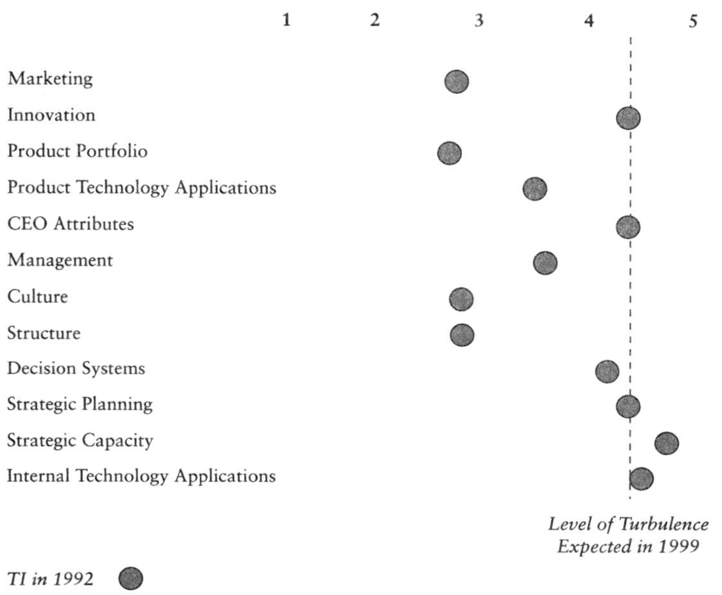

FIGURE 8.1. TI's Strategic Profile.
Adapted from H. Igor Ansoff's Strategic Diagnosis procedures.
Used with permission.

they envisioned for the future. They had to foster risk-taking and creativity that would become a part of the core values of the organization. The culture needed to change to support supersonic agility. The other critical issue that the executives saw was the deteriorated attractiveness of their product portfolio.

Senior leadership's assessment of the company's product portfolio (Figure 8.2) revealed the extreme differences between the company's existing product families and the massive potential that existed in the new digital revolution. Their strategic thinking helped them predict a massive shift in the rules of the game (including the speed of the environment). Their organizational assessment revealed the inadequacies of the existing organization to deal with complexity and speed. The product portfolio assessment helped them understand the need to move their asset base from one of low growth and profit to one of high growth and profit.

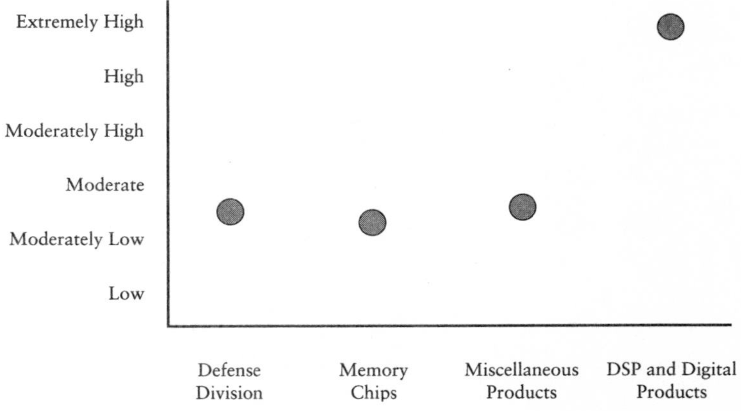

FIGURE 8.2. Future Attractiveness of TI's Product Portfolio in 1992.

High-Speed Environments and Product Portfolios

The Texas Instruments story illustrates the importance of balancing organization and environment. Strategic balancing is a complex process. At TI, for example, the management team had to understand the importance of organizational transformation, the need to reallocate assets out of historic areas of competence, and finally the role of product technology applications in a new environment.

A company needs to be able to manage its risk as well as its future. It does that by having the right combination, or portfolio, of products. But the senior executive—who is often the one who makes these decisions—needs to understand that managing a firm's product portfolio is much like managing a personal stock portfolio: There must be a blending of stable, low-risk products and risky but possibly high-return products. Risk is usually related to product maturity as shown in Figure 8.3.

New products can often be sold at a premium price based on their individual merits, while older products are more commodity-priced because competitors can come out with some-

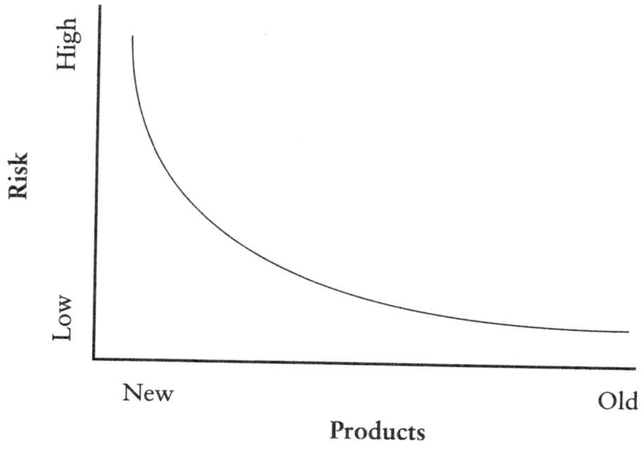

FIGURE 8.3. The Challenge of Managing Risk and New Product Introduction.

thing so nearly equivalent as to make no difference to most consumers. This means that profit margins on new products, especially on those where the firm is the first mover, can be substantial. For more mature products, since competition removes any ability to differentiate, price becomes the deciding purchase issue for the consumers.

Company leadership often becomes risk-averse, deciding to limit higher-risk new product ventures in favor of enhancing earnings in more mature, stable products. Obviously, the reduced investment in new products results in increased profits—for a while. As the old saying goes, "You can pay me now or pay me later." That is exactly what happens to companies that fail to invest in their future.

It becomes apparent that product portfolio balancing is important for two reasons. First, it allows senior management to maximize both future and present profits. Second, it ensures the firm's future. If leaders lose sight of the link between managing future profit and their present portfolio decisions, the organization will be in serious trouble.

Product Portfolio Balancing and E-Chaos

At this point, it's useful to pause and review the 10 forces that were introduced in Chapter One.

Forces Affecting Complexity	*Forces Affecting Rate of Change*
1. Economic	1. Technological
2. Government	2. Market
3. Legal	
4. Media	
5. Climate	
6. Moral	
7. Psychological and Social	
8. Ideological	

In considering the 10 forces at the advent of the new economy, it becomes apparent that both the complexity of the environment and the rate of change in it are soaring. I conducted a number of studies using the Ansoff model in the late 1990s and early 2000 time period, and most of the organizations I observed were minimally at level 4.0 turbulence. Most were higher. In one study done for a small city, the emerging (future) turbulence was predicted to be at level 4.2.

These increasing levels of turbulence change the rules of the game even more. What this means to the manager charged with product portfolio decisions is that the job just became a nightmare. Not only do product life cycles shorten drastically in high turbulence, the level of discontinuous events—surprises—also increases substantially. No longer can an organization allow product portfolio balancing to take a back seat.

Product portfolios must be supervised and monitored on a continual basis.

Turbulence has numerous implications when it comes to a firm's product portfolio. Product life cycles shorten. The ability to be the first mover becomes a critical success factor. The ability to use a differentiated price strategy is limited to short time frames, and then only for the first movers. Products become commodity priced quickly.

Critical mass, the amount of investment it takes a product to break even, increases drastically. The future profit and growth prospects of most if not all products usually change as a result in changes in the rules of the game. The product itself often will undergo radical change. Increased bundling (blending of products and services) will most certainly occur.

This means that the change in the rules of the game results in a major impact on the processes of product portfolio balancing. Product portfolio balancing, of necessity, must emulate the system the firm is competing in. Thus, a systems thinking foundation for product decisions becomes critical to organizational success and survival.

The Temptation to "Manage to the Quarter"

One of the serious problems that grew out of the economic boom of the 1990s was the increase in pressure from the stock market on the boardroom of the average publicly traded company. As fund managers began moving billions of dollars into the stock market they became one of the most serious threats that executives had to deal with. In some cases, fund managers began demanding seats on the board of firms in which they held large blocks of stock. The evolution to this new power base in the market put even higher demands on corporate executives to manage for Wall Street. The result of these pressures was that senior executives increasingly focused on the short-term aspects of the company. Increasingly, the temptation for many senior managers was to "manage to the quarter."

More often than not, managing for Wall Street involves sacrificing the future for the present. It takes almost no analysis to come to the understanding of the long-term implications for a firm if it is managed with only short-term objectives. One of the ways the executives of a firm can avoid sacrificing the firm's future is the use of an effective, systematic, and dynamic product portfolio balancing process.

An effective portfolio balancing system needs to accomplish three basic goals:

- Maximize current and short-term profitability.
- Ensure and maximize future profit potential.
- Enhance the system fit of the firm by understanding and recognizing the macro system implications and relationships with current and new products.

These goals can be accomplished by using a portfolio balancing system that facilitates the integration of the firm's products with the macro system of the future. To accomplish this, I've found that a complex assessment system involving seven passes, that is, seven different tools, is necessary.[1] All seven are important to the process. Any one portfolio-balancing tool has the potential to destroy the future profit prospects for the firm, but you can avoid such traps if you use enough different tools to make up for their individual lapses and shortcomings.

THE SEVEN-PASS PORTFOLIO BALANCING MODEL

In the same way that the macro system (the global marketplace) is a complex interlinking of systems, the product portfolio balancing system must reflect the reality of the larger system. Although most who do portfolio balancing tend to focus on only one or two of the tools, if a firm wants to maximize future profits simple approaches will not meet the challenge. That is why the seven-pass process was developed.

The First Pass: Attractiveness Ranking

Attractiveness involves two dimensions: Future profit potential and future growth. It is possible to position products on a matrix that shows their future profitability (high or low) on one axis and future growth on the other. Obviously the best case would be to have all products with high attractiveness. However, as environmental turbulence indexes exceed level 3.0 profit margins tend to decrease even with explosive sales growth.

This may seem counterintuitive, but remember that the ratio of capacity to demand is one of the major components of environmental turbulence. At level 3.0, the global capacity to produce a product is approximately equal to the demand for that product. As turbulence goes to the level 4.0 to 5.0 range, global capacity becomes significantly larger than demand for the products. At that range of turbulence, products become commodities. For example, the popular processor for computers in the late 1990s and early 2000s was the Intel Pentium, or competitor equivalent. There was little differentiation in the pricing of those chips from one competitor to the next. The reason? Capacity exceeded demand (and that is one of the main reasons that the turbulence level reached the 4.0–5.0 range). So although the profit margins would be relatively low on each chip, the market was so explosive that it was possible to make significant profits based not on margin but on volume.

Realistically speaking, the fact that most industries (globally) are in highly turbulent environments means that it will be rare to find products that have both high-profit and high-growth futures. This also means that high-differentiation competitors (those who try to get a higher price for higher perceived value) will have difficulty competing on a long-term basis. Certainly, first movers will have a short window of opportunity to differentiate based on price, but the agile competitor will realize that almost any product will soon become a commodity-priced item.

Once the products have been analyzed, the next step is to qualitatively rank them from best to worst. It is probable that the firm will have a lot of products in each area, so they will have to be ranked within each area first. Consider a company that makes a lot of computer-related products. Its analysts would assess the revenue potential for each one and rank the products as follows:

Product	*Attractiveness (Growth/Profit)*
Scanner	High/High
Laser Printer	High/Low
Ink Jet Printer	High/Low
Computer Monitor	Low/Moderate

(This process would continue until everything through Low/Low attractiveness had a ranking.)

Once the attractiveness ranking is complete, the firm will have a very important tool for basing future use of investment resources. Of all of the portfolio processes that can be used, the attractiveness ranking may be the most important. The reason? Although a number of products may rank well based on projected future Internal Rate of Return or some other output, if the firm does not have a significant number of highly attractive products for the future, its future does not look very attractive. The future attractiveness ranking is a valuable part of another product portfolio balancing tool, the Boston Consulting Group Matrix.

The Second Pass: The Boston Consulting Group Matrix

The BCG Matrix, as the Boston Consulting Group Matrix is often called, helps balance investment decisions between the future attractiveness of products and a company's position relative

Cumulative Experience

Future Attractiveness	(High)	(Low)
(High)	**The Star** (High future attractiveness; low cost producer)	**The Question Mark** (High future attractiveness; high cost producer)
(Low)	**The Cash Cow** (Low future attractiveness; low cost producer)	**The Dog** (Low future attractiveness; high cost producer)

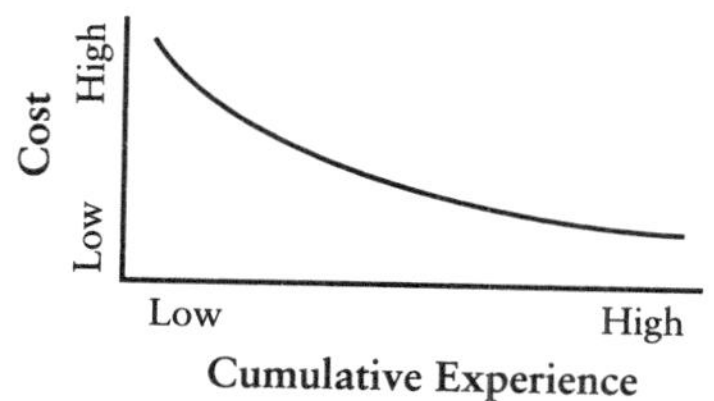

FIGURE 8.4. Adaptation of BCG's Growth-Share Matrix. Used with permission of The Boston Consulting Group. Material adapted from *Perpectives on Experience*, 1968, and *The Experience Curve Reviewed IV—The Growth-Share Matrix or the Product Portfolio*, Bruce D. Henderson, both published by The Boston Consulting Group, Inc.

to competitors' cumulative experience (see Figure 8.4). It's a useful tool, but unfortunately it is commonly misused. Some suggest that it is really a market share matrix, which is not an accurate reflection of how the matrix was developed. The BCG matrix was developed by researchers who studied the relationship between cumulative experience (the number of manufactured units produced) and cost.[2] Notice that as cumulative experience increases, cost decreases. Additionally, the competitor with the most cumulative experience is normally the low-cost producer. Obviously, a company is usually limited in the number of product opportunities it can pursue due to limited capital.

What the BCG researchers discovered was an inverse relationship between the number of units manufactured (cumulatively) and cost. That is, as the number of units manufactured increased, the unit cost went down, as shown in the curve portion of Figure 8.4. This relationship came to be known as an "experience curve." From the data, the researchers concluded that product strategy should be an interrelationship between the future prospects of the product (attractiveness) and its experience curves (managing who would be the low-cost producer). They then named each quadrant of the matrix to represent the type of product that would be positioned in each area.

Star Stars are products in which the firm has the highest cumulative experience. That means that it is the low-cost producer, and other external factors (to be discussed later) are favorable. At the same time, each star product has a highly attractive future, which means that if at all possible, the firm wants to maintain its low-cost-producer position relative to competitors.

The idea here is to determine who is going to be the low-cost producer. So if the firm has the available funds, it should have a *defend strategy* in place for its stars. If a competitor decides to attack the firm's position, the only way to do this is to lose money until it gains the highest level of cumulative experience. The firm must defend its position by investing funds to ensure that its cumulative experience leadership (and thus, its low-cost-producer position) is kept intact.

Question Mark The problem with question mark product is that the firm is trying to catch up. As the low-cumulative-experience competitor, the firm is the high-cost producer. The only way to compete is to take advantage of price elasticity (sell more units so as to make more units) and gain cumulative experience leadership by losing (or *investing,* to put it correctly) money until achieving low-cost-producer status.

Cash Cow The cash cow is a product that has low attractiveness, so the firm would have no interest in investing in it. At the same time, the product is a low-cost leader because the firm has high cumulative experience among the competitors. Usually, no funds are needed to keep this product, so the product strategy is to maintain it.

Dog The dog is a product in which the firm is the high-cost producer (low cumulative experience) for a product that has little or no future attractiveness. The product strategy for a dog is to divest, unless an *economy of scope* reason to keep it emerges in the fourth pass.

The product ranking developed from the BCG Matrix is approached in the following manner:

1. Rank each product area from best to worst (all the stars, for example, then all the question marks, and so on).
2. Complete an overall ranking in the following order:
   - Stars
   - Question Marks
   - Cash Cows
   - Dogs
3. Once the stars are ranked in order (as well as the others) the rankings can be combined such that a "best to worst ranking" can be developed for all of the BCG-ranked products.

The Third Pass: Economies of Scale

This particular ranking may only list one or two products. Economies of scale indicate that the firm with the largest manufacturing plant will have cost advantages. This is due mainly to the ability to divide fixed costs over more units. The idea is to recognize the importance of products where some slight cost advantage might be derived from such differences.

The Fourth Pass: Economies of Scope

This ranking also may list only a few products. Economies of scope are involved when two products have one or more common components. For example, a videocamera and a tape recorder may use the same model of electric motor. The experience curve advantages from such common usage need to be recognized. Ranking those products in order of importance can do this.

The Fifth Pass: Product Life Cycle Positioning

As noted in Chapter Two, products tend to have life cycles. Over the years, studies have found that products have their own four-phase cycle:

Introduction

Rapid Growth

Maturity

Decline

Figure 8.5 gives you another look at the curve that diagrams these phases.

In turbulence level 3.0, it is advisable to have equal distribution of the products in each phase. In lower turbulence environments, it is advisable to skew the distribution to the right, since product life cycles tend to be long. In environments above

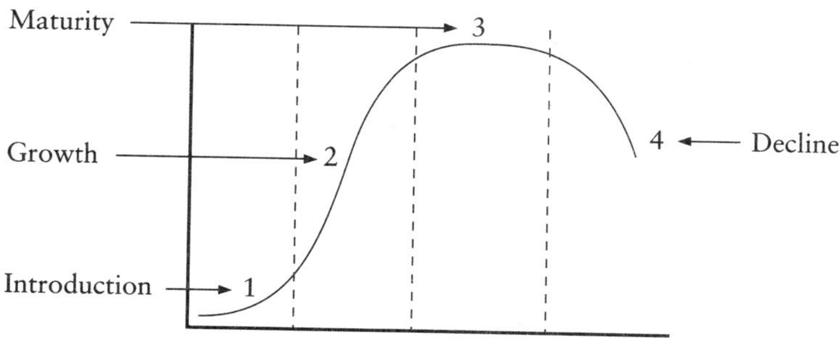

FIGURE 8.5. Product Life Cycle.

level 3.0, on the other hand, it is necessary to skew the distribution to the left (more products in the introduction and the rapid growth stage), because the firm can expect some product failures due to the unpredictable nature of the environment. In addition, the short life cycle at that level of turbulence demands continual and aggressive innovation.

While the weighting of products between each phase might be different for firms in different industries, the following list offers some general guidelines for how a firm might seek to weight product distribution between the different phases.

Product Life Cycle Emphasis and Turbulence

Turbulence	*Phase 1*	*Phase 2*	*Phase 3*	*Phase 4*
Level 1–2	10 percent	25 percent	50 percent	15 percent
Level 3	25 percent	25 percent	25 percent	25 percent
Level 4	30 percent	30 percent	25 percent	15 percent
Level 5	35 percent	35 percent	25 percent	5 percent

Graphed out, these curves would resemble the ones in Figure 8.6. As noted, the percentage distribution might be slightly different

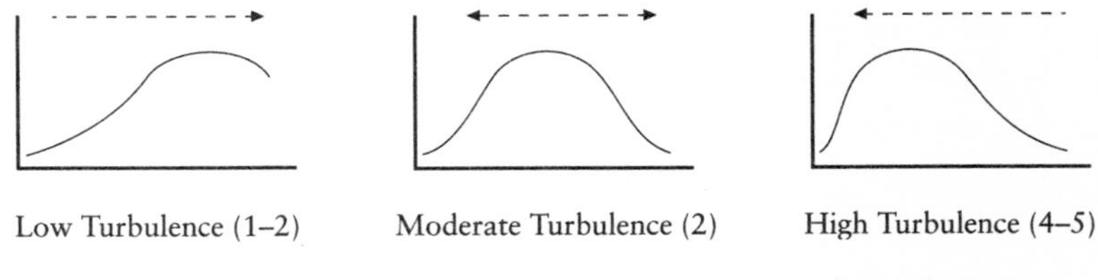

FIGURE 8.6. Skewing Product Distribution to Account for Turbulence.

for each industry. Using a similar distribution approach, the team could compute the number of products needed for each phase of the product life cycle stage distribution easily.

Again, it is important to notice that in low-turbulence environments, it is possible (and most profitable) to limit the introduction of stage 1 products. High levels of innovation are just not necessary. Product life cycles are quite long. As turbulence increases, the distribution of products in each stage of the life cycle must begin shifting from the stage 3 and 4 areas (mature and declining) toward 1 and 2. This is simply a way of recognizing the need to introduce more products in more turbulent environments, since rates of change are accelerated and the length of product life cycles can become extremely short.

The Sixth Pass: Capital Budgeting Tools Ranking

The idea of the time-based value of money has been around for a long time. Most students of finance must learn how to compute the future value of a cash flow stream using a method called present value analysis. Simply put, present value analysis puts a cost on capital and compares an investment with what might be called a sure thing return, like a certificate of deposit. The result is called "discounted cash flow." That is, the future fund flow from a project is discounted to reflect the cost of the capital deployed.

There have been a number of applications of present value analysis, such as IRR (internal rate of return), SVA (shareholder value added), or EVA (economic value added). In all these cases, the basic idea is to recognize the time value of money. IRR projections can be quite problematic for firms entering turbulent environments. The problem is simple: IRR is a linear management tool, so its projections are almost useless unless the future is highly predictable. The use of a linear tool for a nonlinear environment would most likely lead to numerous problems. If the future environment is highly turbulent, it will be anything but predictable. Therefore, the planners of the firm will need to minimize their dependence upon linear models such as IRR.

The ranking process for products with IRR-type assessments is the easiest of all of the rankings since the output is numeric to start with. From a portfolio process standpoint, the highest IRR product would be ranked first with the rest being ranked in numeric order.

The Seventh Pass: X Factors

The seventh pass in a portfolio balancing process based on systems thinking is the development of X factors. X factors are issues that might drastically reduce or enhance the future attractiveness of a product. A good example might be a pending action by the Environmental Protection Agency related to a material included in a product.

Therefore, X factors are issues that must be accounted for. In most cases, when the firm discovers a potential negative discontinuity in the future of a product, a decision must be made as to how this will be anticipated. This can be done using one of three possible approaches:

- Cancel the product.
- Put a hold on the product.
- Put a hold on the product, but continue minimal incremental investment in the product until there is higher predictability in the future prospects for the product.

By using this approach, the firm has a substantially better approach to managing its risk while at the same time making sure it stays in the game for the product.

Strategic intelligence is critical in managing X factors. The ability of the firm's management to understand emerging challenges and prepare for them is extremely important. The intelligence gathered by the intelligence team, as noted earlier, must be linked to the highest levels of the organization. It is the learning that intelligence provides that can have the most beneficial profit impact on product decisions.

The Grand Ranking

Once each product has been positioned during the seven passes, the rankings must be synthesized into a grand ranking. This can be done in two ways—either qualitatively (by simply drawing a line horizontally showing the position of a product in each ranking) or by developing a scoring system that gives the top products in each ranking a number of points (say, 100 for first, 95 for second, and so on) plus adding points for economies of scope or scale advantages (0.05–0.10 points for first, or some similar scaling). In the end, the scores for each product could be added to indicate numerically which product should be the first, second, and so on in the grand ranking.

A SYSTEMS APPROACH TO PRODUCT PORTFOLIO BALANCING: CONCLUSION

Linear assumptions about the future make people comfortable, as discussed earlier. Most people basically dislike thinking about a future that involves high levels of uncertainty. Yet the organizations that sustain long-term success tend to be those that thrive on change and uncertainty.

The problem with most portfolio balancing tools is that they are designed around a linear thinking model. By applying a systems thinking model to portfolio balancing, it is possible to anticipate and account for the uncertainty of the future. Further, by planning from a systems standpoint, the prospects for future profit are greatly enhanced.

High Flyers, First Movers: Southwest Airlines

If there is a company that really understands the word *agility* it is Southwest Airlines. While Herb Kelleher, Southwest's CEO, says he doesn't believe in strategy, the company's performance tells a different story. Yes, Southwest is an agile organization. It can respond to a competitor's moves in a moment, but more often than not, Southwest Airlines is the first mover in innovation.

One of the phrases made popular in the presidential election of 1996 was "It's the economy, stupid." When it comes to the airline business, the popular saying might be "It's the cost, stupid." But Southwest Airlines is much more than the historic low-cost competitor in the airline industry. In fact, over the years, a number of major competitors have been able to get their costs to a competitive level with Southwest's, but they have been unable to take market share. What is the real difference between Southwest and other companies?

A strategic profile of Southwest will point up the differences between that company and other organizations. The turbulence in the airline industry in the early 2000s was over level 4.0. Assuming that 4.0 is a fairly accurate estimate, consider Southwest's profile as presented in Figure 8.7.

Southwest Airlines guards its culture very carefully. This starts at the top. Kelleher has said numerous times, "We try not to take ourselves very seriously." Kelleher lives that principle. The employees are careful in making sure that the company hires the right kind of people. Generally, the company has hundreds of applicants for every job that comes open. That type of culture does not happen by accident.

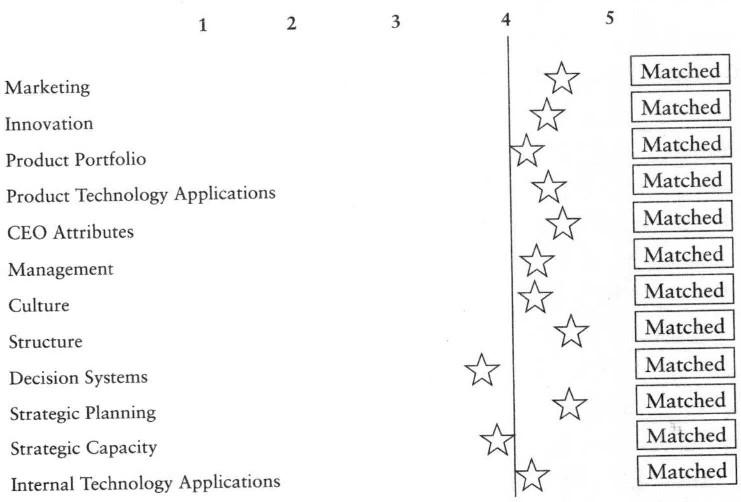

FIGURE 8.7. The Strategic Profile of Southwest Airlines. Adapted from H. Igor Ansoff's Strategic Diagnosis procedures. Used with permission.

A level 4.0 turbulence means that the firm is facing high levels of competition, a lot of uncertainty, and extremely fast change in the environment. Notice also that the company's strategies (marketing and innovation) are just as fast and aggressive as required by the environment. Although Kelleher says that Southwest has no strategic plan, it does have closely held strategic marketing and product innovation plans for the future. In reality, the firm has an excellent strategic plan.

Additionally, notice that the firm's reactive agility or entrepreneurial support systems are excellent for the highly turbulent environment. Observe also that Kelleher is the right CEO for the environment. He's obsessed with being the first mover and challenges his organization to continue to innovate ahead of the competition.

A typical strategy traditionalist would suggest that the company has found its "competitive advantage" and stuck with it. Nothing could be further from the truth. Yes, it was fortunate (and very smart) in avoiding the historic adversarial relationships with labor groups that is so typical in the airline industry. Yes, it is committed to maintaining a position as one of the lower-cost competitors. But it is constantly changing its products. It is constantly innovating in every part of the organization to keep its position on the leading edge of creativity.

Sky High Technologies

As the technology application measurement indicates, Southwest Airlines is not just another staid competitor. Its leadership in the use of technology includes the reality that in 1999, the firm was making 25 percent of its customers' reservations on the Internet. By October 2000, that number was over 30 percent. That was something that Southwest saw coming early in the technology game and that it planned out carefully long before many of its competitors realized the impact of the new economy on the airline business. The firm also has a state-of-the-art computer reservations system that is fully integrated with its operations systems. Southwest's leadership and culture have enabled the firm to effectively take advantage of the new technology-driven market. It has found a way to turn e-chaos into e-profit.

CONCLUSION

Historically, companies have been able to focus most of their energies on production and performance issues. As the new economy has hit the global market like the proverbial tsunami, the rules of the game have changed. Most of that change has occurred in the product area. Companies that do well in the new millennium will be those that understand the necessity of blending technology solutions into product solutions. They will also understand that the "speed of light" changes developing in product portfolios will force changes within organizations. As the new economy takes over, companies will need to increasingly focus on being prolific creators of new products.

W. Edwards Deming's famous saying is appropriate when it comes to product portfolio balancing: "What gets measured is what gets done." Excellent companies constantly assess their product portfolios. Their leaders know that the rapid technological changes of the 21st century are creating rapid shifts in consumer demands in the market. Only by constantly understanding the balance of a company's product portfolio are leaders able to make knowledgeable strategic decisions.

CHAPTER 9

CONTINUE TO LEARN OR CEASE TO EXIST

THE CHANGE OF THE GLOBAL COMPETITIVE ENVIRONMENT from an equilibrium model to a complex, dynamic economic model has implications for the role of management. Complex adaptation must replace the old approach based on linear thinking. This makes it essential to adopt a management process characterized by learning, transformation, and performance.

The excellent organizations reviewed in this book are learning organizations, highly agile, and capable of effective transformation. By contrast, organizations that do not do well are characterized by an inability to learn or to transform.

Excellent organizations emphasize the value of knowledge and learning. At Southwest Airlines, the management culture lives by the adage, "There are no bad ideas." At Enron (as discussed later in this chapter), learning is the norm. The same idea is true at all the organizations that are thriving in the new world of e-chaos.

Dave House, the technology guru who coined the phrase "Intel Inside," places a high value on learning. While he was CEO of Bay Networks (where he turned the company around so it could be sold to Nortel Networks for billions), Dave House received daily information dumps from the company library. It took him an average of two hours a day to scan the information, but he did it to make sure he kept his knowledge of the industry up to date.[1]

As noted in Chapter Three, Dave House was renowned for engaging in animated debates with his subordinates at Bay Networks. Once the debate was finished, House would compliment his opponent. There's no punishment for disagreeing with the chairman in a Dave House organization. The only rule: "If you work for me, you will be willing to challenge anything I say." Not only does Dave House value learning, he ensures that his organization learns by fostering a "challenge everything" mentality.

In looking at successful companies, it becomes apparent that those that are thriving are those that are learning. Obviously they have the ability to convert the learning into action, because those same organizations are excellent when it comes to transformation. But they are more than just good at transformation. They are agile. They are usually ahead of the curve. When hit by the occasional surprise, they use their speed to minimize the damage. The reality is, these companies are able to both learn and respond with speed and efficiency.

INTELLIGENCE AND KNOWLEDGE

Intelligence, as defined by the business community, is "the critical examination of information to distinguish component parts and determine various interrelationships."[2] Jan Herring (the recognized expert in corporate intelligence) defines the conversion of information into meaningful knowledge as "a step in the production of intelligence in which intelligence information is subjected to systematic examination in order to identify relevant facts, determine significant relationships, and derive key findings and conclusions."[3] Another possible definition of strategic intelligence is "the gathering, analysis, and conversion of information about the future into knowledge." It is organizational learning that is designed to provide input for organizational transformation.

Strategic intelligence begins as simple data. Once analyzed, data becomes information—and once translated into a useful form, it becomes knowledge. As Jan Herring puts it, knowledge is output that is the result of careful analysis of information.[4] Once gathered and analyzed, information must then be synthesized. Knowledge reveals the mind of the competitor or the consumer. Knowledge is the gold that is refined out of information.

Companies that understand the value of intelligence and the creation of knowledge have taken the first step toward long-term success. If they surround that knowledge with a highly adaptive organization, they are able to actualize their learning. Companies like Tony & Guy, TMP Worldwide, Texas Instruments, and Enron do this extremely well (as do the other excellent companies cited in this book). Companies that do not do well either gather the wrong information or cannot adapt to the new insights created by their learning. (That's why learning that is not actualized is not really learning.)

It is important to understand intelligence and the role of intelligence in organizational learning, because knowledge ultimately becomes intellectual capital—the stuff of which future profit is composed. An organization may gather intelligence in a variety of ways. Figure 9.1 takes a revealing look at the many ways that organizations can gather intelligence.

Organizational learning is based on both formal and informal processes. If a company is to be successful, it must have both. Informal learning is the outcome of open management

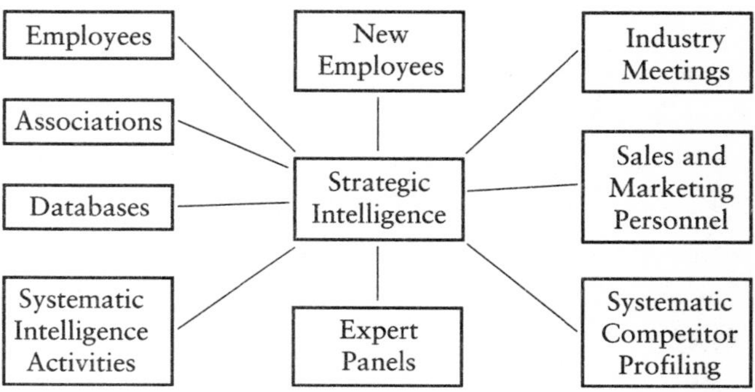

FIGURE 9.1. Resources of Intelligence.

and a culture that values the contribution of every individual. Formal learning processes must be used to convert all learning into knowledge.

INTELLIGENCE SOURCES

Back when I was still an MBA student, I received an unusual challenge. A large company that dealt in numerous defense-related areas wanted to know where every oil field in the Soviet Union was. Additionally, it wanted to know the vital statistics for each field—the formation the field was in, the depth of resources, and so on.

The professor for this course was known for being unmerciful with student teams that did not deliver the goods on their projects. This particular project had some unique problems. It seems that the Russians were quite aware that foreigners would love to have this type of information about their oil fields, and their solution to the problem was simple. They gave the industry press different sets of information about their oil reserves each year, "scrambling" the information and offering entirely different statistics every time. As a result, the global community had some idea of where the Russian oil fields were, but no idea of formations, depth, or reserves.

My student team had four months to complete the project, but as the time for the presentation drew near, we were no closer to the answers than when we started. We even found some of the original geologists who had discovered some of the fields (two were quite elderly and lived in the United States), but could find no reliable source for the vital statistics.

Then, just one week prior to the presentation to the client, we called an oil industry association. Much to our astonishment, we found an American geologist working there who had just done a study of all the Soviet oil fields for the Russians. It turned out that the Russian authorities did not trust their own geologists to conduct a reserve study of their oil resources, so they'd contacted the association, found one of the most reputable geologists in the United States, and persuaded him to conduct the study. We couldn't get him to release the results of the study, but we were able to refer the client to the correct source for the information—and that was good enough to avert the wrath of the professor.

Corporate intelligence specialists are quick to say that it is difficult to predict where critical intelligence will actually be found. In one case in 1996, I was doing research related to emerging technologies. One particular area of the research seemed impossible to capture. The major competitor in the technology space under study was not forthcoming about plans in that area. During a database search session, however, I came across an article from a New Zealand newspaper that quoted a senior executive of the firm—and his comments revealed the critical information the study needed. The following sections discuss some of the intelligence sources that deserve routine use.

Databases

The business intelligence community has long understood the value of some of the major commercial databases. The search routines of the databases allow the researcher to rapidly focus in on key areas. A number of the more prominent database providers include popular publications as well as key speeches in their portfolios. A good database provider and a competent researcher provide the foundation for good intelligence.

Employees and Sales and Marketing Personnel

Leaders of organizations often talk about listening to the customer. Equally important is listening to the employee. Corporate employees read trade journals. They attend industry conferences, and they talk with competitors. They can provide a wealth of information if a formal system of information retrieval is set up. This is especially true of sales and marketing employees. Customers often pass on information that sales personnel from competitors have provided them. Often, the customer will drop vital news into an innocent question: "Is your company going to use the new XYZ technology in its new equipment? The ABC Company representative told me that they were going to have it by December."

New employees can also be a source of information. Some unscrupulous firms will hire their competition's people just to get their information. It is neither ethical nor necessary to go that far. Any new employee—regardless of the reason for the hire—is apt to have industry information that may be extremely important, and a wise company will pay close attention to what newcomers may volunteer.

Systematic Intelligence Activities

Within learning organizations there is an ongoing process of discovering the future. By challenging present assumptions, those organizations are able to identify issues that may be of future interest to the firm. Once those issues are identified, the organization must set out to systematically understand each issue as well as predict, to the extent that is possible, future outcomes related to it.

Segment	Traditional	Non-Traditional	Distance	Wall Street
Classes	Day	Evening	24 hour	Day
Professor	Work experience less important	Work experience critical	Work experience unimportant	Fortune 500 consulting experience
Nature of Courses	Reasonable	Real-world	Interactive, multiple sensory	Take no prisoners; hands on

FIGURE 9.2. Strategic Segmentation of MBA Degree Programs.

Good assessment models are necessary if the intelligence is to be comprehensive and meaningful. The 10 forces model introduced in Chapter One is an excellent starting point for such an analysis, and the Ansoff turbulence model has also been used very effectively in this area. The Ansoff approach involves predictive modeling, so it can be extremely valuable in providing a systems thinking assessment of the future environment—as I've found repeatedly in the more than 100 major studies I've supervised.

Strategic Segmentation and Intelligence

Market segmentation involves dividing markets according to geographic, demographic, or other definable buyer attributes. Ansoff developed a form of strategic segmentation for use with his model that fits the intelligence process very well. Rather than segment according to buyer attributes, Ansoff works with what he calls "critical success factors." Consider how a strategic segmentation of MBA degree programs in the United States, as shown in Figure 9.2, helps the strategist to understand how to design effective intelligence gathering activities.

The MBA market has more segments than the figure shows, but these are enough to illustrate how strategic segmentation can drastically change the way managers look at markets as well as the way an intelligence team would gather information about those markets. The four segments—the traditional student (up to age 24, not working), the nontraditional student (a full-time employee who may be married with a family), the distance learner (who may be anywhere in the world, any age), and the prospective "Wall Street" employee (who is already working at a high level)—have their own critical success factors. Strategy for each segment must be developed independently. Intelligence gathering for each segment will need to attend to the critical success factors for the segment. Strategic segmentation allows intelligence professionals to logically segment data much earlier in the process. It also avoids the interpretation errors that often result from the failure to strategically segment, as when findings relevant to the traditional students are improperly extended to apply to Wall Streeters.

Once the strategic segmentation is complete, the researcher will often begin to develop hypotheses. These hypotheses may be either negatively or positively stated. The idea is to test each hypothesis with the intelligence that is gathered. Researchers often have a bias. That is, they think they know the answer to a question. By developing and attempting to prove or disprove a variety of hypotheses, the impact of researcher bias can be negated.

Systematic Competitor Profiling

Competitor profiling developed from publicly available information can be extremely accurate and vastly useful in developing corporate strategy. The value of such intelligence is obvious—indeed, it can't be overstated; knowing the other side's cards makes it much easier to play your own hand.

The ladder of success is perhaps the most effective way of understanding as well as predicting competitor capabilities and behavior. Consider the profile of Xerox Corporation in September 2000 (discussed in Chapter Five), which appears again as Figure 9.3.

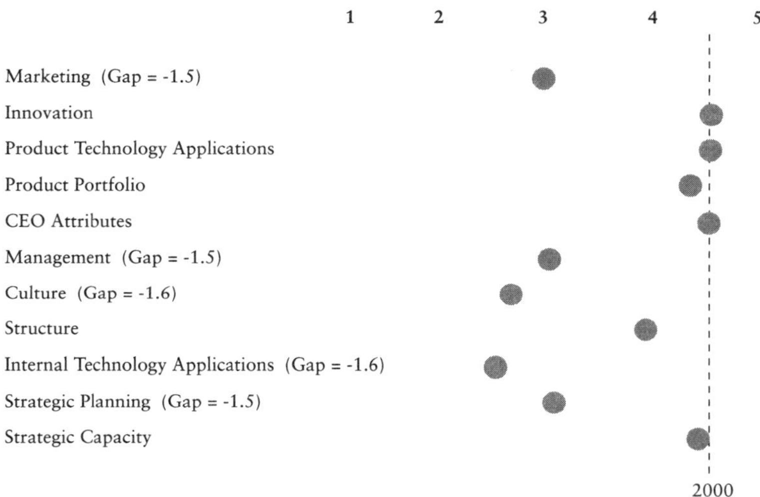

Xerox Gaps

Attribute	Gap	Profit Impact
Marketing	-1.5	Critical
Management	-1.5	Critical
Culture	-1.6	Critical
Technology Applications	-1.6	Critical
Strategic Planning	-1.5	Critical

FIGURE 9.3. Xerox Strategic Profile.
Adapted from H. Igor Ansoff's Strategic Diagnosis procedures.
Used with permission.

For Xerox, the future turbulence of 4.5 (shown by the vertical line in the figure) means that change in the copier/fax segment (an arbitrary division) will be rapid, with high levels of uncertainty. Further, price differentiation will be minimal in that environment. Product life cycles will be relatively short. Generally, competitors will be highly aggressive in all areas of marketing and innovation. Notice also that there are a number of *gaps*—differences between the future turbulence and Xerox's current profile. If left uncorrected, gaps in excess of –1.0 will have a substantial impact on Xerox's bottom line over the next 36 months or so.

This Xerox profile was developed using publicly available sources—it required no underhanded industrial espionage to get the information. In fact, the information about Xerox was gathered in accordance with the ethical standards of the Society of Competitive Intelligence Professionals *(www.scip.org)*. Nonetheless, when people familiar with Xerox understand the information presented, they are quick to agree that the assessment is accurate. Notice that the profile clearly shows the company's deficiencies as well as the magnitude of those deficiencies. From a competitive standpoint, this type of information about a competitor could be extremely valuable not only in predicting its next move in figuring out if its leaders understand how to fix their company.

Notice the five serious profit-impact gaps between where the firm is and where it needs to be. Xerox's marketing aggressiveness was severely undercut by changes in 1998 that changed relationships between Xerox sales personnel and their clients. According to some sources, these changes have serious implications related to Xerox's ability to effectively get products to the client base.

Virtual War Rooms

The phrase "war room" brings to mind *Dr. Strangelove,* the 1960s film that featured scenes set in the Pentagon, in a room covered with world maps. The corporate war room of today is much different. It's digital and it's virtual. The observations in this section are based largely on an interview with Jan Herring, who is (as noted earlier) one of the recognized intelligence experts in the United States. In addition to his background with the CIA, Jan has a distinguished record of developing intelligence functions for the Fortune 1000. At Motorola, he developed what many believe was the most advanced business intelligence system in the world. Later, at the Futures Group, he established the world's leading business intelligence consultancy.

A corporate war room can be a valuable asset. It should be the responsibility of the strategic intelligence team to maintain the following resources for it:

1. Current strategic profiles of key competitors.
2. Major database access capabilities for instantaneous industry or competitor updates.
3. Current intelligence databases as follows:
   - Recent intelligence studies of competitors.
   - Recent industry intelligence.
   - Global competitor country and culture information.
4. The latest in communications equipment, including videoconferencing.
5. The equipment and software to graphically project market maps for discussion and scenario development.

Generally, the war room can be virtual—data can be moved globally as needed. However, to ensure that the intelligence function never gets lost in the shuffle, it is a good idea for the firm's headquarters to have a formal war room that is maintained by the intelligence team on an ongoing basis.

Herring believes that the new millennium is an excellent time for companies to have intelligence capabilities as well as war rooms. Indeed, the electronic war room is the wave of the future, housing relevant data about competitors and markets (including global markets), and providing a basis for assessments the future.

The most important aspects of the war room are the soft processes that are used to manipulate the data. It is extremely important to use intelligence to drive "what if" scenarios and war games that combine competitor profiles with other intelligence in an effort to predict competitor responses to company strategy. Scenarios that use approaches such as the 10 forces model can also be quite helpful in developing strategy to fit changes into the overall environment. (See Peter Schwartz's book *Art of the Long View* for an excellent approach to developing scenarios.)[5]

War rooms can also be very helpful in driving both the quality and speed of decisions. Videoconferencing allows you to bring experts from around the globe to provide country- or industry-specific information, and to share graphic representations of markets, competitors, or other factors. "I've seen global market maps used as a basis for creating very meaningful discussions about market decisions," Herring told me. "They can be used to discuss different possibilities and outcomes. Most importantly, I've seen organizations use graphic presentations (market maps) that were combined with 'what if' discussions to cut decision processes from weeks to hours."

Herring calls this process a "virtual collaborative workplace." In our conversation, he stressed the need to consider all possible factors in the analysis process. In other words, effective intelligence is founded upon systems thinking.

Industrial Counterespionage

Pat Choate (a vice presidential candidate in the 1996 election) is one of the leading experts in the field of global competition, and is the author of numerous books on global competition. He also consults for a number of countries in that area. I discussed industrial counterespionage with him, and his comments are well worth attending to.

During the last four decades of the 20th century, most American companies were unaware of the level of industrial espionage in the United States. U.S. corporate-funded research in

American universities would be in Tokyo before it got from the research labs to the company that had paid for it. In many cases, companies would wake up to find their latest products had been compromised by a Japanese competitor before the Americans could even introduce the product. And Pat Choate advises that this practice is continuing at an even higher pace, with a number of other countries entering the arena. Even the mainland Chinese conduct extensive intelligence activities in the United States.

The few U.S. companies that figure out what their competitors are doing often hesitate to take action. There are a number of reasons for their hesitation. They may be partnered with the offending party in some area, or their executives may fear to take action because of risks to their company or to their personal safety. (In the early 1990s, a major network was interested in having Pat Choate and I appear with a CEO on a network program to discuss the problem. The network could not find a single corporate CEO who was willing to appear. It was apparent that they were fearful of retribution.) In addition, the U.S. government's unwillingness to take appropriate action in such cases discourages companies from proceeding in the matter.

Industrial counterespionage is just as important as effective intelligence. In fact, it should be an active part of the company's intelligence function. It is important to remember that those who practice industrial espionage view it as both a way to avoid costs related to product development as well as a way to gain an advantage over their competitors. In the case of some who gather industrial espionage, there are no rules.

With that in mind, the corporate counterespionage manager must learn to think like his or her opponents. Highly sensitive information must be carefully guarded. In much the same way that government intelligence agencies base access on an individual's security clearance and his or her "need to know," organizations should use similar approaches. Sensitive information should be kept in secure areas. Computers involving sensitive information should likewise be carefully secured. It is also preferable that the personnel working on sensitive information be segregated in secure work areas.

Personnel working on sensitive information need to be periodically assessed. As difficult as it might seem to be, active files should be maintained on all personnel. Drug use, alcoholism, gambling, and other addictive behaviors could all indicate that an individual might be vulnerable to accepting money for information. Also, those with excessive debt problems are equally vulnerable.

It is also important to periodically survey the geographic areas around corporate sites. In one case, an aerospace company discovered that no less than three foreign competitors had located near their main plant. All were conducting active campaigns to recruit key knowledge personnel for the purpose of compromising corporate security.

STRATFOR.COM: 21ST CENTURY INTELLIGENCE

Intelligence work must be done by people who are natural systems thinkers. Highly intuitive people perform the best analysis of intelligence data. Often, people in the intelligence community regard giving intelligence data to the wrong person as the same as wasting it. The native talent is rare, and it is not difficult to conclude that the business intelligence community in the United States is in trouble. Most business intelligence is gathered in one of two ways:

- Outside intelligence consultants
- Internal intelligence teams

In both cases, the individuals doing the work generally gather what might be called "business intelligence." That is, they work with a number of databases, develop a synthesis of the data, and draw a conclusion. Much of the resulting intelligence work is little better than a good high school term paper. What the intelligence community is discovering is that there is a difference between business intelligence and *strategic* intelligence. Business intelligence tells the recipient about the consensus view of a specific topic. Strategic intelligence tells the recipient what is most likely to happen. To put it another way, business intelligence is often a summary of existing views (which may or may not be accurate) while strategic intelligence sifts through the various opinions and predicts the most likely outcome.

If a firm needs either business or strategic intelligence and lacks the resources to develop it, it's possible to buy it as a service. A company called Stratfor.com will do a traditional intelligence-gathering project if a client has a need for a comprehensive look at the information on a specific topic. However, most of the company's work is involved in the strategic intelligence business. Its people are quite good at predicting the outcomes of events. Stratfor (the name stands for strategic forecasting) staff are somewhat iconoclastic in their approach to intelligence:

- They avoid the traditional intelligence sources.
- They develop their conclusions by challenging every assumption, especially the information gathered from traditional resources.
- They are almost exclusively Web-based.
- They understand that the analyst's "mental model" has a lot to do with the quality of the intelligence.

Here's how they do it. Since Stratfor.com is involved in global intelligence (issues in countries) as well as intelligence activities for U.S. companies, its people do not use the traditional sources that might be used by the CIA and others. The Internet is one of Stratfor's best sources. By December 2000, Stratfor had passed the 80,000 mark in subscriptions for its online newsletter. Those 80,000 people also serve as resources for Stratfor intelligence work. It is not unusual for Stratfor to have information that is significantly more accurate than that developed by the CIA.

Stratfor's team of analysts are extremely careful in making sure that their sources (the ones they use) are credible and unbiased. A good example of the quality of Stratfor's work occurred during the Kosovo conflict. Because Stratfor had numerous e-mail contacts in the country, it was much more accurate in getting information about where bombs were dropped and the effectiveness of the bombs.[6] Stratfor boasts many Fortune 500 companies as customers. It also provides intelligence briefings to numerous U.S. agencies.

The second key to Stratfor's success has to do with the mind-set that its people require of themselves. They continually challenge any information that they gather. They insist that there can be no place for any bias on the part of an analyst. That is why their predictions about international events have historically been so accurate.

The third key has to do with their migration to the Web. Historically, Stratfor had a traditional intelligence practice. When George Friedman, the chairman and founder of Stratfor, saw the level of quality coming from the Web (including a number of sophisticated databases), he realized that there was no need to continue competing in the traditional approach to gathering intelligence. In fact, he concluded that the quality of work in the Web-based environment was probably much higher.

The fourth key has to do with the mental model of the analyst. As noted, intelligence people will tell you that some people are capable of doing good intelligence work and that some are not. Good intelligence people are not linear thinkers, they are systems thinkers. Most people in the intelligence business will tell you that excellent intelligence is useless without the right people to analyze it.

Stratfor under George Friedman's leadership has created one of the best intelligence organizations in existence. It hires the right people and they use the right mental models in creating intelligence of the highest quality. Finally, they use their presence on the Web to provide information at digital speed.

Friedman and his team have always known that the primary recipients of their briefings often forward their copies to others. On one specific day, the daily briefing was missent, resulting in only half of the original briefing going out. Shortly thereafter, a call came in from the Israeli Foreign Ministry in Washington, D.C. The caller explained that they had only gotten half of the daily briefing and wondered if it could be re-sent to them. Friedman laughs when he tells the story. "They weren't even subscribers to the service. We suspect we have tens of thousands of people like them who receive forwarded copies of our daily briefing," he said.

ENRON: A LEARNING ORGANIZATION

Companies that are thriving in the 21st century are founded on learning. The leadership of those companies is keenly aware of the importance of learning and its impact on the creation of new opportunity for their organizations.

Meanwhile, a lot of old companies are trying to decide what they will do in the new techno-economy. Deregulation, competition, shifting markets, technological change, and increasing turbulence in the global economy have all combined to create problems in these old-line industries. Actually, that should be restated. Environmental changes have created serious problems for most old-line companies . . . but not for Enron.

Enron has been doing business for almost a century, under a succession of names. In the early 1980s, the company was known as Internorth and owned the largest natural gas pipeline system in the United States. At that time, it merged with Houston Natural Gas. Realizing that it was tied to an old, regulated business model, Enron became one of the first companies in the utility business to promote deregulation. Enron was also in the electric utility business.

CEO Kenneth Lay is known as a strategic thinker. Realizing the problem of being limited to a pure commodity play in the market, he began looking for ways to expand the company's opportunity to make a profit. In 1991, he brought Jeff Skilling on board. Skilling brought the needed tools and creativity to begin realizing the vision that Kenneth Lay had for Enron.

What Skilling did was to create a market model that blended risk and opportunity factors. By balancing the financial, trading, and risk implications of brokering natural gas, Enron created a marketing model with a substantial upside. But there is more to the story.

By the 1990s, Enron had become the largest seller of natural gas and electricity in North America. In 1999, a team of Enron personnel got wind of an idea that was being circulated in England regarding trading commodities on the Internet. Taking advantage of Enron's policy that everyone has the right to create their own future, the team developed a proposal. Within a few short months an idea was presented to the board: EnronOnline.[7] By early 2000, EnronOnline was up and running. The online trading company was developing opportunities to link buyers and sellers of many commodity products.

Rather than buy its telecommunications from others, Enron set out to create its own fiber-optic network, ultimately having up to 18,000 miles in the United States alone. Enron has also begun facilitating the selling and purchasing of bandwidth by securing a number of contracts with major companies in the industry.

What's Enron's Secret?

By 2000, Enron had been named "America's Most Innovative Company" for five years running. In 1999, it was elevated to 23rd on the list of the "Top 100 Best Companies to Work For." In the last 10 years Enron's revenues have grown from $4 billion to over $50 billion. "It didn't happen by accident," says Cindy Olsen of Enron. Olsen credits Enron's success to its ability to balance a number of critical capabilities. She believes that Enron's success is the result of the deployment of the five broad

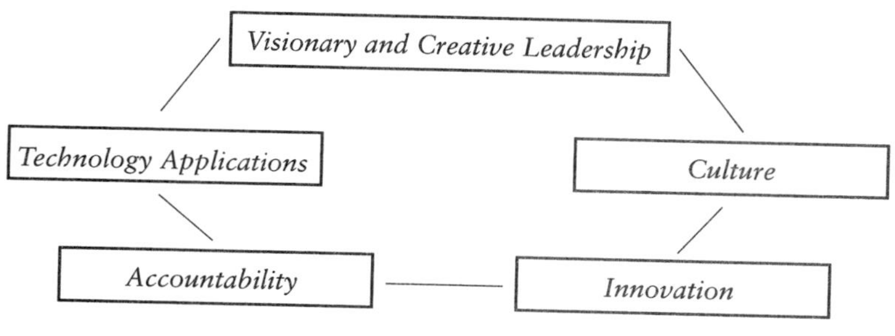

FIGURE 9.4. The Drivers of Enron's Success.

areas of the company shown in Figure 9.4, which are discussed individually in the following sections.

Visionary and Creative Leadership

As with all companies that enjoy long-term success, Enron has a competitive commitment that is driven from the top. CEO Ken Lay and COO Jeff Skilling work closely together to make sure that all of the competitive pieces of the Enron machine mesh well. As Figure 9.4 suggests, success in the new techno-economy is the result of balancing the organization with the external environment. Enron does that by starting in the future. Lay and Skilling live in the future. They constantly concern themselves with the uncertainty of the future as well as the ability of the firm to create a profit position for itself in the future.

Ken Lay views the company as an engine. The fuel for that engine is the talent, the intellectual capital of its people. One insider said that Kenneth Lay has an uncanny ability to find the "best and the brightest" people around, and cited the hiring of Skilling as one of those successes. Lay spends more of his time involved in the future and external perspectives than most other executives. Add to that the fact that he is a real people-oriented leader, and you have an executive who is able to focus an organization on excellence.

Jeff Skilling is often characterized as the creative leader of the organization. "Basically, he leads by creating businesses for the company to go into," said one person. Skilling created the business model that has enabled the company to so successfully profit from the commodity-type markets of electric power and gas. Using Skilling's approach, the company profits regardless of market levels, since it occupies the role of facilitator in a lot of transactions. Skilling "knows how to take an old business and create value out of it."

Technology Applications

Technology affects an organization in two ways. First, technological change in the external environment can change the company's prospects in the product area. That is, technology can change the way in which the product is marketed or delivered. A good example of this is the way that the Internet has changed product marketing.

Second, technology changes can affect the speed and efficiency at which the firm moves. Technological changes in the external environment can change the internal levels of speed and efficiency required to keep pace with the environment. The internal processing capability (as seen in the Oxford Healthcare Plans situation) must be able to meet standards imposed by the competitive market.

Enron uses technology to its fullest. Its internal systems must be leading edge to support the level of accuracy and speed required in the numerous markets they serve. And the company uses technology as a competitive tool. Its people have creatively used their understanding of changes in the global technology market to create new and highly profitable spaces for the firm. They use their technology systems to sell technology products, facilitating the purchase and sale of bandwidth across North America. Additionally, they are using their creative skills to develop numerous other technology-related products for the future.

Culture

The senior executive team at Enron spends a lot of time protecting the firm's culture. Enron's culture fosters creativity. People there thrive on iconoclastic behavior. Enron competes with other major organizations such as the consulting firms to make sure of hiring the very best. At the same time, it expects excellence from its people. Excellence at Enron is more than performance. Excellence means that every one of the 17,000-plus employees is a member of the creative team at Enron. As Cindy Olsen put it: "We leverage our open, empowering leadership culture with our innovation-driven culture and combine that with the best fresh talent we can find. In the end, that enables us to creatively make markets."

Accountability

Olsen likes to refer to Enron as a "meritocracy." Every employee of the firm is annually evaluated using a 360-degree assessment. Additionally, a peer ranking is completed on all employees each year. Those at the top of the ranking receive highly attractive financial rewards. Those at the bottom receive little or no incentives. The idea is to reward those who feed the wealth creation of the organization. Further, Enron wants to make sure that its most creative and innovative people, its intellectual capital, want to remain a part of the firm.

Innovation

"We don't know what we will be in the future. We do know that we are positioned to become an absolutely new company every day," said one executive. That same executive suggested that Enron is a true learning organization. More than that, Enron is an "out of the box" thinking company. That is true for its old markets as well as for the emerging technology markets it targets.

"If it makes financial sense, we will go wherever we think we can make a profit and we will usually make it a point to get there first," said one executive.

Enron's culture is designed to foster high levels of innovation. "Everyone has equity" is the idea behind the ability to drive high levels of innovation. That means that making mistakes is OK. Rewards and personal growth opportunities are oriented toward keeping the firm pointed toward innovation.

Everyone's the Next CEO Until Proven Otherwise

Enron makes sure that it thrives on uncertainty. In fact, in many ways the leaders of Enron work very hard to create much of the uncertainty that its competitors must deal with. It might be fair to say that the company has no core business. At the same time, whatever Enron is at any point in time will be different the next day. Enron is successful because it has rejected the old ways of doing business and decided to create entirely new ones. It is apparent that as long as it continues to do that, it will continue to grow and profit from the changing global environment.

ORGANIZATIONAL LEARNING

Learning organizations do not just happen. They must be created and nurtured. There must be accountability that continually supports the learning process within the organization. It is important to understand that learning organizations cannot exist in a vacuum. Companies that lack strategic balance will generally be unable to create an effective learning environment.

Organizational learning is the fuel that fires the company engine. Learning provides a framework for effective transformation. Effective learning develops a map to the future in a complex adaptive environment.

CHAPTER 10

MANAGEMENT AND DYNAMIC SYSTEMS

MANAGEMENT INVOLVES MORE THAN JUST PLANNING AND executing. It is more like the role of the conductor of an orchestra, evoking the skills and instruments needed at each point in the developing production. Indeed, many of the disappointing, alleged perfect solutions that have emerged over the past years take on new meaning when viewed within a systems context. Even though none of them offer the promised last word on ensuring profitability, they can be valuable tools for solving an identifiable problem.

Of course, the usefulness of a tool always depends on the circumstances in which it is used. In fact, even though TQM initiatives have been reported as carrying an 80 percent failure rate and process reengineering initiatives a 70 percent failure rate, both these management tools do have real value. The failures related to these initiatives have little to do with the value of the tools and much to do with the misunderstanding of when and how to use them.

High-speed, chaotic environments require complex thinking and as a result they require the use of a range of tools able to address the proliferation of challenges the firm faces or will face. When tools such as TQM are used alone or on the wrong problems, they often damage the organization they were intended to help. Nonetheless, in the context of a systems approach to the organization, many of these same business tools can be as beneficial as their creators could wish. This chapter presents a few of the more important tools in two batches, interrupted by an account of one of the excellent companies that uses them, to point out where there is value (that is, potential for enhancing profit) as well as where there is no value.

THE USUAL SUSPECTS

In this section, I discuss the tools that generally come to mind first when a consultant gets called in: teams, scorecards, TQM, Kaizen, open-book management, vision statements, and process reengineering.

Teams

As noted earlier, it seems that for most consultants, the first prescription is for a client to form teams. The team approach often does make sense—research has identified two consistent benefits from its use:

- Enhanced quality of decision making
- Increased propensity for risk-taking

Note that consensus building is not on the list, even though consensus does sometimes develop when teams are used. Whether or not the group reaches a consensus, it is the group learning achieved from the interaction of ideas that improves the quality of the ultimate solution. (Consensus tends to be overrated—it feels wonderful to work in a group where everyone enthusiastically supports the current course of action, but it can mask real problems because no one wants to look too closely and perhaps see something that will rain on the general parade. It's often asserted that the Japanese have problems because of their preference for working on consensus and making sure no one loses face, which makes individuals reluctant to engage in R&D on products that might ultimately be viewed as mistakes.)

M. Scott Meyers was one of the pioneers in the use of teams for decision making. He concluded that the people doing the job knew a lot more about solving the problems in their own work area than those supervising them knew. He took the concept into Texas Instruments with extremely positive results.

Increasing the levels of risk-taking is often a challenge for leaders. As firms enter environments of high rates of change and high levels of uncertainty, it is risk-taking (with the obvious result of some mistakes) that can lead the firm to success. Teams allow people to pool their knowledge and assess the results of both action and inaction, and can thus help increase the willingness of employees to take appropriate risk.

Teams cannot solve all of a company's problems. Helpful as they can be, they need to be matched to the problem being targeted, both by their composition and by their authority to do something about it. Otherwise, like the change teams at the bank I described in Chapter Seven, they're apt to be a waste of time—or worse.

Scorecards

Scorecards involve compiling the best practices for all areas of a firm's operations (either industry-wide or from specific competitors), then comparing the current status of the firm to the collected practices in each part of the scorecard. This approach presupposes that it is important to maximize the whole firm—that is, all components of the firm—and that the world will stay put long enough to do so. The process can be used very effectively, as the Lexus product team did when they took 500 engineers and benchmarked the best aspect of every car made in the world at that time and then designed the Lexus around the resulting profile.

Unfortunately, much of the effort in using scorecards is directed toward strategic alignment, which is founded in the traditional strategic model. The first problem with this approach is that the firm is attempting to align itself around a strategic construct that lacks any performance linkages.

The second problem with the scorecard approaches may be even more troublesome. In most cases, there are no ROI linkages with the various aspects of the scorecard that the firm is supposed to match. Many of them are great ideas, but—as the little old lady used to say in the commercials—"Where's the beef?" Or, to put it another way, "Where is the statistically validated link between emulating this behavior and profit?" The answer is simple: There is none.

In principle the scorecard idea has some merit. It suggests that the entire firm's profile be addressed. The problems with the approach are the referent profiles. Just because something worked for someone, somewhere, sometime, that does not necessarily mean that the same practice will be appropriate under different circumstances. Additionally, there are ample examples of situations where supposed best practices were adopted and within a short period of time the company was in serious trouble—thus calling into question the relationship between the practice and the performance of the organization. Absent a systems-based, future-oriented strategic paradigm and metrics from which to achieve system fit, the approach can create a lot of dissatisfaction with the current operation and no hint of how to fix it.

Total Quality Management

Total Quality Management (TQM) is a process designed to ensure that a firm's products and services are always at their optimum level. This is a worthy goal, but—as I've pointed out repeatedly—quality is only the table stakes to get into the game. It's not strategy. Even though its absence will lead to the demise of the firm, quality is still only an aspect of operating management. It is an internal process to ensure the minimum standards of the product that the firm seeks to provide to the customer.

The most serious problem with TQM is the fervor with which it's presented as the ultimate solution. The proof is in the pudding: How many Baldrige award winners have gone on to experience serious problems? The Baldrige is far from a guarantee that a firm will catapult to the top of its industry. Obviously, quality can significantly enhance the future prospects of the firm, but it's not the only thing or even the main thing a firm needs. It is *strategy*—strategy based on the future competitive environment—that provides the fuel for the future profit fire. It is the entrepreneurial behavior of the firm that creates the need for quality. For without the creation of products from a dynamic strategic foundation, there will be no need for quality . . . for there will be no products.

Kaizen

Kaizen—continual improvement—is a great tool. But it is a great *linear* tool. In organizations where the culture encourages empowerment, it can help harvest substantial profits from the intellectual capital of the operating team. The thing to bear in mind about Kaizen is that it's oriented toward improving existing processes, not creating entirely new processes. It is a concept that can flourish in an empowered organization. It can also drive linear innovation if the internal system is in place to allow it. But it can't help an organization that is not in sync with its environment, because doing the wrong things better only gets you more quickly to where you don't want to go.

Open Book Management

Another approach that has gained popularity in some areas is what is called "open book management." The idea is for senior management to frequently and openly share financial information with the entire firm, and withhold nothing from employees.

Sharing information does a great deal to build trust between various levels of the organization, and many researchers have attributed all the improvements observed in open-book firms to that development. However, it seems likely that there is something more subtle going on: a Hawthorne effect. This phenomenon is named for studies conducted at the Hawthorne Works of the Western Electric Company between 1924 and 1932, which produced a fascinating insight into human productivity.[1] The researchers were attempting to find the optimal light level for the production area, so they set up an isolated line that they could control. But they couldn't find an answer, because *every change* in the lighting in the test area, either up or down, tended to enhance productivity. These enhancements continued until the light became so poor that people could not see their work.

The positive performance variance was more than likely related to the attention the workers were getting from the researchers. As recent research has demonstrated, worker productivity may be more related to soft issues of an interpersonal nature than has ever been understood before.[2] In fact, the same relationships appear to directly effect employee retention as well.

Open book management may well lead to improvements in employee performance, but it needs to reflect genuine trust and attentiveness. Just hanging the numbers on an intranet database won't do the job on its own, and neither will telling people things and then paying no attention to their reaction.

Vision Statements

The idea of mission statements and goal setting was discussed earlier. Corporate vision statements have been in vogue for a number of years. Executives will often suggest that mission and vision statements provide common purpose and direction for the employee team. In the strictest sense, vision statements have little value to the organization. Entrepreneurial vision statements (as a reflection of the need to respond to emerging environmental turbulence) are more desirable, but will probably have little if any impact on the direction or success of the firm.

What type of a vision statement could have a major impact on a firm? A vision that was in harmony with the way senior leadership treated its people would have impact. In other words, if the senior team "walked the talk" of an entrepreneurial vision, there could definitely be an organizational impact.

Process Reengineering

Process reengineering is perhaps the most misused and misunderstood of the management tools. For good reason, employees who hear the words "process reengineering" immediately think "downsizing." Nonetheless, process reengineering and process engineering (understanding how to design new processes for new ventures) is a critical skill, and one that few organizations possess.

In its purest form, process reengineering compares existing processes with what might be called "absolute processes." In other words, it compares how long a current process takes to how long it would take if only the actual activities of the process are considered. To better understand the concept, consider how long it takes to get something from a typical old-fashioned mail-order company.

You order a simple product and are told that you can expect to receive it in 60 days. How long do you think the actual time to process your order might be? One month? One and one-half months? More often than not, the actual time is probably one to two days to ship the order. So what's the problem? Well, it sits in the "received orders" box for a week, and then it goes to "inventory control," which takes two weeks. From there, it goes to the warehouse and then to invoicing, and so on and on . . . you get the picture. In most cases, about 90 percent of the elapsed time in such processes is wasted time.

The failure of organizational leadership in the early 1990s to recognize the implications of strategies employed by Japanese competitors and others led to failure to understand the drastic impact such strategies would have on selling margins. Their solution was to cut people—under the facade of "process reengineering"—to the tune of 40,000 middle management jobs per month.

But real process reengineering is not downsizing. It is the streamlining of processes. It is a critical skill in developing time-to-market capabilities if the firm wants to meet the levels of innovation of the emerging competitive environment. Simply put, process reengineering is a skill that (listen carefully) *the internal organization* (not external consultants) must be able to use effectively. Process reengineering is a key corporate skill that enables organizations to achieve system fit.

STANDARD AERO: MANAGING THE ENTIRE ENTERPRISE FOR PROFIT

One company that understands how to combine a number of management tools effectively to achieve strategic balance is Standard Aero of Canada. Standard Aero competes in a highly turbulent environment, doing required periodic maintenance on aircraft engines. Clients include major airlines as well as corporate aircraft owners. The company's leaders have systematically used a number of practices to change the competitive nature of the entire organization.

Standard Aero is owned by BTR, a diversified global conglomerate based in England, which views wise risk-taking as its lifeblood. For Standard Aero, this willingness to foster creativity and risk-taking has enabled it to thrive during a time when its industry was undergoing massive consolidations worldwide.

Here is its story, based on an interview with Paul Soubry, EVP for Marketing and Business Development (based in Montreal, Canada), and Paul Goffredi, a regional director in the Dallas office. This interview was developed with the idea of getting two points of view within the same company. Watch the dynamics between the two—Soubry (the senior) views his job as being a resource, and Goffredi (the junior) is the one with the job of creating real growth in his area of responsibility.

"The environmental turbulence on your scale would be at least a 4.5 on a scale of 5," Paul Goffredi told me. "Most of our competitors are being absorbed by the OEMs [Original Equipment Manufacturers]. The good news for Standard Aero is that we are not only growing, but we are growing in the profit area as well. Our basic business is engine overhaul. It just makes sense to try to grab that piece of the business if you're the manufacturer in a vertically integrating market."

Paul Soubry makes a point of calling Goffredi to ask, "What can I do today to help you do your job better?" He is quite serious in his question. Rather than being the enforcer in a control-driven organization, Soubry fulfills the role of encouraging entrepreneurial risk in the organization. The question reveals an organizational commitment to aggressive innovation as well as marketing. It reveals an attitude of dynamic renewal, the continual rebirth of a firm so that it fits its environment.

Rather than engage in the mindless pursuit of the "fad of the month," Standard Aero has systematically changed the organization with the precision of a Swiss watchmaker. It began by investigating various processes that resulted in numerous cycle time reductions. (Interestingly, it also did a very wise thing with its process reengineering program. Although the work began with the help of a dependable consulting firm, Standard Aero management soon realized that they needed to move the process inside the firm. Now they have their own team that helps all parts of the firm in process analysis and improvement.)

"I've got the power to do just about anything that will help the firm," says Goffredi. "I came from a hyper-control environment at another firm. The change has been phenomenal for me. Now the only pressure is to consistently find ways for Standard Aero to stay at the head of the pack."

According to Goffredi, Standard Aero's conversion to a Type III firm is a story in itself. (As introduced in Chapter Five, a Type III firm is adaptive: future-focused, creative, entrepreneurial.) "We went from a nice, quiet [competitive] environment to your worst nightmare in less than three years. Most people did not see this coming." The reality is that many firms in other industries have been destroyed by changes that took as much as a decade to occur. Standard Aero's industry went through a drastic shift in 36 months. How is it that Standard Aero had the flexibility and aggressiveness to move to the leading edge of the "wave of change" that totally changed its environment in only three years?

"Like I said, I've got the corporate empowerment to be an innovator," Goffredi continued. "We have a saying: We'll do anything if it makes sense." When I asked whether or not Standard Aero would venture outside of core business areas, Goffredi's response said a lot about the foundations of Standard Aero's success: "It's my opinion that we have no boundaries. I am firmly convinced that our people are ROI-focused. That means that where we compete—or in what industry—is less important than recognizing the opportunity to sustain profitability."

That attitude has apparently served Standard Aero well. In an environment that usually waits for innovation to be passed down from the OEMs, Standard Aero has involved itself in some unique innovation. It has developed its own diagnostic tools for engines, and has come up with some new and exciting compounds to protect engines. Its people are in many cases out-innovating the large OEMs. So while the firm is taking a systems view of the external environment, it also tends to take the same approach in looking at the inside of the firm. "We'll do anything if it makes sense" is alive and well throughout Standard Aero's organization.

One of Goffredi's most important points is related to the driving force behind Standard Aero's ability to engage in what might be called "dynamic renewal." He described some key factors behind Standard Aero's success in being innovative:

- It all starts with the senior executive.
- Innovation must be driven.
- Quality must be a part of everything the firm does.
- Organizational culture supports and encourages success.

Goffredi believes that the fostering of innovation, creativity, and risk-taking is driven from the top office in the firm—the CEO is responsible for setting the firm's sights on success. In addition, he believes that the firm takes a very methodical approach to hiring managers who meet two qualifications: First, they are people who know how to run a business (according to Goffredi, they come in with the basic skills to run a business in about any industry). Second, they tend to be "frame breakers." That is, Standard Aero hires and promotes people who thrive on being involved in frame-breaking change.

Quality—TQM—is a part of every process at Standard Aero. In a highly regulated environment such as aviation where quality standards are extremely high, quality must be the foundation for every process. While TQM can sometimes slow an organization down, Standard Aero balances that with an internal emphasis on process reengineering. The result is a high-speed organization that achieves the highest levels of quality.

It is also no surprise that Standard Aero fosters a culture that values team goals above individual goals. "Our regional sales team asked to be compensated as a team, instead of individually. They realized that each person had some unique skills. Now, they can help each other with key account issues and feel like they're not only helping themselves, they're helping the team. That's worked out quite well."

Soubry's comments were quite similar to Goffredi's. When asked about the fact that Standard Aero's culture appeared to drive a lot of nonlinear thinking, he replied, "BTR is ROI driven. They have never been tied to historic business areas. If we deliver, they're happy."

Another philosophy Soubry talked about was the company's marketing approach. Its first thought on markets is what he called "organic market growth." Implicit in Soubry's comments is the idea of growing horizontally as well as vertically. This explains some of the innovations developed by Standard Aero as it moved into realms formerly controlled by the OEMs. The second principle he cited was what he called "innovation by growing market opportunities." One of Standard Aero's keys to growth has been the way innovations have led to new internal systems that could be used across diverse markets.

Perhaps the true key to Standard Aero's success was revealed in Soubry's comments about balance. "One of the real issues we focus on is balancing short-term and long-term opportunity. One of the keys for any company is to have the fortitude to be willing to sacrifice some short-term profit in favor of long-term growth and profit."

In discussing growth, Soubry naturally got into the issue of risk and how it relates to opportunity. "We make some mistakes," he admitted. "We try to use contingency planning to help us make good decisions and to prepare for the high levels of uncertainty we face in a lot of markets. If you are going to be successful, you are going to make a few mistakes along the way."

Standard Aero's success has led to some unexpected challenges. The redesign of the entire firm created growth and profit opportunities that were quite good. It also led to the need for

Standard Aero to develop its own internal training program to introduce the use of empowered teams and new concepts such as agile manufacturing. With its internal training program and completely redesigned processes, Standard Aero has achieved some astounding results. "We've reduced cycle times on some processes from 90 days to 28 days," Soubry told me. "On certain engines, we reduced our manhours from 1,500 to 1,000. What we have discovered is that consistency and repeatability must be built into all of our processes."

Standard Aero's new self-managed teams now do their own scheduling and hiring. If a process needs to be changed, they do it. "Our team leaders' view is that managers are resources which help teams be successful," said Soubry. "In a number of cases, the teams take the initiative to remove poor performers. It seems that when people are valued by their superiors, they seem to take a different attitude toward their work and their company. We're extremely pleased with our new organization."

CHAOS, RISK, AND PROFIT

Standard Aero exemplifies the principle that firms that focus on ROI instead of "core business area" or "core competencies" will usually be the most successful firms. As an executive from another firm suggested: "There is smart risk and stupid risk. The key is to encourage smart risk and discourage stupid risk." Standard Aero successfully encourages smart risk. Or, to put it another way, it encourages people to "do anything if it makes sense."

As the turbulence of the environment increases, the need to accelerate the frequency of risk-taking in an organization becomes more and more important. As I've noted, there is a direct link between the matching of risk-aggressiveness with turbulence and the profitability of the firm. That is why firms that foster creativity and risk-aggressiveness are also engaged in dynamic renewal.

Standard Aero exemplifies the principle of strategic balance, which it achieves by using appropriate tools that focus on addressing specific problems. The next group of sections address some additional sharp-pointed tools: management by objectives (MBO), flattening the organization, staying close to the customers, conducting 360-degree reviews, pursuing growth strategies, value migration and value chain analysis, scenarios and war-gaming, and knowledge functions. As with the first set, some of them work better than others, and some don't work at all in most cases.

Management by Objectives

MBO became popular a number of years ago. It has managed to resurface under a number of names. In principle, MBO advocates proposed that if a company adopted a top-down cascade of objectives, and if all the subordinates achieved their promised objectives, then the firm would achieve its objectives (that is, profit and performance).

There are some good points about MBO. Measured objectives are a form of goal-setting, a positive activity for a firm to engage in. Goal-setting has been proven valuable in enhancing performance. So the basics of MBO are good.

Unfortunately, MBO also has a number of problems. First, it usually ties employee rewards systems to short-term goals (quarterly or annual profit). That practice tends to encourage the sacrifice of long-term profitability for short-term success. Another main problem is the weakness of contingency linkages (that is, the actual links between a certain objective and the profitability of the firm). MBO tends to focus on outcome rather than input, but it is input factors—creativity, entrepreneurship, risk-taking—that produce long-term profitability. MBO tends to ignore those critical inputs in favor of "what have you done for me lately?"

MBO can be helpful in providing direction for organization members. The critical role of MBO is the linkage to profit-producing behaviors. If MBO is directed at strategic gaps in the organizational profile (strategic balance), it can be quite effective in changing the firm's profit profile. Absent that linkage, the long-term prospects for the firm will be minimal at best.

Flattening the Organization

Flattening the organization—reducing the number of reporting levels—has often been an excuse for downsizing. To put it another way, it's become a great excuse for getting rid of overhead, that is, people. The most vulgar form of this idea is called *rightsizing,* which translates to "Aren't you glad we're firing you?" It's time to be honest about rightsizing, downsizing, and similar euphemisms. They all amount to a public declaration that the organization failed to develop effective strategies in the past.

Flattening the organization *does not change* the communications processes of the organization. It does not create an organic monolith that can leap tall buildings in a single bound. In 1996 I interviewed Philip R. Thomas, the process reengineering guru of the Thomas Group, and he pointed out that through the use of effective process analysis and reengineering, a hierarchy could communicate just as rapidly as a "flattened" organization. So it is really (if the truth were told) an issue of flattening the organization to cut overhead—just another excuse for the failure to plan (strategically) for the future.

Staying Close to the Customer

Understanding customer needs—understanding customer expectations—forming strategic partnerships. All are great-sounding ideas, but one question remains: "Does the customer have a clear vision of the future?" In fact, research suggests that when we ask customers what they need, much of the answer is influenced by who is asking the question. What we really need to know is, What do the customers expect in the future? What systems dynamics will come into play to change current customer expectations and profiles? Often that question must be, What currently unrealized needs will the customers have in the future?

A number of years ago, someone proposed the "pooled ignorance theory." If you carefully collect input from the various constituencies of an organization related to any matter, the synthesized output from the stakeholders will often be worth less than the input that might have been obtained from any one of them individually.

It is not an issue of asking the right people. It is an issue of asking the right questions, in the context of a systems thinking paradigm. In fact, as a lot of theorists are pointing out, the key is not staying close to the customers *now,* it is anticipating future customer needs and expectations. Those are two radically different approaches with radically different outcomes from a profitability standpoint.

Rather than staying close to the customers as a single strategy, it makes more sense to combine this concept with another: staying close to the future. Staying close to the customer has its role from a systems standpoint, but it's also essential to discern future customer needs, trends, and attitudes. To be effective, especially in turbulent environments, the firm must be able to learn about the future as well as the present. Learning about the future enables the firm to anticipate changes in customer preferences and needs as well as competitors' strategies. At the same time, customer relationships enable the firm to gather intelligence related to current issues, including those of a discontinuous nature.

Conducting 360-Degree Reviews

In principle, 360-degree reviews have merit. The idea is that all people in the firm are stakeholders, and thus should have input in evaluating an individual's transactional style. When it works, it works well. For example, a consultant acquaintance recently created a subordinate review assessment instrument for supervisors and managers at a Fortune 100 firm. Prior to the study, the consultant told management personnel about the transactional aspects of the evaluation (they understood not only what they were being measured for but that the measurement involved *how* they treated people). The results were quite positive from the client's standpoint, because the assessment clearly made the managers accountable for how they treated their subordinates.

Unfortunately, although most 360-degree assessments could be categorized as "nice" and "informative," it is unusual for such evaluations to be so effective. They are rarely tied to external competitive issues, such as the pressing need for the team members of an organization to engage in high levels of creativity and risk-taking. More than that, it is rare for the 360-degree review to have enough consequences for the manager to make it really meaningful for the evaluatee. As a result, the reviews often degenerate into a pro-forma exercise.

Growth Strategies

Growth can be good, and it often is good. Even with declining margins, growth can drive the profitability trends of a company in positive directions. So what could be bad? What are the negatives to a myopic growth approach?

Unless the organization's leadership understands the capacity/demand ratios of the future environment, it cannot see what type of growth is necessary. If the future environment is under turbulence level 3.0, then growth may be nice but it is certainly not necessary, except to maintain market share. At turbulence levels around 3.0, growth equal to industry growth is a necessity—but only at the level of market growth itself. At turbulence levels of 4.0 and above, since the industry capacity substantially exceeds product demand, market share growth becomes critical to the survival of the firm. To restate it, above turbulence 4.0, increasing the firm's percentage of market share becomes critical to its survival.

Although it is good to recognize the need for growth, much of the current thinking fails to recognize the issues related to capacity/demand ratios. Only when growth strategies are contingently linked to these ratios will the logic underlying growth be beneficial from a profitability standpoint.

Value Migration and Value Chain Analysis

A senior analyst for a major firm recently commented, "I bought the book [on value chains] and was greatly disappointed. There's just not a lot new there for someone who understands business." Value migration is relatively useless to study because it is an effect, not a cause. It occurs when the overcapacity in an industry, with its related turbulence in the 4.0–5.0 range, drives product-pricing to the commodity level.

Thus the issue is not value migration at all, it is the macro system. When conditions become extremely turbulent and include a lot of excess capacity, decreases in pricing begin to force competitors out of the segment. At such high levels of turbulence, value is created by discontinuous innovation and little more. (At such high levels of turbulence and overcapacity, innovation must bring genuinely new products and services—simple product improvement doesn't work anymore.)

Scenarios and War-Gaming

Shell Oil brought the concept of scenarios to the business public's attention when it used the technique to prepare for various pricing levels of crude oil.[3]

Scenarios are much more suited to change management than they are to strategic work, although they do support strategic work in some cases. This support derives mostly from their ability to drive learning (and the possibility of linking learning with organizational power) for the purpose of responding to or anticipating change. Scenarios are valuable tools, especially in turbulent environments. What scenarios lack is the required "whole system" view of the future. In either case, scenarios should not be discounted as important weapons in the organization's planning arsenal.

War-gaming is a variant of scenario planning that was first developed by the U.S. military for the purpose of strategy development. War-gaming and systems thinking are often mentioned in similar contexts. War-gaming differs from scenarios in that war-gaming engages planners by requiring teams to emulate the anticipated behavior of the different competitors. War-gaming has been used in a number of instances to successfully anticipate competitors' moves and preemptively develop effective strategies.

War-gaming's effectiveness can be enhanced through the use of a comprehensive metaphor, such as environmental turbulence, from which to define the future competitive drivers of an environment. With significant accuracy behind it, the turbulence metaphor offers confidence to the planner when competitors' moves are gamed so that they can be tested against the future turbulence index.

Knowledge Functions

A lot of companies are forming what they call "knowledge organizations." Many are even designating a "chief knowledge officer" to be responsible for organizational learning. This can be useful, but many of these initiatives fail for lack of attention to some of the key principles related to the Five Personalities of Change presented in Chapter Seven, as well as to some of the other research on resistance to change. Additionally, the knowledge functions need to be defined and organized with a view toward future-based systems thinking; if they only look to past experience, they are unlikely to prove helpful.

THE HEART OF THE PROBLEM

The core issues with many of the approaches discussed in this chapter are revealed in the concept of Learning-Transformation-Performance. Often theorists mistake accidental management for brilliance. Just because a company happens to do well in its current circumstances, that does not mean that what the firm is doing at that time is the reason for its success. For example, consider the way demand for oats and oat-based products soared after a book came out suggesting that oat consumption could reduce cholesterol. Had Quaker Oats assumed that its TQM program was responsible for the dramatic increase in revenues it enjoyed, it would have been deceiving itself. The failure to learn from a systems view means that the observer will be unable to understand the reasons for any successful endeavor. The ability to learn with a systems perspective means that the observer will be able to understand the performance within the context of what really contributed to the firm's success.

Learning, in a systems thinking context, provides powerful understanding of the links between an activity and its applicability. Transformation, in a system accountability context, provides the framework through which performance-generating change can be accomplished. When system fit is finally accomplished, the organization will become a top performer.

CONCLUSION: TAKING A SYSTEMS LOOK BACK

The purpose of this investigation is not to be critical of any one individual or tool, but rather to challenge mental models. The ability to think as nearly as possible in harmony with the external macro environment is something almost everyone involved in the field of management would agree upon. It is only when their personal paradigms are challenged that they will take offense. In the same way that Galileo felt compelled to challenge the status quo in the interest of community learning and betterment, each person who engages in conveying management theory and thought should view their highest duty not as one of defense but as one of honest investigation. The outcome of honest investigation should be the betterment of society, whether it be business, social science, or theology. It is with that intent that his book was developed. As a testament to the principles suggested here, I sincerely hope that my own understanding and views of management have also been changed by the endeavor to learn and to grow.

CHAPTER 11

THE PROCESS OF STRATEGIC BALANCE

MANAGEMENT THEORY IS GREAT. IT IS FUN TO DISCUSS AND TO debate, but the real benefit of any theory is when it can be translated into action that benefits the bottom line of an organization. Strategic balance—rather than being just another theory—is an approach that can be used to significantly change the future prospects of an organization. It is also logical and practical. This chapter will develop the process that can be used to continually reinvent an organization by means of the systematic application of each of the approaches discussed in this book.

THE PROCESS

Implementing and maintaining strategic balance is a matter of taking some specific and concrete steps:

- Bringing the CEO attributes in line with what the firm needs—it all starts with a chief executive who understands the process and cares about it
- Determining the strategic segments the firm is competing in
- Conducting a future turbulence assessment and 10 forces analysis
- Analyzing the product portfolio so the firm is creating the right products at the right time
- Preparing an organizational profile to get a reading on strategic balance
- Developing a transformational plan to manage change as it occurs
- Conducting accountability assessments to ensure that change really happens
- Developing and monitoring a corporate strategic plan that deliberately builds success

The CEO

The board of directors of a company is responsible for selecting the CEO. In the case of a lot of privately held corporations, the CEO also happens to be the single largest shareholder. Either way, the position is pivotal when it comes to creating a company that is designed to thrive in chaotic environments. It is important to understand the general level of emerging environmental turbulence if this match is to be achieved. A one-size-fits-all ap-

CEO Attributes

Factor	1	2	3	4	5
Attitude Toward Change	Reject	Resist	Slow Adaptation	Drive Change	Aggressively Drive Change
Attitude Toward Creativity and Risk	No Value	De-Value	Necessary Evil	Drive Creativity	Aggressively Promote
Attitude Toward Subordinates	Expect Performance	Expect Efficiency	Meet Objectives	Respect and Value	Encourage as Team Member

FIGURE 11.1. Matching CEO with Environment.
Adapted from H. Igor Ansoff's Strategic Diagnosis procedures.
Used with permission.

proach would be problematic, since there are a few firms that are still competing in lower levels of turbulence. Once the turbulence level is known, it's easy to define the type of CEO leadership that the firm needs. Success begins with the right leadership for the specific environment the firm faces in the future. For ready reference, Figure 11.1 reproduces the assessment for CEOs that was presented in Chapter Two.

Michael Tushman suggests that about 80 percent of the time, when organizations encounter frame-breaking change, it's essential to replace the CEO and executive team to get the organization to respond to the changes in the environment.[1] But Tushman's statement is an observation, not a recommendation. Usually, a firm's leadership fails to respond to environmental signals as the firm enters the stagnation phase. That ultimately results in the firm's reaching the crisis phase. That is when boards finally change the CEO and executive team—but it is often not necessary for things to go so far.

The CEO profile provides an excellent metric that can be used in the selection of a new CEO. However, replacing the CEO shouldn't be a hasty step—it could be detrimental to the future of the organization, costing it valuable knowledge about the industry. So the question is, "How do you get someone to change?" The answer: Accountability.

There are a number of ways to bring accountability to bear on leaders. At Southwest Airlines, the leadership culture is intolerant of leadership styles that would interfere with the firm's ability to continually learn and transform itself. A number of organizational cultures have such accountability built into them.

At a seminar a few years ago, someone came up at the break and told me the story of a telecommunications firm that had just been split into two separate organizations, with a president heading each one, at the order of the company's chairman. The visionary chairman clearly communicated the reality that the firm had to move out of historic telecommunications markets into the next wave of technological opportunity. One of the group presidents, call him John, made it known that all the talk about the Internet exploding and the convergence of wired and wireless communication was just a bunch of junk. He had no intention of leading his side of the organization out of the business segments it knew so well (its historic competencies).

After hearing of John's comments a number of times, the chairman sat down and crafted a short, simple letter that went something like this:

Dear John:

It has come to my attention that you do not support our organization's objectives of becoming a technology leader in our industry. I would like to offer two opportunities for you to consider:

1. *Leave the company.*

2. *Lead the technology revolution for our company.*

Please advise me of your decision by next Monday at 9:00 A.M."

The following Monday morning, a transformed employee reported for duty. John advised the chairman that he did want to lead the transformation of the company. From that point on, he was the technology evangelist in the company, and went on to lead his group to the forefront of the industry.

What is the lesson in this story? Quite simply, by imposing accountability standards, it is often possible to change the behavior of an individual. TMP Worldwide has had similar experience. When TMP acquires a company, it does not take long for the management of the acquired company to realize that TMP expects its managers to think out of the box, and to aggressively create the future rather than become comfortable with living in the past. One manager said it was an interesting process to watch. "It doesn't take long for them to figure out that we're a creative, aggressive competitor," she told me. "In our case, the managers at the acquired companies either jump at the opportunity to be part of a thriving organization or they leave and find a company that fits their personality more closely. We rarely have to get rid of anybody. They realize that they must either get on the team or off real quickly."

There are few Jack Welches and Carly Fiorinos in this world. For those who are not born with that level of intuitive skill, it is possible to commit to change by becoming accountable to a new set of leadership standards and behaviors. The bottom line of leadership is this: The senior executive of an organization is the key to creating and supporting the behaviors that result in the formation and continuation of Type III, adaptive organizations.

Strategic Segmentation

Once an organization has a committed CEO, the next step is to understand the numerous strategic segments in which the firm is competing. As earlier pointed out, even a single product can have different segments. Consider the problem in segmenting the personal computer market:

Critical Success Factors

Home Computer	*Home Office*	*Corporate*	*Educational*
Price (low)	Reliability	Speed	Price (low)
Bundled software	Price (moderate)	Repair	Simplicity
Minimal connectivity speeds	Moderate to high connectivity speeds	Network + high connectivity speeds	Some network requirements
Low memory requirements	High memory requirements	High memory requirements	Low memory requirements

Even this simple segmentation reveals different competitive segments for what is superficially the same product. And each of the segments can be at a different level of turbulence. That means that it will be necessary to have different strategic profiles for each of the segments. Different types of leadership and different rewards systems will be necessary to maximize profit in each specific segment. What works in the retail home computer market will be totally ineffective in the corporate work station market.

That means that a one-size-fits-all approach may not work, even when it comes to corporate culture. In companies like Hewlett-Packard, it has worked because most product lines have been in similar levels of turbulence. Since HP competes in two distinct segments, the consumer technology segment and the corporate technology segment, the failure to understand the turbulence in either segment and balance the organization for each segment could result in reduced profitability.

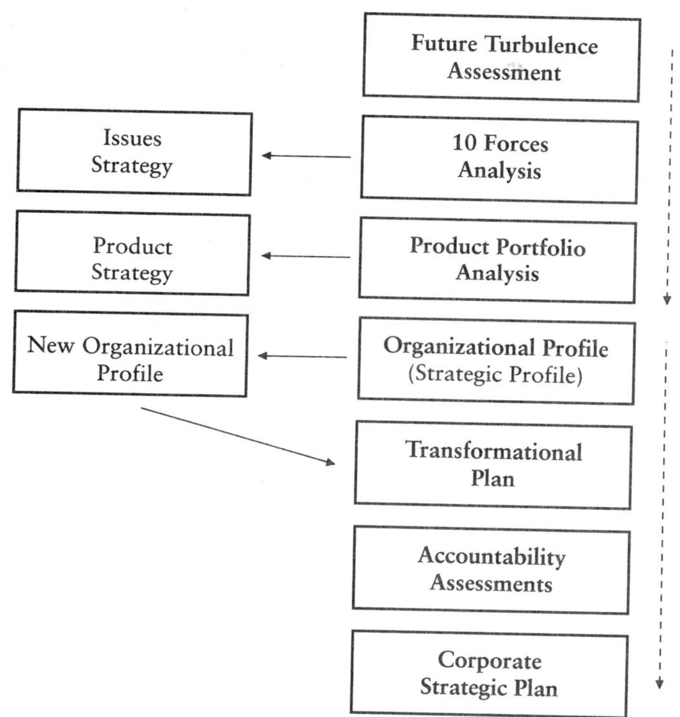

FIGURE 11.2. The Strategic Planning Process.

Strategic segmentation is critical. It lays the foundation from which organizational strategy may be developed. That process begins with understanding the future turbulence of each strategic segment. To provide an overview of the entire process, the flow chart in Figure 11.2 shows the stages of effective strategic planning.

Predictive Modeling: Future Turbulence

Normally, it takes three separate assessments to determine future turbulence in a segment.

- Internal management
- Published literature
- Outside experts (Delphi panel)

A typical assessment of the future will often reveal different views of the future among the three different groups. Figure 11.3 presents a typical assessment of the future, showing projected marketing and innovation turbulence as seen by internal management (the squares), a review of publications on issues related to the future of the industry (the triangles), and a panel of outside experts (the circles). The dotted line connects the values the researcher selected as the most accurate in this case, and the tables below the charts show how a simple average can be computed to determine future turbulence.

Choosing the most accurate view of the future is a key step in this process. For example, there were three diverse opinions regarding the "future sales aggressiveness" of competitors, ranging from 3.3 to 4.9. In this situation, determining the final level is not a matter of splitting the difference but of assessing all the estimates and making an educated choice. For Figure 11.3, the researcher chose 4.9 as the most accurate number. When using multiple estimates of the future, it is not unusual for the researcher to perceive that one source's understanding of the future is significantly more accurate than another's. In this case, the researcher believed the experts. Once each driver of future marketing and future innovation turbulence is derived, the job becomes fairly straightforward from that point on. It involves the computation of an average of the responses.

Environmental turbulence usually serves as the benchmark profile for the entire organization, but it doesn't always work. For one defense industry client in 2000, the future marketing turbulence came in at 4.3, but the future innovation turbulence was 3.5. As a result, the research team recommended that the firm's marketing strategies be developed to match the 4.3 turbulence and the firm's innovation strategies be developed to

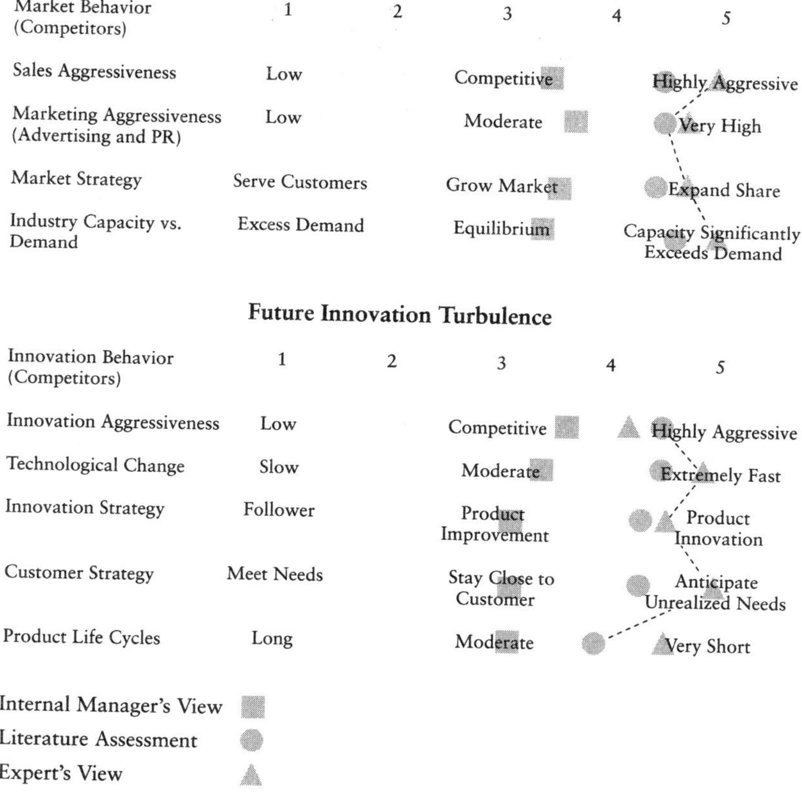

Turbulence Assessment

Expected turbulence 3 or less:	Use five-year future assessment
Expected turbulence 3 to 4:	Use four-year future assessment
Expected turbulence 4 to 5:	Use three-year future assessment

FIGURE 11.3. Computing Future Turbulence.
Adapted from H. Igor Ansoff's Strategic Diagnosis procedures.
Used with permission.

Future Marketing Turbulence

Sales Aggressiveness	4.9
Marketing Aggressiveness	4.5
Market Strategy	4.8
Industry Capacity/Demand	5.0
Future Marketing Turbulence	**4.8**

Future Innovation Turbulence

Innovation Aggressiveness	4.3
Technological Change	4.9
Innovation Strategy	4.4
Customer Strategy	4.9
Product Life Cycles	4.2
Future Innovation Turbulence	**4.5**

FIGURE 11.3. *(continued)*

match the 3.5 turbulence. For the balance of the organization, an environmental turbulence of 4.0 was used. (That meant that the support system for the firm's marketing was capable of supporting it in the higher level of competitiveness characteristic of turbulence of 4.0 or higher.)

In assessment after assessment, I've found that internal management tends to view the future turbulence approximately one level lower than the literature reveals or the experts view it. This has serious implications for the strategic planner. The tendency of internal managers to see the future as significantly calmer than it is going to be explains why internally developed strategies so often fail.

The next assessment is the literature review. There are numerous databases available for searches of relevant journal articles, trade publications, press releases, and speeches. Basically, the literature review involves assessing each article and overlaying the information onto the turbulence chart.

Finally, a Delphi panel is convened. Six experts are polled to obtain their view of the future. Ideally, some interaction between views is encouraged to see if the experts will ultimately end up with near-identical ratings for each area. Generally, the panelists will have quite similar views of the future if experts of sufficient quality are used. Experience has shown that the expert panel is usually the most accurate of the three assessments. The researcher must be extremely careful in that, however, since there have been a few instances in which the internal management had the best understanding, and many more where the literature proved to be quite accurate.

Understanding future environmental turbulence provides the basis for a systems thinking approach to designing the firm's strategies and organization. To account for all eventualities, however, a more global assessment is required. That investigation involves pending legislation, competitor profiles, political issues, and such. A comprehensive study of the 10 forces introduced in Chapter One provides specific issues that the firm must account for in the development of its strategy. The provision of that information is the job of the organization's strategic intelligence team. That team has different names at different companies, but the role is the same.

Product Portfolio Analysis

Next, the analysis of the firm's product portfolio is completed, as described in Chapter Eight. With the 10 forces analysis and the future turbulence of each segment, the planning team has the tools to employ the seven-pass portfolio approach to develop a high-growth, high-profit product portfolio for the firm.

Organizational Assessment

At the same time that the product portfolio is assessed, the organizational strategic profile must be developed. The assessment provides not only the gaps, but the level of urgency that each gap has attached to it. (The bigger the gap, the higher the impact on future profit if it is not corrected). Once the assessment is complete, both the product portfolio changes and the organizational changes (strategy and organization) are blended into one set of strategic initiatives. Synthesizing a number of gaps into one initiative accomplishes this objective. Figure 11.4 provides a simplified example of how this is accomplished.

The organization illustrated in the figure has gaps in management (Leadership Style = –1.5; Attitude Toward Risk = –1.6) and in its culture (Values = –1.5). The lower part of the figure shows how those gaps can be corrected with one specific strategic action.

Once the managers are trained, the organization provides coaching that will help them encourage subordinates to be more creative and risk-taking. Notice also that an assessment must be developed that makes the managers accountable for the behaviors that produce profitability. This type of synthesis is completed for the entire organization. The result should be 8–10 strategic initiatives that, if accomplished, will significantly change the future profit prospects of the organization.

Transformation Plan

The first aspect of a transformational plan is to recognize the personality of change each employee brings to the process. Early in the transformation, you want to emphasize the use of pathfinders and listeners, along with a limited number of organizers. This is because the early transformation strategy must be designed to achieve the 25 percent diffusion goal (the point of no defeat) for major changes in the organization. As a corol-

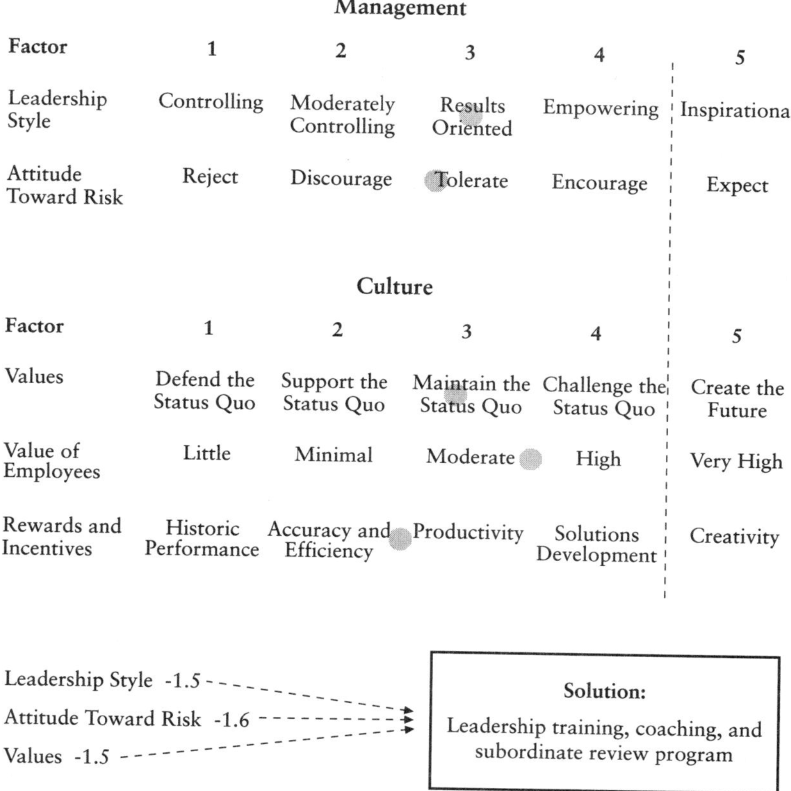

FIGURE 11.4. Combining Management and Culture Assessments into a Common Initiative. Adapted from H. Igor Ansoff's Strategic Diagnosis procedures. Used with permission.

lary, followers and patriots must not be used in transformation activities until the process is too far advanced to be stopped. The effectiveness of the transformation is maximized by involving the right personalities of change at the appropriate times in each change, and implementing with a modular approach.

If the turbulence assessment was for three years in the future, a three-year modular implementation plan needs to be developed. Ideally, each year the firm would set interim targets of transformation that would lead to the ultimate transformation of the entire organization. The use of intermediate goals is critically important in managing resistance to change.

The use of modular implementation accomplishes two goals. First, it minimizes the magnitude of change that must be accomplished each year. Second, by minimizing the magnitude of change each year, it decreases the level of resistance to change.

If the firm engages in a turbulence assessment and an organizational profile each year (assuming that the firm uses a three-year future target for turbulence), two important events will occur at that time. First, adjustments to future turbulence will be made annually. Second, the success of organizational transformation will show up in the changes in the firm's strategic profile. Preparing a new strategic profile gives the firm an opportunity to make midcourse corrections incrementally.

Accountability Assessments

W. Edwards Deming's oft-quoted line, "What is measured is what gets done," is generally accepted as true. In the case of strategic balance and transformation, the idea is to make the corporate system accountable for the behaviors that will produce maximum profit. The strategic profile assessment of the organization reveals gaps within the organization that will have marginal, serious, or critical impact on profit. If those gaps are to be corrected, there must be accountability for the resolution of each one.

Leaders of organizations understand the importance of maintaining certain types of leadership style, culture, and the like—but this is easier to decide than to measure, and accountability requires measurement. One attempt at measurement is the 360-degree assessment. Generally, the idea is to get an idea of a manager's relationships with subordinates, peers, and superiors. There are two keys to making any such assessment effective: First, it has to involve real accountability. When a

Leadership Style Index	Interpersonal Skills Index
The Leadership Style Index (LSI) is a subordinate review assessment that measures the types and quality of transactions between a manager and his or her subordinates. The LSI uses a five-point scale with 5 indicating the highest level of leadership empowerment and significance-building behavior.	The Interpersonal Skills Index (ISI) is a peer review instrument that measures transactions between individuals. The ISI focuses on transactions that foster high levels of cooperation and support of corporate objectives.
Executive Teams Skills Index	**The Five Axis Assessment**
The Executive Teams Skills Index (ETSI) is a peer assessment that measures senior managers' behaviors. Managers, especially SBU managers, are assessed by their peers. The ETSI is designed to eliminate silos and to foster team-oriented focus on corporate objectives.	The Five Axis Assessment (FAA) is addressed to the senior executive of an organization. The FAA includes the LSI and incorporates that assessment into a number of assessments that measure how an executive's activities create strategic balance, meet corporate objectives, and drive organizational renewal.

FIGURE 11.5. The Carter-Underwood Accountability Assessments.

company is in trouble, it is not uncommon for assessments on managers to be completed only to be ignored by low-scoring managers' superiors. Second, the assessment itself must measure transactions.

Often, assessments are little more than smile sheets—the sort of assessments given at the end of a training class that have no meaningful measurements. A number of years ago, I teamed up with Dr. Les Carter (my coauthor on *The Significance Principle)* to develop a number of transactional assessments. Carter is a nationally recognized psychotherapist who often works with senior executives in the area of work and family balance. As a result of that collaboration, we developed the four assessments shown in Figure 11.5.

All four assessments are designed to be used in conjunction with a coaching program. At the senior executive level (CEO, chairman), the coaching should be from an outside source (a member of the board plus an external coach is appropriate).

For other senior executives, an outside coach working in conjunction with the individual's superior (who also functions as a coach) best accomplishes the coaching.

For most of the internal team, an internal coaching program is recommended. In every case, the individual's superior must be a part of the coaching team. The other member of the coaching team would be a trained individual who serves as a part of the organization's training group. The training coach needs to be of the same rank as the individual who is being coached. Additionally, the training coach must sign an agreement with the individual who is being coached to ensure the confidentiality of all matters related to the coaching.

To date, the LSI (subordinate review) and ISI (peer review) have been employed in a number of organizations. While we haven't yet gathered sufficient data to allow statistical analysis, some important observations have already come out of the use of the assessments.

There appears to be a very high correlation between ISI scores and individual performance in a team setting. Those who score high are consistently viewed as high performers by their managers. Those who receive low ISI scores from peers tend to be low performers in groups. Additionally, those who score low on the ISI appear to have negative relationships with subordinates.

The LSI is enjoying a similar pattern of success. Managers with subordinate assessments of 4.0 and above have organizations that are high performers. Managers with subordinate assessments of 3.0 or less tend to lead low-performing organizations. The higher LSI managers often have waiting lists of employees that want to go to work for them. The low LSI managers have significantly higher turnover rates.

The ISI and the LSI have been used as a basis for coaching individuals, both managers and individual performers (often management-level individuals with no direct reports). The experience to this point has been quite positive in that participants understand the transactional issues that have been measured. Further, since the measurements are transactional in nature, the individuals have a path for changing transactions and thus their interaction with others.

In the case of other areas such as marketing, innovation, and such, there are no existing assessments that can be used. In those cases, gap-oriented assessments must be developed to ensure that the level of required behavior is achieved. A good illustration of this type of assessment is in the area of public relations. PR involves the generation of stories about a company's products and people. Those articles often appear in major publications as well as trade-specific journals. If an organization fails to generate a steady supply of PR articles that point to the superiority of its products compared to those of its competitors, the firm's customers will ultimately come to believe that the competing products must be better. And as the adage suggests, "Perception is reality"—especially when it comes to PR.

Accountability assessments measure organizational behavior. They offer metrics that can be used as a basis for effective coaching. They can also measure progress. The most important thing to remember is that appropriate assessments can be the catalyst for changing the behaviors of the entire organization.

CONTINUALLY CREATING STRATEGIC BALANCE: THE LAUCK GROUP

The Lauck Group, a relatively new entrant into the commercial interior architecture field, exemplifies the principles developed in this book. It is one of the most dynamic and exciting companies around, and its progress has been astounding. "We see major shifts in our industry over the next 60 months," a Lauck executive told me. "We're already in the process of completely re-creating our entire organization, from top to bottom." That statement is typical of those made by companies that thrive over long periods of time.

History

Alan Lauck started the company in 1984. The company's beginnings are a far cry from the technological marvel that is the current world headquarters. The first office was a spare room in Alan's house, but Alan Lauck had a far greater dream for his company. He had a vision of a company that thrived on creativity and discovery of the future. He had a vision of a company where people would love to work. He also wanted a company that was not just his company. He wanted everyone involved to have an entrepreneurial interest in the firm.

It only took the Lauck Group twelve years to gain national acclaim. By 1996, the firm was nationally recognized for its work and was still experiencing substantial growth. In the mid-1990s, Alan Lauck decided to embark on another venture as his full-time focus and limit his work at the Lauck Group. Early on, Alan Lauck decided that he wanted an organization that was not dependent upon one person as owner and leader. When he decided to decrease his involvement in the daily operations of the firm, the mechanisms were already in place to allow the firm to continue and to thrive. As testimony to the foundation that Alan Lauck laid, in 1998 the firm received an industry award that recognizes the "International Top 40" companies in the field. Additionally, the firm was named to the "Industry Giants List" in 1997–99. There is more to the story. Between 1996 and 1999, the Lauck Group doubled in size. That growth reveals the true impact of focused leadership, learning, and organizational agility.

Organization and Leadership

The Lauck Group is organized into six teams. Those teams direct all the activities of the firm, both current and future. Figure 11.6 illustrates the loose organization of the six Lauck Group teams. The absence of lines and arrows is deliberate—the Lauck Group avoids hierarchy at all costs.

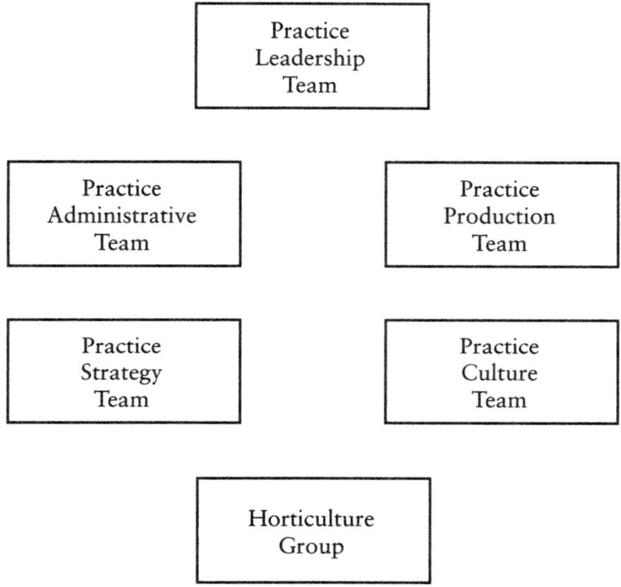

FIGURE 11.6. The Lauck Group: Designed for Adaptability and Speed.

Although organization charts often convey little more than who holds the power and how to communicate within the organization, that is not the case with Lauck. The Lauck "Tribe" (as its people call themselves) has little time for ego and power trips. At the top of the Lauck priority list is the client. Next on the list is the practice itself. Third come the people of the organization.

The Practice Leadership Team comprises the seven principals and an executive coach. The principals are the senior executive team of the organization. Four of the principals hold ownership in the company, but when it comes to how the company operates, whether or not one is an owner is of little importance. The principals coordinate the various aspects of the firm. They are proactively involved in making sure that the key components for excellence and winning remain the focus of the organization. The leadership team sets extremely high standards for the organization. They are also involved in major decisions that affect the whole firm.

The leadership team provides direction for the rest of the teams. The administrative team is composed of both principals and presidents, and its role is to guide the various administrative functions of the organization, including finance, recruiting, facilities, and human resources.

The Practice Production Team, also composed of principals and vice presidents, is focused on the "Lauck of today," which means it is continually trying to improve the firm's products and processes. The production team monitors ongoing projects, client relationships, and pending business. The Lauck process is consultative in nature—leveraging intellectual processes and solutions that target achieving clients' business objectives. At the same time, Lauck never loses sight of the final goal: maximizing client satisfaction.

The Practice Strategy Team is a group of principals and vice presidents that is concerned with the "Lauck of tomorrow." Lauck is committed to carrying its core business principles forward, but has no ties to the past when it comes to strategy. Lauck is constantly in the process of becoming something different. That process is under the leadership of the strategy team.

The Practice Culture Team is a popular group, because it is responsible for a number of very important aspects of the Lauck culture, including "Focal Shifts." Lauck guards its culture with the same tenacity that Coca-Cola guards the formula for Coke. Lauck's culture thrives on change and creativity—and on communicating the value of each contributor to the organization. The culture team realizes that the culture of Lauck is what creates its "sustainable iconoclastic advantage." It also realizes that if the culture ever begins to lose its focus on entrepreneurial behavior, the Lauck Group will cease to be a leader in its field.

Then there is the Horticulture Team. So what is this team all about? It is about the art of planting, harvesting, and growing seeds of creativity and fun within a nurturing, self-sustaining environment. It is devoted to fun, zany ideas and activities that challenge people to be playful and creative. This brings out the genius in the firm's people.

The Process

While the process is not extremely formal, the Lauck Group's teams spend a lot of time learning about the future. As commercial interior architects, its people have the responsibility of understanding the impact of management trends as well as technology developments. When designing a floor or a building interior for a Fortune 1000 firm, their task is to anticipate both external changes in the environment and internal changes in the organization. For example, a lot of the design work done by the Lauck team involves technology. Walls and ceilings are often designed around technology requirements. As broadband applications, both wired and wireless, begin to develop, Lauck's clients expect it to be ahead of the curve in understanding those changes and how they will affect the organization.

Focal Shift

Early in its history, the company's leadership understood the importance of organizational learning. They also understood the reality that every member of the team had an important contribution to make to the Lauck Group's success. They decided that they needed an enjoyable yet formalized approach to fostering learning. That began as something called "Beer Thursday." It is now known as "Focal Shift."

Once every month or so, the organization shuts down its operations around 4:30 P.M. Each event has a different theme. Once it was a high school prom, and everyone had to go out and find clothing to wear, just like they had worn to their high school prom. On another occasion, they invited the SPCA to

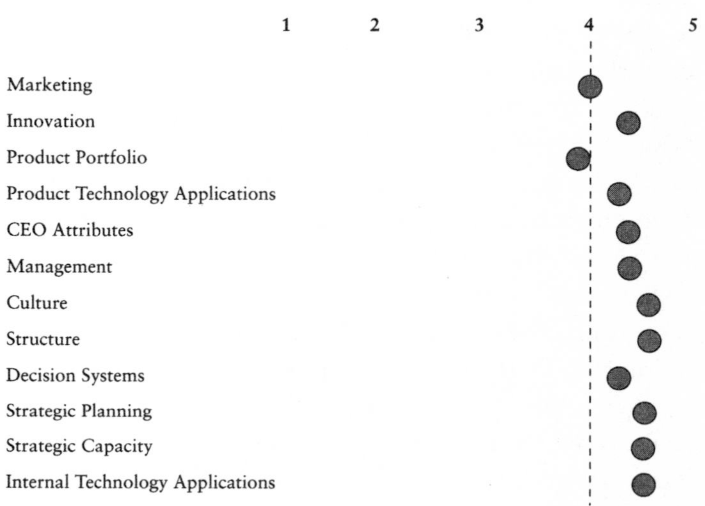

FIGURE 11.7. Strategic Profile of the Lauck Group. Adapted from H. Igor Ansoff's Strategic Diagnosis procedures. Used with permission.

come and explain their service to the community, and on still another, a Lauck team member exhibited photographs she had taken of architecture in India. Behind each event is the idea of challenging tradition. By fostering an iconoclastic attitude in the firm, the Focal Shift helps Lauck be a true learning organization.

The Lauck Practice Leadership Team oversees and coordinates many of these direction-defining activities. It works in conjunction with each of the other teams to create a seamless approach to learning and transformation. The results of this work is revealed in a strategic profile of the organization shown in Figure 11.7.

It should be no surprise that the Lauck Group has doubled in size since 1998. This explosive growth may be directly attributed to the firm's leadership. "One of our commitments is to live out of the box," says Bridgitte Preston, one of the principals of the firm. "We're a future-focused organization," she adds, "and one of our objectives is to totally redesign every key component of the business every three to five years."

The Lauck Group is technologically savvy. It has a state-of-the-art local area network that includes a computer for every employee. When it was unable to find employee coaching and feedback software that met the firm's needs, it designed its own. Every employee of the firm gets daily feedback on personal performance. As part of that system, employees are encouraged to set high goals. "We want people who want to achieve great things," says Judy Pantello, another of the principals of the firm. "If you want to be the next CEO, every member of the team will mentor you, regardless of your position. We use our daily feedback system to help every individual to achieve their objectives."

The strategy process is based on the open culture and the tradition of learning at the organization. Commitment to learning is evident at all levels. While the strategy team is responsible for the development of the strategic plan, the entire organization partners with it in developing an understanding of the future. It is the organizational learning process that establishes the basis for the strategic plan.

Product Portfolio Analysis

The Lauck Group spends a great deal of time understanding future changes in its products. The problem is, numerous forces in the environment drive Lauck products in one direction or another. The open learning environment of the organization has served the firm well. It usually tends to be a leader in its industry. In 1998, the *Wall Street Journal* featured a story about a company that had used curvilinear walls in their interior architecture. The story talked about how this new approach in design had broken new ground in the design of workplaces. The Lauck staff found the article quite interesting and amusing—they had introduced the same concept 13 years earlier.

The challenges of new management approaches (which change interior architecture), new materials, new design concepts, and rapidly changing technology puts the Lauck Group on a fast track. Since it has created a fast-track organization, it is certainly capable of leading in its field.

Organizational Profile

As the organizational profile of the Lauck Group reveals, it is positioned for success in a highly competitive, rapidly changing world. The Practice Leadership Team actively manages each attribute of the firm. Its members constantly challenge the status quo to ensure that the firm will be positioned to maintain its growth and profit profile. An interesting part of the competitive profile of the company is its commitment to technology leadership both internally and externally. It makes extensive use of technologies such as PDAs (personal digital assistants), cell phones, and pagers. The company has a policy that the first focus is always the customer, and the widespread use of such technologies makes sure that its people can communicate on a timely basis.

As a company that works around the world for the Fortune 500, the Lauck Group uses virtual work platforms on the Web to serve customers more effectively. On one project in 1997, the client wanted offices built in 10 different countries and needed the work done quickly. The Lauck Group committed to meet the client's deadlines.

It met the commitment in an extremely creative way. First, it realized that it needed to work with local associates in each of the countries. Rather than spending time learning the local laws and ordinances, the Lauck Group partnered with the best commercial interior architecture firms in each country. That did not solve the problem. As good as their counterparts were, the Lauck team in the United States had to be the driving force behind the entire design program.

The time differences between the United States and the 10 countries could have been a problem. The Lauck teams realized that by using virtual work platforms, they could use the time differences to their advantage. Each day, the various teams at Lauck would complete their work and post it on the virtual work platforms for their counterparts in each country. The foreign associates would begin their work at around 1 A.M. U.S. time, using the virtual work platforms as the basis for their day's work. As the foreign counterparts neared the end of their work day, the U.S. teams would be arriving at work to begin theirs.

Accountability

As with almost all the companies that thrive in e-chaos, the Lauck Group has employees who uniformly love working there. In an industry characterized by turnover rates of 20–25 percent per year, Lauck's turnover is just 7.71 percent. That obviously has a lot to do with the people-oriented management approach and with the culture. It also has to do with the accountability approach at the company.

It matters a great deal that every employee has the right to choose personal goals. For those with outside demands, such as young children to care for, a lot of flexibility is provided. The only stipulation is that each individual meet their objectives. "We're not into bureaucracy," Judy Pantello told me. "If someone has other priorities, they can pretty well self-manage their schedule as long as their contribution meets the standards of the firm." For those who have high aspirations, people at all levels coach them to help them achieve their goals. And since each person at the company gets feedback every day via an automated system, accountability is a continual process.

The Lauck Group is a true learning organization. It is also designed to operate in the high speeds of international competition for clients who expect excellence. By using a systematic process that begins with learning, the firm's leadership is able to develop transformational plans for its products and the organization. Out of that comes a strategic plan for the future. From its origin in Alan Lauck's spare room in 1984, the Lauck Group has joined the International Top 40 in its industry in a few short years. The Lauck Group is clearly a Type III organization. It should be no surprise to see the firm continue to grow and thrive in the new economy of the 21st century.

THE PROCESS OF CREATING SUCCESS

Success is never simple in a complex world. Success in e-chaos must be more than using just one management tool. Certainly, success will not generally find an organization whose leadership is consumed with historic competencies. Success in a complex, dynamic environment will only be achieved by an organization operating as a complex, adaptive system. That means that the firm's leadership must use a holistic approach, understanding the future of both the environment and the firm.

The creation of success is a choice. The leaders of the successful companies featured in this book understand that reality. That is what sets their companies apart from others. There is more. The world as we know it in 2001 is going to change. It will probably change radically.

The major shift in the rules brought about by the digital revolution has just begun. As technological change accelerates (which it will), and as the digital revolution diffuses globally, more dramatic shifts in the rules of the game are to be expected. Managers entering this new world will have serious choices to make, and the implications of those choices will be substantial.

In the new world of continual shifts in the environment, management and not technology will be the key to survival and success. Those who wonder what happened or watch what happens will be left behind. Only those who make things happen will be able to lead organizations that find the future and profit from it.

CHAPTER 12

WINNERS AND LOSERS IN THE NEW DIGITAL WORLD

LOOKING AT THE FIRST DECADE OF THE 21ST CENTURY, I HAVE some good news and some bad news. The good news is that the technological revolution is going to continue. In fact, it's going to accelerate. It's going to be a brand new world of communication and services. The bad news is that if you thought the 1990s brought about a lot of change, you haven't seen anything yet!

WE'VE ONLY JUST BEGUN

One of the hit songs of the 1970s was titled "We've Only Just Begun." That song might be more appropriate for the first decade of the 21st century. As the century turns, the Internet is a baby from a technology standpoint. When it comes to e-commerce, the changes of that decade may create a new opportunity for even more robust growth and profits.

Computing is going to rapidly change, both short term and long term. That 1.4 gigahertz rocket ship of a computer processor of 2000 will soon seem slow—speeds of up to 4.5 gigahertz are expected by 2002 or 2003.[1] But don't forget: We've only just begun. Take a look into the future, just a few short years further on.

The next wave in computing will involve light technologies. Using this new technology, optoelectronics, computers will operate like the computers of today but will run at much faster speeds and much cooler temperatures. They will also be smaller and take a very different physical form. Here's what the computer of 2010 might look like:[2]

- Hard Disk: 1 terabyte (Approximately 1,000 times more than today)
- Processor: 100 gigahertz (Approximately 100 times faster than today)
- Memory: Significant changes in clock speed will match CPU speed (current memory speeds usually result in the CPU spending up to 70 percent of the time waiting for data from the memory or cache)

Add to all this the reality that greatly improved and enhanced voice recognition applications will be able to make the keyboard unnecessary, and the real impact of these changes will be substantial. Perhaps even more exciting is the introduction of quantum computing. Quantum computing, or nanotechnology, offers the prospect of creating computers that will make today's supercomputers obsolete.[3]

At the same time that computing is changing, so are telecommunications and networking. New developments in optical networks will change the bandwidth available to the end user. Basically, the supply of bandwidth will become almost infinite with the new all-optical technologies soon to leave the drawing board for the manufacturing plant and store shelves.[4] To the ultimate consumer this will mean that video streaming on the Web will approach television quality. This development alone may entirely change many of the ways that organizations do business with each other as well as with customers. Other developing technologies that focus on wireless transmission, including optoelectronic technologies, can further drive the coming changes in the telecommunications sector.

MEDIA FUSION: NOT EVEN A BLIP ON THE RADAR SCREEN

Consider the fact that over 70 percent of the people in the world do not have access to telephone service. What would happen if—almost overnight—those people got high-speed access to the Web? One company believes that it has discovered how to do that.

It turns out that most homes and businesses in the world have electricity even if they don't have telephone service. One company, Media Fusion of Dallas, Texas, believes it has found a way to use electrical lines to carry data transmission anywhere those lines go.[5] The idea behind Media Fusion's approach is based on theories developed by William "Luke" Stewart. Basically, what he believes is that it is possible to send communication via the magnetic wave that surrounds each power line. That magnetic wave is fairly consistent, according to Stewart, all the way to the power outlet inside the house.

Stewart claims that his application will offer unlimited broadband capability on a network that already exists around the world. Speed is another issue. Since the transport medium is the magnetic waves surrounding the electrical power lines, Stewart believes that the signals will travel at 186,000 miles per second—the speed of light.

There are skeptics regarding Stewart's ideas, even though Media Fusion was recently granted a patent on this technology.[6] Numerous experts suggest that the approach will simply never work. At the same time, a lot of companies are interested in staying close to Media Fusion—especially the power transmission companies.

One engineer at a major power transmission company told me that he believed that the Media Fusion technology would work. When I asked why he was so confident, he explained that his company had tested the idea over 15 years earlier. It worked then, he said, and it ought to work now.

If the Media Fusion plan really works as well as the company's founder believes it will, it will drastically change the world of communication. The same is true of companies like Terabeam, which is using a wireless light signal to transmit broadband applications. There are a number of companies just like those. The bottom line: Don't expect the e-world to reach a point of stability for a long time.

IF WE'VE ONLY JUST BEGUN . . . WHERE ARE WE GOING AND HOW DO WE GET THERE?

The increasing level of technology innovation will have a highly predictable outcome: More complexity and more chaos. If that is true, and it is, the real issue is, "How do we get there?" To some extent, the answer to this question has already been provided, in that companies that balance leadership, learning, and agility with the environment are going to be the real winners in the future e-chaos world. These are the ones that understand the performance secrets of balancing the people and the technology aspects of their firm. To conclude this book, the rest of this chapter discusses a number of projected winners—and one loser—in the new world of e-chaos.

Telecom Technologies, Inc.: Winner

So you would like to go out for a quiet dinner but have to leave your cell phone on because your CEO said you'd better be ready to answer if the Jones contract comes through. The only problem is, at least fifteen thousand people (at least it seems like that many) have your cell phone number because you let your teenager borrow it last weekend. And what about that e-mail you are waiting on, do you dare leave the office before it comes in?

Thanks to Telecom Technologies and its successor company, in the very near future you will not have to worry about any of those things.[7] Instead, just before you go out to dinner, you go onto the Web and in a few short moments you make sure that only your boss's call and that important e-mail message will make it to your cell phone. Everything else—calls to your office, calls to your home (and your kid), faxes, and more—will be stored until you decide you are ready to get them all.

In the late 1980s and the early 1990s, the world witnessed the convergence of computing and telecommunications. The result of that convergence was the explosive growth of the technology business sector and the emergence of firms such as Cisco Systems and Amazon.com. A lot of people who invested wisely at the beginning of that cycle became millionaires. What would happen if a similar shift happened a second time? It is quite possible that is exactly what will occur.

Telecom Technologies was started in 1994 by Anousheh Ansari and her husband Hamid, both immigrants from Iran. The company did well from the beginning, but often struggled to stay afloat because its Fortune 500 clientele was often slow to pay.[8] The company managed to get through those early struggles and by 2000 was the leader in a technology called "soft switches."

Soft switches, according to Terri Griffin, Telecom Technologies' vice president of marketing, are going to change the communications landscape. Historically, the telephone companies positioned large switches at their central offices to route calls. Special features like call forwarding had to be programmed into a number by the telephone vendor before it could provide a service. With soft switches, that will no longer be the case. Soft switches bring IP (Internet protocol) to the application and allow customers to control their own communications devices. It is a simple matter of going to a Web site and telling the system how to handle all incoming communications. Paging, office phone, home phone, e-mail, faxes, streamed video messages—all can be directed with a simple click. In the future, conversion programs will allow e-mail to be converted to voice mail and sent directly to the cell phone. In the same way, the cell phone can be used to generate a voice message that is converted to text and sent as an e-mail message. The possibilities are endless. "The communications industry is in the same stage that the computing industry was in 15 years ago when they moved from mainframes to networks," Terri Griffin says.

Telecom Technologies should be one of the big winners in that explosive shift in the market. The company is not just on the leading edge from a technology standpoint, it is designed to maintain high levels of creativity and speed in that market. Consider the corporate profile shown in Figure 12.1, which was developed from information gathered about the company. It quickly becomes obvious that the company is designed for leadership in the new millennium.

The current environmental turbulence in the industry is only about 3.7, but it is expected to shift to 4.5+ over the 2000–2002 time period. The current profile of Telecom Technologies is much more flexible and aggressive than needed for level 3.7 turbulence. Such positive gaps can be problematic—overprofiling often indicates wasted resources—but they're what a strategically balanced company will show when turbulence is expected to quickly shift to a much higher level.

Innovation (Aggressiveness)

Factor	1	2	3	4	5
R&D Spending	Low	Moderately Low	Competitive	Moderately High	Highly Aggressive
Product Life Cycles-Plan	Very Long	Long	Moderate	Short	Very Short
Customer Focus	Respond To Demands	Meet Demand	Stay Close to Customer	Anticipate Needs	Anticipate Unrealized Needs

Product Technology Applications

Factor	1	2	3	4	5
Technology Applications (Product)	None	Limited	Moderate	High	Very High
Technology Philosophy	None	Last In	Adapt with Competition	Seek Early Adaptation	First Mover

CEO Attributes

Factor	1	2	3	4	5
Attitude Toward Change	Reject	Resist	Slow Adaptation	Drive Change	Aggressively Drive Change
Attitude Toward Creativity and Risk	No Value	De-Value	Necessary Evil	Drive Creativity	Aggressively Promote
Attitude Toward Subordinates	Expect Performance	Expect Efficiency	Meet Objectives	Respect and Value	Encourage as Team Member

Culture

Factor	1	2	3	4	5
Values	Defend the Status Quo	Support the Status Quo	Maintain the Status Quo	Challenge the Status Quo	Create the Future
Value of Employees	Little	Minimal	Moderate	High	Very High
Rewards and Incentives	Historic Performance	Accuracy and Efficiency	Productivity	Solutions Development	Creativity

FIGURE 12.1. Telecom Technologies:
Designed to Thrive in E-Chaos.
Adapted from H. Igor Ansoff's Strategic Diagnosis procedures.
Used with permission.

It should be no surprise that many of the values of TTI are quite similar to those of other thriving companies profiled in this book. Terri Griffin, like a lot of others at the company, has no interest in working anywhere else. "I've never been treated like this at any other company, and I've worked at some great companies," says Griffin. She went on to discuss the open attitude and supportive approach of the CEO, Anousheh Ansari, and to share a number of the principles of the firm:

- Solutions sell, technology doesn't.
- Never let egos get in the way of doing the "right thing."
- Great culture + great people = great company.
- You never achieve real success unless you like what you are doing.

Telecom Technologies should be expected to outperform most of its multibillion-dollar competitors. The reason is, competitors like Lucent and Nortel lack the management and culture profiles to support such high-speed change. One company that will probably do well in the soft switch space is (surprise) Cisco Systems. As the profile of Cisco and its CEO in Chapter Three demonstrates, Cisco is a highly aggressive, adaptable organization. Its support systems (culture, decision systems, and so on) are ideally designed for the emerging soft switch market.

Fidelity Investments: Winner

Fidelity Investments is a closely held private corporation that has built an enviable track record of performance, becoming the nation's largest mutual fund company. Chairman Edward C. Johnson III has been faced with losing some of his top fund managers to even more lucrative opportunities outside Fidelity. That may be the price a company pays for success, but in Johnson's case, he's taking an aggressive approach to developing financial incentives that will help Fidelity keep its intellectual capital.[9] Although Fidelity's loss of a few key fund managers has been widely reported, other aspects of life at Fidelity have not been so well publicized—particularly the company's technology strategy.

Fidelity Investments emphasizes excellence. Its managers believe that how people are treated—and how they treat each other and the customer—are critical to their success. They are unwilling to compromise those principles. The same level of commitment to excellence is revealed in their technology strategy.

Fidelity uses multiple redundancy in all aspects of its computer applications. If bad weather approaches one of its U.S. computing centers, generators automatically come on line and supply the power for the computers until the storm has passed. In some cases, the processing of customer accounts is automatically switched to one of the other centers. A tour of one of Fidelity's computer centers reveals the lengths to which its people will go to make sure that their customers never lose access to their system.

A tour of the facility also reveals a beautiful swimming pool. What is not obvious to the casual observer, however, is that the pool is part of a water reservoir that will supply 15 days of water for cooling the computers if the local water supply is disrupted. The centers are pictures of redundancy. If a system has a problem, a second system will immediately take over. If the backup system fails, the processing is automatically switched to one of the other computing centers. How good is this system? As one Fidelity insider put it: "You could be online checking your account when the computer center got wiped out by an explosion and you would never be aware that there was a problem. The system is that good."

When Fidelity became concerned about year 2000 readiness with one group of computers, rather than risking a problem, it replaced all of the systems with new Y2K-compliant systems. Integrity means dependability to Fidelity. The company views any possible interruption in service to its customers as a potentially catastrophic event. That is why it stays at the leading edge in computer and telecommunications technology as well. Unlike Oxford Health Plans, Fidelity never lets trouble in a computer application ride until it becomes a crippling problem.

Fidelity spent over $1.5 billion on technology in 1999 alone. That is significantly more than most of its competitors.[10] It took the leadership in online trading and formed Powerstreet, an online trading company. As with most of the thriving companies featured in this book, Fidelity's leadership is paranoid about leading their industry. They expect to lead with the best funds, and they expect to lead in the technology arena. The firm's CEO is a fan of Kaizen, or continuous improvement (briefly described in Chapter Ten). He expects everyone to continually improve the firm. But Kaizen has little to do with the firm's success. On one hand, Fidelity is the picture of dependability and stability. On the other, it is excellent at discontinuous improvement (as opposed to Kaizen's continuous improvement). Rather than following, the Fidelity team focuses on leading the pack.

Fidelity Investments spends a lot of time in the future. It does that with its investment portfolios and it does that with its people as well as its technology. The company works hard to have a culture that resembles Southwest Airlines and other thriving, people-focused organizations. Succinctly put, Fidelity Investments is a company that understands and applies the principles of strategic balance. It will definitely be a winner in the new millennium.

TMP Worldwide: Winner

Most people wouldn't use the words *exciting, creative,* and *lucrative* when asked about the business of yellow pages advertising, but Andy McKelvey, founder and CEO of the world's largest yellow pages advertising agency, would—and he'd argue that *fun* and *inspiring* need to be added to the list. In 1967,

McKelvey founded Telephone Marketing Programs, now TMP Worldwide, a billion-dollar-a-year public company that has found a way to make the mundane world of yellow pages advertising an exciting and extremely profitable business.

When Andy McKelvey entered the yellow pages advertising business more than 30 years ago he had two goals. First, he knew he wanted to grow, because the alternative was not attractive. Second, McKelvey thought that if he could get to $2 million in billings (net revenue to an advertising agency) it would be a monumental accomplishment. McKelvey reached $2 million long ago and hasn't looked back since. Now, more than three decades later, he heads a multinational company with three core businesses, more than 3,500 employees, and offices in 12 countries.

A history of entrepreneurs shows a common pattern. First, many entrepreneurs go into businesses that are familiar to them. Second, 90 percent of them fail within the first five years. After the poor ideas and incompetent managers get winnowed out, the failures are usually due to either of two factors: inability to cope with success and inability to deal with change.

Many entrepreneurs hit the "$2 million wall"—the revenue level at which a business owner must make the conversion from being a hands-on manager who can engage in very high levels of controlling behavior to that of a true, empowering leader—and fail to adjust. Others find themselves unwilling to move outside their area of comfort, or familiarity. They forsake the very behavior that helped them achieve their early success: entrepreneurship. Entrepreneurial behavior creates organizations that thrive on change. That is why the 10 percent of new firms that pass the five-year test tend to be led by charismatic leaders who view change as their opportunity to grow and to succeed.

TMP's Andy McKelvey fits that description. In a yellow-pages world that others would call boring and repetitious, he fosters an exciting work environment with an attitude of strategy, growth, innovation, and leadership.

Strategy at TMP "Personally, I believe the vision concept is very overrated," suggests McKelvey. "Understanding your universe, or what is best described as your competitive environment, is the one true vision that business leaders must concern themselves with today."

At the heart of Andy McKelvey's concept is the idea of systems thinking—the process of making reliable inferences about complex environments. "Profit begins with change leadership at the top," says McKelvey. "If you don't understand your universe, when an opportunity comes along you won't be able to take advantage of it because you simply won't recognize its real value."

The strategy process at TMP obviously has little to do with mission statements. Although TMP closely defends and maintains its attitudes toward customers and employees, the strategy process allows for no mission-type limits. The senior management team at TMP views its strategy process as a highly intuitive one.

"We have a lot of impromptu strategy sessions," McKelvey notes. "If someone identifies an opportunity we like to move quickly. We don't wait for an annual planning session."

Jim Treacy, chief operating officer and executive vice president, believes there is real value in TMP's impromptu strategy sessions. "We often get pretty intense in our debates, but we all realize that if our ideas won't get past a little internal testing, they certainly won't last on the outside. We also have an unwritten rule about those meetings, you can challenge and argue all you want, but there are no hard feelings. Andy's that way, we all are. We participate in healthy debates and the results of those discussions are significant opportunities."

According to Treacy, you don't need to look any further than TMP's entrée into the online recruitment market to see this philosophy at work. Seven years ago, at a time when traditional companies were paying little if any attention to a new and little-known phenomenon called the Internet, TMP was exploring ways to take its business online.

In 1994, TMP acquired Adion Information Systems, owners of the Monster Board *(www.monster.com)*, now the largest and most successful career center on the World Wide Web. About the same time, the company acquired Online Career Center *(www.occ.com)*, the Internet's earliest career site, and TMP Interactive was born. Today more than 34,000 companies post jobs on TMP's recruitment Web sites. The company added the content power of About Work *(www.aboutwork.com)* and the strength of college-focused StudentCenter *(www.studentcenter.com)* in early 1998.

For reasons like this and many others, Jim Treacy strongly supports McKelvey's idea of "understanding your universe." He believes that strategy that focuses on the present capabilities of the firm has little to do with organizational success and growth. "You have to look ahead and jump the curve," says Treacy, who moved from executive vice president to chief operating officer in the first quarter of 1998. "We have to ask the question about 'what other businesses should we be in?' if we are to effectively meet future customer needs and demands. It's the only way you meet corporate growth and profitability objectives."

It was this thinking that also led TMP into the executive search and selection marketplace early in 1998. According to McKelvey, clients were approaching TMP about providing a wider range of staffing services including executive search and he felt it was critical to develop an in-house capability to meet their demand. In April 1998, TMP acquired Johnson Smith & Knisely, Inc., the 12th-largest executive search firm in the United States. Just two months later, the company announced it had entered into an agreement in principle to acquire TASA Holding AG, an international executive search firm. And, just as the company did with its traditional recruitment business, TMP plans to jump the curve again by introducing executive search and selection to the Internet—and doing it sooner than most people think.

TMP's Approach Sustained profitability requires firms to address two critical issues. First, as environmental turbulence climbs, the type of leadership style used throughout the firm has a greater and greater effect on ROI. Second, in a turbulent environment sustained profitability can only be achieved by a firm that continues to foster high levels of empowered innovation. That might also be described as strategic balance.

"He's from the school that says 'go solve the problem, then ask for forgiveness,'" says Treacy of Andy McKelvey. McKelvey realizes that TMP's success is founded on its people. "A lot of firms talk about how their employees are their most important assets," he says, then points out, "Reality is, it's difficult to build a culture which supports that type of behavior on the part of management. Everyone agrees it's a nice idea, but the real issue is whether or not the employees are really being treated like that."

When Andy McKelvey visits one of TMP's offices, he likes to ask one particular question of the senior manager: "What do you like most about working for TMP?" "There's one answer that makes my day," says McKelvey. "If I get that one, I know that our senior leadership is doing its job well." The answer he likes to hear? "I like working at a company where I can be my own boss."

"A lot of people talk about empowerment, but it's still rare at companies," says McKelvey. "Empowerment at the client level is absolutely critical if our people are going to not only exceed customer needs, but additionally make them feel that they have the freedom to set their own standards of excellence. [McKelvey also said that TMP gets 99 percent of new product ideas by listening to clients.] That's why I believe that 'how you treat your people' is where profit starts."

When it comes to people, McKelvey sees some serious flaws in the way many companies manage certain areas of their business. "Many companies fail to recognize the critical strategic role that the human resources function plays in driving corporate success. The failure to anticipate not only the quantity of people you need in the future but also the quality of these people can devastate a company. We see this as a major opportunity for us—helping companies fill those strategic needs. The expansion of our traditional recruitment advertising business, first to the Internet and then into executive search and selection market, is all part of it."

Innovation at TMP It is difficult to completely separate strategy and leadership from innovation. Absent effective strategy and appropriate leadership, an organization has little hope for success. At the same time, firms that have excellent strategy and leadership place a high value on innovation.

The idea of "discontinuous innovation"—innovating outside current core competencies and current product areas—is at the heart of TMP's success. Perhaps Andy McKelvey said it best: "We constantly look to introduce more products and to uncover brand new areas of opportunity." Echoing McKelvey, one TMP manager said: "I believe Andy McKelvey would go into almost any business if it made sense. He's not tied to any arena of competition. He's a lot more concerned about 'arenas of opportunity.'"

It's probably no accident that Jim Treacy's views are so thoroughly in tune with McKelvey's. "We foster a 'create your own opportunity culture,'" says Treacy. "If someone sees an opportunity for the firm, we want them to go for it. We firmly believe that's another reason TMP is always at the forefront of innovation."

TMP doesn't stop with its people; it has also made great strides in the area of technology applications. Its managers have taken what could have been an old-style company and put it right at the head of the technology movement.

TMP's Performance Getting past $2 million in billings (McKelvey's early goal for the company, and a wall for many entrepreneurs) was apparently no problem for TMP. The company reported 1997 gross billings of more than $1.05 billion. TMP has gone from being a privately held company to a publicly traded firm (NASDAQ: TMPW). Under McKelvey's leadership, the company has grown to become the worldwide leader in its three core businesses:

- Yellow pages advertising (the original business)
- Recruitment advertising
- Interactive services

But there's a lot more to the story than just the fact that TMP has now diversified into other businesses. Consider the following:

- By 1997, TMP had become the world's largest yellow pages advertising agency and was larger than its next ten leading competitors combined.
- TMP's recruitment advertising business—which did not exist in 1993—had become the largest recruitment advertising agency network in the world by 1997. The network also includes a growing executive search and selection business.
- TMP's interactive business would rank (if it were ranked in the Web Publishing Ranking of companies) eighth among a group of familiar names like Microsoft and Yahoo! (1998)

TMP's Revenues ($ million)

2000	*1999*	*1998*	*1997*	*1996*	*1995*
$1,200	$765	$657	$541	$227	$123

TMP: Winners in a Turbulent Environment It is difficult for companies involved in old-line businesses to engage in strategic renewal. It is even more difficult when high levels of turbulence enter the historic business segment of the firm. More often than not, such firms are ill-equipped to deal with the complexity and the rate of change characteristic of turbulent environments.

TMP Worldwide is an exceptional firm in many ways. Its response to the technological change of the 1990s was one of leading rather than following. Its management recognized the need for systems thinking approaches to strategy and the profit power of thinking about the universe. They also demonstrated the critical links between effective strategy, fostering innovation, entrepreneurial behavior, and people-focused leadership.

Rather than its historic businesses and competencies, TMP is preoccupied with what it needs to become. It is also preoccupied with its people and its customers. As many companies have demonstrated, it is not nearly as difficult to achieve one success as it is to repeat that success over long periods of time in environments of high uncertainty and rapid change. TMP has provided that example. Figure 12.2 shows the reasons for TMP's success, making it easy to see why the firm will do exceptionally well in the e-chaos of the new economy. It is truly a company that maintains its strategic balance. TMP's strategic profile reveals the secret to its success.

The Promotion Network, Inc.: Winner

"Roger's at least one French-fry short of a happy meal," says one. "Not really," says another, "He's at least half an order short of a happy meal." So it goes every day at TPN. There sits Roger at a lunch table, listening to smile-softened insults. Roger is undaunted—he takes the barbs in stride and quickly delivers a few of his own. Much like a pack of sharks at a feeding frenzy, the group takes random shots at each other. That's The Promotion Network: a crazy, "no holds barred" company that's one of the top eight sales promotion firms in the United States.

Roger, by the way, is Roger Winter—the CEO of TPN—and the people making those remarks work at TPN. What kind

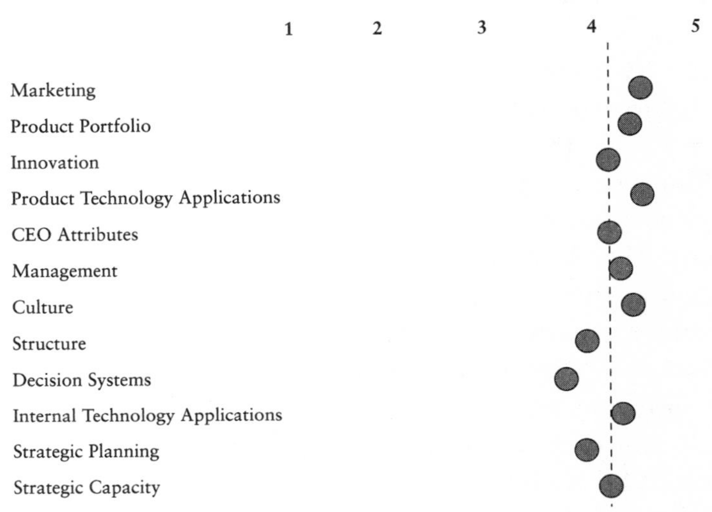

FIGURE 12.2. TMP's Strategic Profile.
Adapted from H. Igor Ansoff's Strategic Diagnosis procedures.
Used with permission.

of a CEO would tolerate that type of behavior? Actually, in Roger's case, he encourages it. Working at TPN is a little like working in a police station—you only worry if someone's not kidding around with you.

TPN's client list reads like a who's who of the Fortune 500. Competition for such prestigious clients is high—and their requirements can be even more demanding. "In the business of ideas, it's important to have a thick skin," says Winter. He goes on to explain how he believes the "fun based" culture at TPN supports high levels of productivity and quality. "We have a lot of fun at TPN. We also work very hard. I believe our employees as well as our clients benefit from the way we do business," says Winter.

The sales promotion industry is truly chaotic. Sales promotion items are typically point-of-sale materials such as posters or giveaways. It's a small community as industries go, because of the very special nature of the products and the high levels of urgency most clients attach to their needs. Often, in response to a short-term lull in revenues, a client will turn to the sales promotion experts to develop a creative idea for increasing traffic in a retail location. Needless to say, the delivery date for a lot of the projects is "yesterday."

Winter, who got his start in the corporate arena at McDonalds, says he learned some important lessons about performance and the value of a highly productive "family" type atmosphere there. He often quotes Ray Kroc, the founder of McDonalds: "Take care of the people and the rest will follow." Taking care of his people, that's what Winter does.

The hectic pace and demanding nature of the sales promotion industry is known to drive high levels of turnover—often in excess of 17 percent annually. At TPN, the turnover rate is more like 6 or 7 percent. The reason? This "creative machine" has a big heart. The company also pays a lot of attention to who gets hired. If someone doesn't fit the mold in the beginning, no matter how good they are, they don't get a second look.

TPN's people are paid highly competitive salaries, according to Roger Winter. In addition, the firm has a very good 401(k) plan that has 97 percent participation by the staff. It also has an excellent insurance and benefits package. But those are not the real drivers behind this highly creative machine.

"I cannot tell you how incredibly hard our people work," says Winter. "Yes, we take very good care of our people, because as a company, we have a reputation for taking exceptionally good care of our clients. The two go hand in hand."

A tour of TNP would have to begin at the center of the company, the lunchroom. A lot of things take place in that open, friendly environment. In addition to having a gourmet cook on staff to provide lunch for the TPN team each day, the lunchroom serves as the creative pit for the organization. It's where a lot of the friendly harassment takes place as the pressures of the morning are discussed. It's also the site of a lot of impromptu brainstorming sessions. As a company, TPN is organized around the clients. So each day, as client needs change, the organization of the firm changes. It's the lunchroom that serves as the focal point for a lot of the creative solutions that drive out of TPN.

Next to the lunchroom is the company gym. The room includes aerobics equipment, weights, and professional trainers. Each team member is invited to develop a personal fitness plan with the professional trainers. Next to the gym is the massage room. Yes, any member of the team can take a break for a massage any time they want. It should be noted that massage, aerobics, and weight training have all been shown to decrease the impact of stress in a person's life.

Last but not least is the on-site child care facility. Not only are team members encouraged to bring their children to work, they are encouraged to take breaks and spend time with their children. The facility is staffed with qualified, trained personnel. It should be of no surprise to learn that all these benefits—from lunches to massages, personal trainers, and child care—cost the employee nothing. TPN takes care of its clients and its employees, but it does more. It even takes good care of the team members' parents.

Periodically, TPN has a "parents' day" celebration. This is a time when every member's parents are invited to gather for a special two-day event. For the most recent occasion, a two-day event was planned at Roger Winter's Texas ranch. Team members from TPN's Chicago and New York offices were brought to Dallas along with their parents for the event. The parents of the Dallas office team members were also flown in from around the country. It was a real Texas weekend, complete with a Saturday evening barbecue. The focal point of the weekend was the four-hour company employee meeting, where each employee had to explain their job and what they did—to their parents.

"It was a blast," says Winter. "We had people who make corporate presentations to Fortune 500 CEOs and their knees were shaking. This was a wonderful opportunity for the team members and their parents." For TPN, it was an expensive weekend, about $150,000. Roger Winter had an answer for those that might ask, "Why spend so much money to bring the team members' parents together?" At the closing of the weekend, Winter answered that question as he spoke to the parents: "When your son or daughter calls you and says 'I'm thinking about taking a job with another company,' I'm trying to make sure you know exactly what advice to give them," he said with a chuckle.

As for marketing, TPN rarely has to engage in an all-out effort. (Roger Winter points out that business lost due to a few client mergers has caused the company to scramble a few times.) "We are extremely aggressive when we get the opportunity to get new business," says Winter. "However, our business growth is about as fast as we can handle. We get most of our new business opportunities from people who have moved from an existing client to another company. That's just about the highest compliment a sales promotion professional can pay us." Winter goes on to explain that the firm has a compounded growth rate of 36 percent per year for the last five years.

When a company is consistently in the condition that it can hardly accept new business, it must be doing some things well. TPN prides itself on putting the client first. The TPN team organizes around client needs and client excellence. Its people do not question client timetables for the delivery of a project, they change their own arrangements to meet client needs. From time to time, almost everyone at TPN has to work long, late hours. (The company chef keeps meals available for those who work late, by the way.)

As for strategy, the company has a "challenge everything" mentality. The open nature of the organization provides an environment that promotes learning. As technology has changed, TPN has stayed at the leading edge of that change. That's because the firm's strategy is about learning from the future.

Across the board, leadership, structure, innovation, marketing, culture, all the key drivers of success have been meticulously planted and grown within the TPN organization. It is that attention to the "behaviors that produce profit" that will lead TPN to even higher levels in the future.

AT&T: Loser

AT&T began a voluntary break-up in 1995 by spinning off NCR and Lucent.[11] The objective was to become a premier video, voice, and data company. The problem was, AT&T's competition was increasingly agile and aggressive. At the same time, the company had spent little time in changing its strategic profile. By the year 2000, the company was plagued with numerous strategic imbalances. Figure 12.3 shows the profile of AT&T.

It is readily apparent from the figure that AT&T is in trouble. It has developed numerous strategic gaps in excess of –1.5.[12] As previously indicated, such gaps are bound to have a substantial impact on the ability of the organization to perform in the level of turbulence indicated. Not only do the gaps show the reason for AT&T's problems at the time of the study, they also indicate that unless the gaps are corrected, the company will operate well below optimum in the future. (This conclusion assumes that the turbulence does not decrease—which seems safe enough as a prediction. It is, in fact, expected to increase in the 2001–2004 time period).[13]

At the same time, it becomes apparent that AT&T has had serious problems in the strategy area for a number of years.[14] That was pointed out in the analysis of the NCR acquisition, back in Chapter Two. The bottom line: Absent appropriate organizational as well as strategy changes, AT&T will produce profits that are well below optimum. In essence, the company is a Type I organization and needs to become a Type III organization.

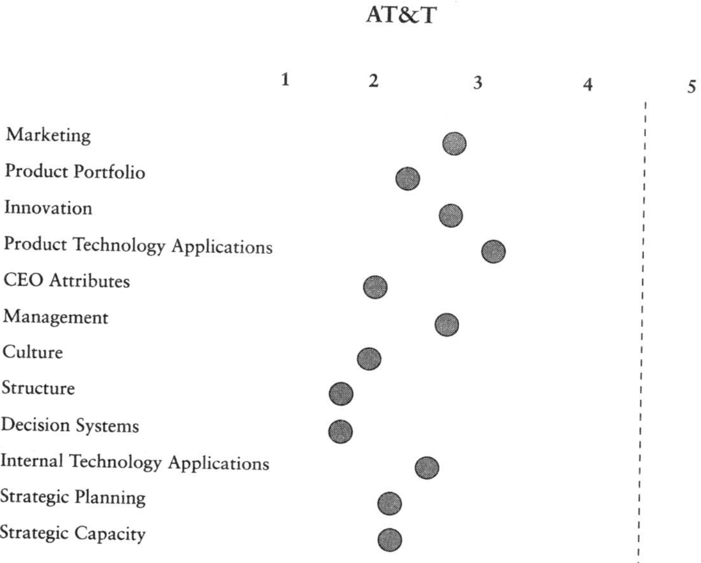

FIGURE 12.3. Strategic Profile of AT&T: December 2000. Adapted from H. Igor Ansoff's Strategic Diagnosis procedures. Used with permission.

Dell Computer Corporation: Winner

Dell Computer is characterized by a number of excellent attributes including customization, leading-edge technology, customer value, and service and support.[15] Simply put, Dell is designed to deliver leading-edge value that fits customer needs.

Michael Dell, the company's founder and chairman, pays a great deal of attention to maintaining the balance of the firm. He insists that the organization be committed to excellence—not only with the end product that the company delivers, but with customer service as well as the employees and their environment. As with other successful companies, hard work is the norm at Dell. Its management believes that if the company is to do well, every member of the Dell team must strive for excellence.[16]

As a direct marketer, Dell had a business model that was a perfect fit for the emerging digital economy of the late 1990s and early 2000s. By adapting its business to the electronic marketplace, Dell has been able to effectively maintain its customer relationships while keeping costs down.[17]

A strategic assessment of Dell Computer reveals that the firm is extremely well profiled for the future. It aggressively focuses on the future and at the same time maintains an organization that is capable of efficient, rapid transformation. Add to that a wonderfully customer-focused organization and you have a company that will continue to thrive in the 21st century.

Oracle: Winner

Oracle is a company that seems to thrive on change. In 1997, when the company's existing software seemed to be approaching a mature stage, Larry Ellison insisted that the firm take the lead into the new e-commerce age.[18] In actuality, Oracle in 1997 was faced with the type of product portfolio decision that often leads firms into disaster. On one hand, existing products were producing extremely high profits. On the other, it became apparent that the firm was going to have to invest heavily in the future if revenues and profits were going to continue on a long-term basis. That is what Oracle under Ellison's leadership decided to do.[19]

An assessment of Oracle reveals marginal gaps in the areas of management (–0.6), culture (–0.6), and strategic planning (–0.7). It is reasonable to conclude that much of Oracle's historic success has been due to Ellison's ability to make strategic decisions effectively, and further to maintain a stable of gifted, intelligent people to execute those strategies.[20]

Oracle should continue to thrive subject to three conditions: The level of entrepreneurial behavior characteristic of Ellison needs to be maintained; the management and culture must not deteriorate to the point where the company reaches a stage of imbalance; and the softness of the firm's strategic planning must continue to be offset by Ellison's ability to drive effective learning into the organization.

THE SECRET TO PERFORMANCE?

If a company applies the principles developed in this book, will that guarantee exceptional success? No. E-chaos by its very nature involves high levels of uncertainty. Poor product strategy by itself can devastate a company. Additionally, as the fourth quarter of 2000 revealed, prospects can change quickly in a turbulent economy.

Nonetheless, a number of conclusions can be made about companies that do (and do not) achieve strategic balance as it is developed in this book. First and foremost, it is important to remember that companies that enjoy long-term success tend to be quite similar.

- They are led by a succession of CEOs who value iconoclastic behavior, are preoccupied with discovering the future first, and insist on leading companies that are consistent first movers.
- They are led by a succession of CEOs who understand the concept of strategic balance. Those CEOs understand that sales or products or service alone will not ensure success. They understand that success is achieved by balancing all of the complex aspects of the firm with the external, emerging environment.
- They have managers who value their people and lead them instead of trying to control them. Great strategies do not sustain success. Great strategies supported by a management team that values its people proactively are what allow the firm to execute great strategies. Is it any wonder that the list of the "Top 100 Companies to Work For" often includes many of the top-performing companies?

- Finally (and again), they are balanced organizations. They focus on quality, but it does not consume them. They make sure that their leadership and culture create high-speed learning environments. They reject bureaucracy and self-importance in favor of teamwork and humility. To high-performance organizations, what the company used to be hardly matters. Their product portfolio efforts and their strategies focus on allocating assets to the highest areas of return, without regard to historic competencies.

A number of the executives featured in this book are admittedly gifted, intuitive people. They do as a matter of instinct what the principles of this book guide all managers to do, whether they have the same type of intuitive skills that Jack Welch has or not. Once the principles of strategic balance are understood, any manager should have the ability to see how to maximize a company's performance. Just bear in mind one simple statement: Companies in strategic balance tend to significantly outperform those in imbalance. As the new techno-economy continues to emerge, that reality will become even more obvious. Certainly, all companies will go through ups and downs in the new economy. But some will emerge as even better companies, while e-chaos will eliminate others.

ENDNOTES

Chapter One

1. "Slow Learner," *Forbes Magazine,* 4 May 1998, p. 1.
2. Michael L. Tushman and Philip Anderson, "Technological Discontinuities and Organizational Environments," *Administrative Science Quarterly,* 1986, *31,* 439–465.
3. Ralph D. Stacey, *Managing the Unknowable.* San Francisco: Jossey-Bass, 1992.
4. Sumantra Ghoshal and Christopher A. Bartlett, "Changing the Role of Top Management," *Harvard Business Review,* January-February 1995.
5. ABC, *Sixty Minutes* interview with Jack Welch on 29 October 2000. All references to Welch in this chapter were taken from that interview.

Chapter Two

1. H. I. Ansoff and Edward McDonnell, *Implanting Strategic Management.* New York: Prentice Hall, 1990. All references to Ansoff's work in this chapter are taken from this reference unless otherwise noted.
2. Alfred O. Lewis, "Strategic Posture and Financial Performance of the Banking Industry: Strategic Management Study." Unpublished Ph.D. dissertation, US International University, San Diego, Calif., 1989.
3. Roman Lombriser, "Impact of General Manager Leadership Behavior on Success of Discontinuous Strategic Changes in Thirty Swiss Business Firms." Unpublished Ph.D. dissertation, US International University, San Diego, Calif., 1992.

4. Mamoudh Chafie, "The Relationships between Top Management Information Systems Profiles, Managerial Capability, and Environmental Turbulence." Unpublished Ph.D. dissertation, US International University, San Diego, Calif., 1992.
5. W. R. Ashby, *Introduction to Cybernetics.* New York: Wiley, 1956.
6. Thomas J. Peters and Robert H. Waterman Jr., *In Search of Excellence.* New York: Harper & Row, 1982.
7. Erica Rasmusson, "Five Companies to Watch," *Sales & Marketing Management,* 2000, *152*(7), 84–85.
8. "Rebuilding the Garage," *Economist,* 5 July 2000, *356*(8179), 59–60.
9. "Rebuilding the Garage."
10. "A Wake-Up Call for HP," *Technology Review,* May/June 2000, *103*(3), 94–100.
11. Phaedra Hise, "HMO, Heal Thyself—Starting with Thy Computers." *Forbes ASAP,* 21 August 2000.

Chapter Three

1. Andy Serwer, "There's Something About Cisco," *Fortune,* 15 May 2000.
2. Serwer, "There's Something About Cisco."
3. J. P. Donlon, "Why John Chambers Is the CEO of the Future," *Chief Executive,* July 2000, *157,* 26–36.
4. Donlon, "Why John Chambers Is the CEO of the Future."
5. Donlon, "Why John Chambers Is the CEO of the Future."
6. "John Chambers: Internet CEO & MS Hero." Speaker introduction on the Northern California Chapter National Multiple Sclerosis Society Home Page. Available online: *www.msconnection.org/events/dinner/chambers.htm.* Access date: 26 February 2001.
7. Dave House, "Off-Line," *Telecommunications,* 1998, *32*(7), 86.
8. Bob Wallace, "Nortel's Departing President Discusses Bay Experience, Future Plans," *Computerworld,* 18 June 1999.
9. Rosanne Maeck, "Interview with Dave House, CEO, Bay Networks." *FaultLine,* November 1998, *19*(2).
10. Jean-Rene Gonthier, "Interview with Dave House," 2000. Available online: Informatique Bureautique, *www.home.ch/~spaw1116/Bay/Interview.html.* Access date: 26 February 2001.
11. Maeck, "Interview with Dave House."
12. Dave House, "The Unified Network of the Future: Voice, Data, Cellular, and More Over a Single Integrated Network." Guest

Editorial on the Novell Web site, 21 June 1999. Available online: *www.novell.com/news/leadstories/1999/jun21/index.html.* Access date: 26 February 2001.

Chapter Four

1. Henry Mintzberg, *The Rise and Fall of Strategic Planning.* New York: Free Press, 1994.
2. Richard D'Aveni, *Hypercompetition.* New York: Free Press, 1994.
3. Eugene R. Fama, "Agency Problems and the Theory of the Firm," *Journal of Political Economy,* April 1980, *88*(2).
4. John O. Burdett, "The Magic of Alignment," *Management Decision,* 1994, *32*(2), 59–63.
5. Charles Bruno, "Wal-Mart Casts Wide Router Net," *Network World,* 27 March 1995, *12*(13), 69–73.
6. "What Comes Next?" *Inc. Magazine,* October 1997.
7. Roman Lombriser, "Impact of General Manager Leadership Behavior on Success of Discontinuous Strategic Changes in Thirty Swiss Business Firms." Unpublished Ph.D. dissertation, US International University, San Diego, Calif., 1992.
8. Ralf F. P. Schulze, "Differences of Corporate Management Behavior to Foster Success of Intrapreneurs in Charge of Incremental or Discontinuous Innovations." Unpublished Ph.D. dissertation, US International University, San Diego, Calif., 1994.
9. Heather Haverman, "Between a Rock and a Hard Place: Organizational Change and Performance Under Conditions of Fundamental Environmental Transformation," *Administrative Science Quarterly,* March 1992.
10. "Study Suggests Downsizing May Not Increase Performance," *Dallas Morning News,* 20 August 1995.

Chapter Five

1. David K. Hurst, *Crisis and Renewal.* Cambridge, Mass.: Harvard Business School Press, 1995.
2. Ichak Adizes, *Corporate Lifecycles: How and Why Corporations Grow and Die and What to Do About It.* Englewood Cliffs, N.J.: Prentice Hall, 1988.
3. Ralph D. Stacey, *Managing the Unknowable.* San Francisco: Jossey-Bass, 1992.
4. Henry Mintzberg, *The Rise and Fall of Strategic Planning.* New York: Free Press, 1994.

5. Dawn Kelly and Terry Amburgey, "Organizational Inertia and Momentum: A Dynamic Model of Strategic Change," *Academy of Management Journal,* 1991, *34*(3), 591–612.
6. Michael L. Tushman and Philip Anderson, "Technological Discontinuities and Organizational Environments," *Administrative Science Quarterly,* 1986, *31,* 439–465.
7. Rebecca M. Henderson and Kim B. Clark, "Architectural Innovation: The Reconfiguration of Existing Product Technologies and the Failure of Existing Firms," *Administrative Science Quarterly,* 1990, *35,* 9–30.
8. Michael L. Tushman and Elaine Romanelli, "Organizational Evolution: A Metamorphosis Model of Convergence and Reorientation," *Organizational Behavior,* 1985, *7,* 171–222.
9. Jay Mendell, *Nonextrapolative Methods in Business Forecasting.* Westport, Conn.: Quorum Books, 1985.
10. Robert H. Waterman Jr. *The Renewal Factor.* New York: Bantam Books, 1987.
11. Danny Miller and Peter Friesen, "Innovation in Conservative and Entrepreneurial Firms: Two Models of Strategic Momentum," *Strategic Management Journal,* 1982, *3,* 1–25.
12. Daniel A. Leventhal and James G. March, "The Myopia of Learning," *Strategic Management Journal,* 1993, *114,* 95–112.
13. Alan D. Meyer, "Adapting to Environmental Jolts," *Administrative Science Quarterly,* 1982, *27,* 515–537.

Chapter Six

1. "Many Firms Flying by Seat of Pants," *Dallas Morning News,* 4 September 1993.
2. "Navigators Without a Map or Compass," *Financial Times,* 20 October 1993.
3. Eric D. Beinhocker, "Strategy at the Edge of Chaos," *McKinsey Quarterly,* 1997, (1), 24–39.
4. Beinhocker, "Strategy at the Edge of Chaos."
5. Thomas Kuhn, *The Structure of Scientific Revolutions.* Chicago: University of Chicago Press, 1970.
6. Ron Davison, Internet chat room posting on the topic of systems thinking, 1996.
7. Barry Richmond, "System Dynamics/Systems Thinking: Let's Get On With It," speech delivered at the International Systems Dynamics Conference in Sterling, Scotland, 1994. Quoted in G. Richardson, *Feedback Thought in Social Science and Systems Theory.* State College: U. of Pennsylvania Press, 1991.

8. Katz and Kahn, 1966. "The Social Psychology of Organizations."
9. Henry Mintzberg, *The Rise and Fall of Strategic Planning*. New York: Free Press, 1994.
10. Henry Mintzberg, "Crafting Strategy," *Harvard Business Review,* July-August 1987.
11. Jay B. Barney and Ricky W. Griffin, *The Management of Organizations*. Boston: Houghton Mifflin, 1992.
12. David Ricardo, *The Principles of Political Economy and Taxation*. 1817.
13. Michael Porter, *Competitive Advantage*. New York: Free Press, 1985.
14. Michael Porter, *Competitive Strategy.* New York: Free Press, 1985.
15. Michael Porter, "How Competitive Forces Shape Strategy," *Harvard Business Review,* 57(2) (March–April 1979), pp. 37–45.
16. Porter, *Competitive Strategy.*
17. Jay B. Barney, "Firm Resources and Sustained Competitive Advantage," *Journal of Management,* 1991.
18. Robert C. Hill, "When the Going Gets Rough: A Baldrige Award Winner on the Line," *Executive,* August 1993, 7(3), 75–29.
19. Robert C. Hill and Sara M. Freedman, "Managing the Quality Process: Lessons from a Baldrige Award Winner—A Conversation with John W. Wallace, Chief Executive Officer of the Wallace Company," *Academy of Management Executive,* February 1992, 6(1), 76–88.

Chapter Seven

1. William Finnie, "Strategies, Systems, and Organizations: An Interview with Russell L. Ackoff," *Strategy & Leadership,* 1997.
2. Richard Bartlett, "A Growth Culture," *Executive Excellence,* 1997.
3. Program announced on the AOL UK Web site. Available online: *www.aol.co.uk.info/corporate/press/releases/2000/pr000720.html.*
4. Paul Whitfeld, "Faster Food," *Marketing,* 1 June 2000, p. 22.
5. Deni Connor, "QuikOrder Brings Domino's Pizza to You in 30 Minutes or Less," *Network World,* 6 March 2000, *17*(10), 20.
6. E. M. Rogers, *The Diffusion of Innovations*. New York: Free Press, 1983.
7. Jim Underwood, "Making the Break: From Competitive Analysis to Strategic Intelligence," *Competitive Intelligence Review,* 1995, 6(1), 15–21.
8. Abraham H. Maslow, "A Theory of Human Motivation" *Psychological Review,* July 1943.

9. Lon Roberts, *Process Reengineering,* ASQC Quality Press, 1994.
10. Peter Drucker, *Innovation and Entrepreneurship.* New York: Harper & Row, 1985.
11. Michael L. Tushman, William H. Newman, and Elaine Romanelli, "Convergence and Upheaval: Managing the Unsteady Pace of Organizational Evolution," *California Management Review,* Fall 1986, *29*(1).
12. Les Carter and Jim Underwood, *The Significance Principle.* Nashville, Tenn.: Broadman & Holman, 1998.

Chapter Eight

1. Jim Underwood, "Strategic Portfolio Balancing," in *The Handbook of Business Strategy.* New York: Faulkner & Gray, 1998.
2. Boston Consulting Group, *Perspectives On Experience,* n.p., 1983.

Chapter Nine

1. Dave House, "Off-Line," *Telecommunications,* 1998, *32*(6), 86.
2. Leo Carl, *CIA Insider's Dictionary of U.S. and Foreign Intelligence, Counterintelligence, and Tradecraft.* Washington, D.C.: NIBC Press, 1996.
3. Jan Herring, "What Is Intelligence Analysis?" *Competitive Intelligence Magazine,* July-September 1998, 1(2).
4. Herring, "What Is Intelligence Analysis?"
5. Peter Schwartz, *Art of the Long View.* New York: Doubleday, 1991.
6. "The Intelligence War Moves Online," *Industry Standard,* 21 June 1999.
7. David J. Wallace, "One-Stop Energy Shop," *Business 2.0,* 13 June 2000.

Chapter Ten

1. E. Mayo, *The Human Problems of Industrial Civilization.* New York: Macmillan, 1933.
2. Les Carter and Jim Underwood, *The Significance Principle.* Nashville, Tenn.: Broadman & Holman, 1998.
3. Peter Schwartz, *Art of the Long View.* New York: Doubleday, 1991.

Chapter Eleven

1. Michael L. Tushman, William H. Newman, and Elaine Romanelli, "Convergence and Upheaval: Managing the Unsteady

Pace of Organizational Evolution," *California Management Review,* Fall 1986, *29*(1).

Chapter Twelve

1. "Speed Demons," *Popular Science Magazine,* May 2000.
2. "The Computer of 2010: Building It," *Forbes ASAP,* 21 August 2000.
3. Neil Gershenfeld and Isaac L. Chuang, "Quantum Computing with Molecules," *Scientific American,* 1998. Available online: *www.sciam.com/1998/098issue/gershenfeld.html.*
4. Eric W. Pfeiffer, "Gilder on Optics," *Forbes ASAP,* 21 August 2000.
5. "Media Fusion, L.L.C." *World Business Review.* n.d. Available online: *www.wbrtv.com/underwriters/mediafusion/.* Access date: 28 February 2001.
6. Stacey R Closser, "Media Fusion Seeks Strength of Powerline System," *Dallas Business Journal,* 5 June 2000.
7. Late in 2000 (after this chapter was written), Telecom Technologies agreed to merge with Sonus Corporation in a $700 million acquisition, and the deal went through early in 2001. Sonus has a strategic profile quite similar to that of Telecom Technologies, and as a result there should be no negative impact on the future performance of TTI.
8. Cheryl Hall, "Electrical Engineer Builds Award-Winning Company," *Dallas Morning News,* 7 November 1999.
9. Jack Egan, "The $13 Billion Honey Pot," *Forbes Magazine,* 15 May 2000.
10. Danny Hakim, "A High-Tech Vision Lifts Fidelity." *New York Times,* 17 September 2000.
11. I thank Kevin Albaugh, Tiffany Hsieh, and Savanna Tsang for their assistance in developing the AT&T profile and information.
12. Brian Quinton, "Is the Dream Dead?" *Telephony,* 30 October 2000, p. 26.
13. Brian Quinton, "A Hail Mary Play," *Telephony,* 4 September 2000, p. 12.
14. Peter Elstrom, "AT&T: Breaking Up Is Still Hard to Do," *Telephony,* 6 November 2000, pp. 173–174.
15. I thank graduate students Kari Cain, Linda Shirley, and Janet Wilson for their assistance in analyzing Dell Computer.
16. Betsy Morris, "Can Michael Dell Escape the Box?" *Fortune,* 16 October 2000.
17. Michael Dell, "Building the Infrastructure for 21st Century Commerce," 12 May 1999.

18. I thank graduate students Michelle Ozymy, Bruce Taylor, and Stony Gwitira for their work in developing the Oracle research.
19. Andy Serwer, "The Next Richest Man in the World," *Fortune,* 13 November 2000.
20. David Stiress, "Power to the People," *Fortune,* 13 November 2000.

INDEX

Q

R

U

V

W

X

Y